Computing Bodies

Claude Draude

Computing Bodies

Gender Codes and Anthropomorphic Design at the Human-Computer Interface

Claude Draude
Kassel, Germany

Dissertation Ruhr University, Bochum, 2015

The research in this book was funded by the German Research Foundation (DFG), as part of the training group "Gender as a Category of Knowledge" at the Humboldt-Universität zu Berlin, Germany.

ISBN 978-3-658-18659-3   ISBN 978-3-658-18660-9 (eBook)
DOI 10.1007/978-3-658-18660-9

Library of Congress Control Number: 2017943838

Springer VS
© Springer Fachmedien Wiesbaden GmbH 2017
This work is subject to copyright. All rights are reserved by the Publisher, whether the whole or part of the material is concerned, specifically the rights of translation, reprinting, reuse of illustrations, recitation, broadcasting, reproduction on microfilms or in any other physical way, and transmission or information storage and retrieval, electronic adaptation, computer software, or by similar or dissimilar methodology now known or hereafter developed.
The use of general descriptive names, registered names, trademarks, service marks, etc. in this publication does not imply, even in the absence of a specific statement, that such names are exempt from the relevant protective laws and regulations and therefore free for general use.
The publisher, the authors and the editors are safe to assume that the advice and information in this book are believed to be true and accurate at the date of publication. Neither the publisher nor the authors or the editors give a warranty, express or implied, with respect to the material contained herein or for any errors or omissions that may have been made. The publisher remains neutral with regard to jurisdictional claims in published maps and institutional affiliations.

Printed on acid-free paper

This Springer VS imprint is published by Springer Nature
The registered company is Springer Fachmedien Wiesbaden GmbH
The registered company address is: Abraham-Lincoln-Str. 46, 65189 Wiesbaden, Germany

"One of the problems is this – the heart is not heart-shaped."[1]
Julian Barnes
A History of the World in 10 ½ Chapters

---

1 Excerpted from *A History of the World in 10 ½ Chapters* by Julian Barnes. Copyright © 1989 Julian Barnes. Reprinted by permission of Random House Canada, a division of Penguin Random House Canada Limited.

Contents

Figures 9

Introduction 11
    A Personal Assistant 11
    Notes on Research Material and Approach................................. 16

1. The Interface 25
    1.1. Reconsidering the Interface 25
    1.2. Human-Computer Interface:
          Bridging the Gap – Establishing the Gap........................... 31
    1.3. The Embodied Agent Interface 40
        1.3.1. Interface Metaphors 40
        1.3.2. New Functionality, New Look:
              The Embodied Agent Interface.................................. 43
        1.3.3. The Spark of Life 48

2. Reflections 55
    2.1. Mirrors and Windows: Amplifying the Imaginary 55
        2.1.1. The Changing Role of the Screen 55
        2.1.2. Entering a Mathematical Wonderland 58
        2.1.3. Mirrors and Identities... 66
    2.2. "The so-called mirror is always already coded." 76
        2.2.1. The Interface as a Place of Sign/Signal Mediating ... 78
        2.2.2. Principles of New Media Objects 85
    2.3. Between Science and Fiction 90
        2.3.1. Boundary Objects 90
        2.3.2. Narrations 96

3. Realizing the Agent Interface 105
    3.1. The Return of the Body 105
        3.1.1. Addressing the Body.. 105
        3.1.2. Bodies in Action 114
        3.1.3. Agency: Embodiment and the Ability to Act......... 121
        3.1.4. The Gender Generator.. 128

3.2. "Once more with feeling": The Role of Emotions 134
    3.2.1. The Computer as Affective Device 134
    3.2.2. "The Agent that Walked Out of the Display…" 142
    3.2.3. The OCC Model of Emotion 148
    3.2.4. Alternative Approaches to Emotion 153
3.3. "The object stares back" 162
    3.3.1. Beyond the Screen 162
    3.3.2. Gaze Behavior in Embodied Conversational Agents 169
    3.3.3. The Object Stares Back? Summing Up Thoughts on Gaze 176

4. Passing as Human **183**
4.1. Uncanny Doppelgängers 183
    4.1.1. The Uncanny Valley 183
    4.1.2. Doubles 187
4.2. Counting as Machine – Counting as Human:
    Rereading the Turing Test 190
    4.2.1. The Gender Imitation Game 190
    4.2.2. Ambiguous Positions at Peril:
        The Case of Olimpia and the Virtual Human 194

Appendix **203**

Bibliography **205**

Figures

Fig. 1 The Knowledge Navigator 12
Fig. 2 The Semantic Web 14
Fig. 3 Siri Interface 15
Fig. 4 Seven Stages of Action 33
Fig. 5 Gulfs of Interaction 34
Fig. 6 Information Processing Cycle 36
Fig. 7 Seven Stages of Action II 37
Fig. 8 iPad Multi-touch 56
Fig. 9 Alice Entering the Looking-glass 61
Fig. 10 Alice as a White Pawn 63
Fig. 11 Robot Boy with Robot Teddy 96
Fig. 12 Greta Bridging the Gap between User and System 115
Fig. 13 Greta in Interaction 118
Fig. 14 Max in Interaction 119
Fig. 15 Max System Architecture Overview 120
Fig. 16 Simplified BDI Overview 123
Fig. 17 Communication Protocols 126
Fig. 18 BDI-architecture of the MAX Model 127
Fig. 19 Gender Module 132
Fig. 20 Gendered Character Evaluation 133
Fig. 21 Virtual Human MAX at the Heinz-Nixdorf Museum, Paderborn 144
Fig. 22 Max System Architecture with Emotion System 144
Fig. 23 Max as the Guide at the Heinz-Nixdorf Museum Gets Angry
        and Leaves the Display 146
Fig. 24 Overview OCC Model of Emotion Structure................................ 151
Fig. 25 Typical Architecture 156
Fig. 26 Alternative Implementation of Emotions 156
Fig. 27 Speech Act Table (Excerpt) 157
Fig. 28 CAVE Overview.. 166
Fig. 29 ECA Greta Playing a Game of Dice with Two Humans............... 171
Fig. 30 "Diagram for two people talking" 173
Fig. 31 "Detail of eye gaze state transitions" 174
Fig. 32 The Uncanny Valley 183

Introduction

A Personal Assistant

In the middle of my research project, I sit at a laptop computer. I am surrounded by books and stacks of journals, papers, and articles. Some are printed out, while some are bookmarked on the screen, which is a gateway to thousands of on-line resources that might be equally important. As I try to sort the research material – aided by the use of a word processor, literature annotation software, and several web tools – a passage from a science fiction novel comes to my mind. In Neal Stephenson's *Snow Crash*, we read of one possible scenario for human-computer interaction:

> "'Okay. Let's get some work done. Look up every piece of free information in the library that contains L. Bob Rife and arrange it in chronological order. The emphasis here is on free.'
> 'Television and newspapers, yes, sir. One moment, sir,' the Librarian says. He turns around and exits on crepe soles." (Stephenson 1992, p. 109)

The Librarian in this scene is not a human. He, or "it", is an advanced piece of software that mimics human appearance and that acts, for the most part, as if it were human. He – and this pronoun is relevant, for within the story the three-dimensional embodiment is pictured as an older man with gray hair and concomitantly addressed as a man – is able not only to compile and sort information autonomously, but also to adapt to the user's preferences. As the interaction proceeds, the Librarian learns what is of potential interest for the specific user. This ability is continuously enhanced through conversations between user and artifact. The ideal of an interface agent as the *user's little helper*, who offers non-obtrusive assistance, is also depicted in William Gibson's novel *Idoru*. Here, the character of the Music Master not only "provides musical variety" but also serves to "keep [...] company" (Gibson 1996, p. 43). Both the Librarian and the Music Master are perceived as social entities with whom the human spends time and conducts conversations. In a depicted world of information overload, where seemingly all knowledge is accessible in digital form, these assistants obtain and deliver a structured overview. They perform a task that is perceived by the human as either tiring or overwhelming.

The Librarian and the Music Master are examples taken from fiction. They indicate that embodied entities, as visions and concepts for new interface solutions, have been objects of consideration for quite some time. The Librarian invokes the concept of Apple's *Knowledge Navigator*, a computer-as-personal-helper scenario that was first described by John Sculley in 1987 (Sculley, Byrne 1987). The vision for this technology was inspired by Vannevar Bush's *Memex*[2] and Alan Kay's work on *agent technology*[3]. Sculley viewed the building of the Knowledge Navigator as dependent on further development of important technologies, such as: a highly elaborated communication technology infrastructure; three-dimensional visualizations in real-time; enhanced data bases and information retrieval; hypermedia technology; and, of course, advances in artificial intelligence research, especially regarding intelligent software agents. Sculley did not necessarily tie the Knowledge Navigator to a specific embodiment. Still, he wished for speech recognition and the generation of synthetic speech, as well as for advanced graphics and appropriate displays (Sculley, Byrne 1987). Also in 1987, Apple produced a visionary video of the Knowledge Navigator. In this scenario, the software is impersonated by a white man, dressed as a servant, who answers to a white, male university professor.

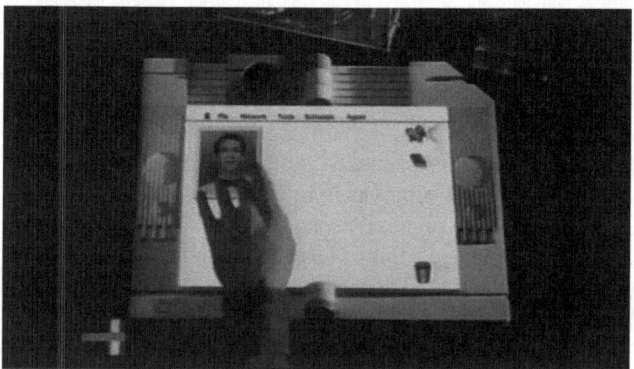

Fig. 1 The Knowledge Navigator
(Source: Screenshot from *http://www.youtube.com/watch?v=9bjve67p33E&feature=related*, checked on 10/12/2014)

---

2 "Consider a future device for individual use, which is a sort of mechanized private file and library. It needs a name, and, to coin one at random, "memex" will do. A memex is a device in which an individual stores all his books, records, and communications, and which is mechanized so that it may be consulted with exceeding speed and flexibility. It is an enlarged intimate supplement to his memory." (Bush 1945, p. 5)

3 See Chapter 1.3.

The futuristic technology in the video[4] is contrasted by the modernist setting and interior of the professor's office; the atmosphere – chamber music, a dark wooden interior, old paintings and photographs, and an antique globe – is almost Victorian. The video gives the impression that old knowledge is meeting new technology. The professor's research project is "Deforestation in the Amazon Rainforest" – a fitting topic for the 1980s. In a wise move, the Apple Corporation links prospective technology to topics like ecology and sustainability. The Knowledge Navigator replaces the professor's human assistant or secretary. Not only does the software help with office work, it keeps track of the professor's personal life by taking phone calls and arranging appointments. The Knowledge Navigator, a device that was never actually built, demonstrates how science and fiction interlink to form a narrative. The Knowledge Navigator is reminiscent of two other technologies or scenarios: Tim Berner-Lee's early vision of the Semantic Web, and Siri[5], a virtual assistant software that became available to the broader public with Apple's iPhone 4S.

Similarly to the Knowledge Navigator, the *Semantic Web* offers assistance to human users in their delegation of tasks to software agents. Tim Berner-Lee states: "The Semantic Web will bring structure to the meaningful content of Web pages, creating an environment where software agents roaming from page to page can readily carry out sophisticated tasks for users" (Berners-Lee et al. 2001, p. 25). The Semantic Web differs from the Knowledge Navigator regarding the envisioned form of embodiment.

As Figure 2 shows, the Semantic Web does not provide one anthropomorphic interface agent that the human user interacts with. Instead, several software agents, which form a multi-agent-system, execute tasks on behalf of the human user.

---

[4] The Knowledge Navigator video is available online at *http://www.youtube.com/watch?v=umJsITGzXd0*, checked on 12/11/2013.

[5] "Siri. Your wish is its command. Siri on iPhone 4S lets you use your voice to send messages, schedule meetings, place phone calls, and more. Ask Siri to do things just by talking the way you talk. Siri understands what you say, knows what you mean, and even talks back. Siri is so easy to use and does so much, you'll keep finding more and more ways to use it." See the company website at *http://www.apple.com/iphone/features/siri.html*, checked on 10/11/2013.

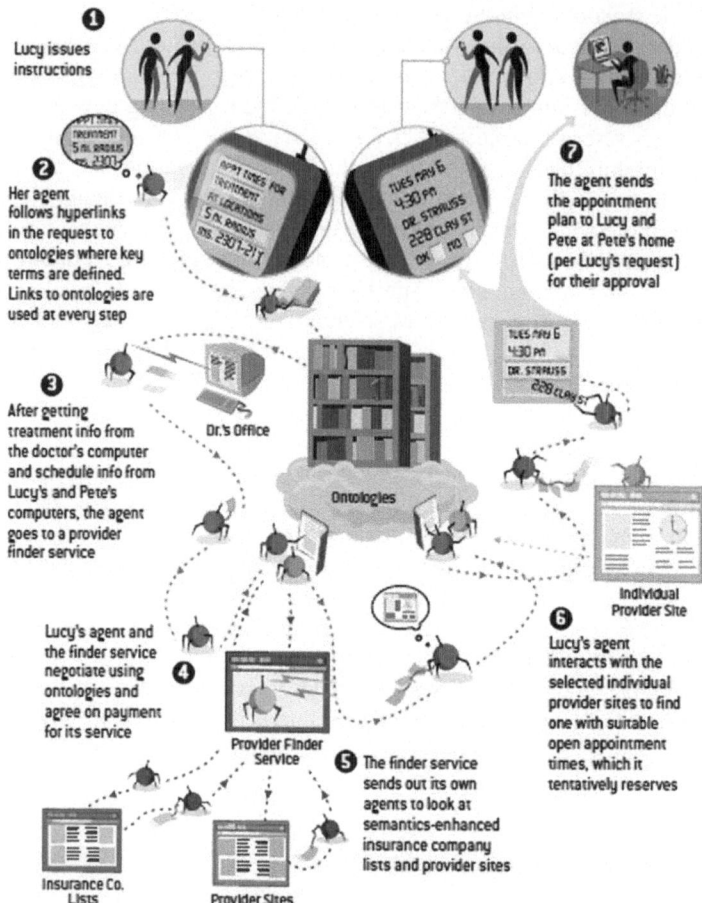

Fig. 2 The Semantic Web
(Source: Berners-Lee et al., 2001)

The above figure presents two siblings, Peter and Lucy, who want to find a doctor with whom they can book an appointment for their elderly mother. The figure shows that knowledge and information are stored on and distributed through computers, specifically by means of databases and cloud services. In the course of the usage scenario, the execution of tasks is delegated from the human user to software agents. The figure shows disseminated software robots that look like insects crawling around the web. Relevant information or status updates are sent from these software robots or, put differently, software agents[6] to the humans for approval.

In a way, the Siri application for the Apple iPhone combines the scenarios indicated by the Knowledge Navigator and the Semantic Web: like the former, it impersonates a human; as the latter suggests, it brings semantic technologies together with web-based or cloud-based knowledge and adapts to the user's preferences. Siri does not come with a human counterfeit – as with navigation systems found in automobiles, it works through voice recognition and generation. Although the user can typewrite commands, the novelty of Siri is that it brings oral interaction to an everyday device. Users can not only touch the display, they can also talk to it.

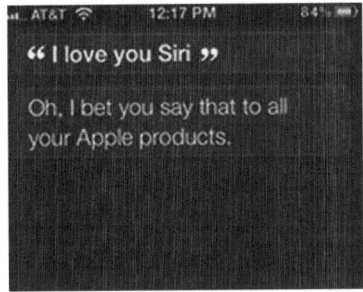

Fig. 3 Siri Interface
(Source: *http://cdn.antenne.com/media/uploads/thumbs/siri-topteaser_jpg_200x1000_q95.jpg*, checked on 10/6/2014)

To a far greater degree than the multi-agent concept of the Semantic Web, Siri anthropomorphizes technology. This anthropomorphization puts gender on the agenda in a very obvious way[7]. On the corporate website, the application is referred to as *it*, yet both the name "Siri" and the voice code *it* as female[8]. This is noteworthy in so far as it contrasts with the male impersonation of the Knowledge Navigator, but it remains unsurprising given the female coding of assistance or care work in society in general (Wetterer 2002).

---

6   The term and concept of "agents" is explained in Chapter 1.3.
7   For an excellent full analysis on gender and Siri, see Both (2011).
8   The human user can also pick a male-coded voice. But, as in car navigation systems, the default setting is the female-coded voice.

Notes on Research Material and Approach

The examples given so far – the fictional Librarian, the semi-fictitious Knowledge Navigator, the Semantic Web, and finally Siri – describe scenarios that introduce a new interaction concept, namely that of a virtual character/embodied agent interface. Ideally, this agent is smart: it incorporates a higher level of functionality than do previous human-computer-interface solutions and is therefore of more substantial assistance to the user. It does not just free the user from repetitive, boring tasks – it helps to steer across an ocean of data and it manages personal obligations. Depending on the approach that is followed, this happens by implementing various degrees of intelligence and animation.

The focus of my analysis is the proclaimed coming-to-life of the interface (Prendinger, Ishizuka 1998). This coming-to-life indexes a turning point at which the software changes from being conceived as an object to being acknowledged and addressed as a subject. The new qualities that the "agent technology"[9] brings to the interface – including animation, pro-activity, autonomy, intelligence, and embodiment – actively pursue or result in *life-likeness*. With this, the interface not only is perceived as anthropomorphic, it also contributes to the anthropomorphizing of the whole machine.

The key traits and technologies of this concept of the personal helper are illustrated by embodied interface agent systems: MAX and Greta are two examples of these very ambitious projects. MAX, developed by the Artificial Intelligence Group at the Technical University of Bielefeld, Germany[10], was initially designed to assist users in Virtual Reality assembly constructions. A model of MAX currently serves as a virtual museum guide at the Heinz-Nixdorf Museum in Paderborn, Germany. I first encountered Greta[11] at a conference, in 2005[12], where the model substituted for the third human player in a game of dice. Systems like MAX and Greta are most commonly referred to as Embodied Conversational Agents, or simply as ECA. There exist a variety of terms for virtual assistants: Embodied Contextual Agents, Virtual Personal Service Assistants, Virtual Humans, and avatars[13]. These artifacts are viewed – especially by those who engage

---

9 See Chapter 1.3., particularly 1.3.2. and 1.3.3.
10 For a more detailed description of MAX and Greta, see Chapter 3.
11 Greta's design and architecture was constructed, amongst others, by Catherine Pelachaud, University of Paris. See: *http://www.iut.univ-paris8.fr/~pelachaud*, checked on 04/01/2013.
12 AMAAS: International Conference on Autonomous Agents and Multiagent Systems, June 2005, Utrecht.
13 See Magnenat-Thalmann (2004), Pelachaud et al. (2002), Lee et al. (2002), Cassell (2000a), Livingston et al. (2002).

in their design engineering process – as the next step in human-computer interaction after the graphical user interface (Ball, Breese 2000, p. 189). Embodied agents as virtual counterparts are presented as the most natural way of making computer technology accessible and manageable, in particular for non-expert users. Here, *natural* means mirroring the human user. The gist is that, since human face-to-face interaction uses verbal as well as non-verbal behavior, embodied forms of communication should be taken as a model for human-computer interaction as well. The research goal for the personal assistant is therefore to design a human-like machine as alter ego.

Accordingly, these Virtual Humans (Magnenat-Thalmann 2004) form a nodal point where threads from various fields of knowledge interweave and result in the production of technological artifacts. Against the background of artificial intelligence research, anthropomorphic interfaces present a zone for the contestation of what passes as human and what does not. They describe borderline territory between humans and machines. Furthermore, they demonstrate how concepts of self, nature, and intelligible identity get realized in accordance with technology.

By denomination, the embodied interface agent is a special kind of embodiment of the interface. Here, embodiment means invoking the body of a human – or, more precisely, simulating the shape of the human body, the movements and actions that are noticeable, from the outside, when looking at or interacting with the interface-agent. For instance, the inside of the body – organs and bodily functions – is not simulated, whereas facial expressions and emotions are. The Virtual Human, as a light-projected form of visualization or as an image on display, goes further than Siri by embodying not only voice synthesis but also non-verbal expressions of the body. The ambitious goal of mirroring the human through the machine is interlinked with embodiment. As the examples above show, anthropomorphizing the interface couples technology with the gender order in an obvious way: Siri's default voice is coded as female, MAX – the construction helper – has the shape of a man, and Greta impersonates a virtual woman.

In this analysis, I presume that the gendering of the artifact operates in ways that go beyond the given images. The coding of the Virtual Human at the level of identity is consistent with gendered codings on more abstract levels of the technology. The co-construction (Boehner et al. 2005) of gender and technology, I contend, is so powerful because the symbolic gender order is linked to theories, methods, and procedures of computing technology.

Gender studies research has shown that gender and gender interdependencies – such as ethnicity, social positioning, and sexual orientation – are relevant to all levels of technology production. To name just a few examples: Cecile Crutzen writes about gender dynamics in the object-oriented approach to programming, which carries "illusions of objectivity and neutrality of representation, the negation of power and dominance by its translation into something "natural" and "obvious"' (Crutzen 2003, p. 102). In a research project at the University of Bremen, Kamila Wajda, Susanne Maaß, and I developed a model that addresses gender and diversity aspects along all phases of research and development in informatics (Draude et al. 2014). Heidi Schelhowe (Schelhowe 2005) also pleads for an integration of gender perspectives within the construction process of software in order to make technological choices discussable and to avoid a naturalization of normative settings. She refers to a guide for *Digital Media in Education* in which recommendations for gender-sensitive software design are given (Wiesner et al. 2004). Another example is Justine Cassell's "feminist approach to software design," where storytelling is used to disclose stereotyped identity constructions in game software for children (Cassell 1998). Göde Both analyzes the concepts of human and machine agency from a gender studies perspective and uses Siri as a case study (Both 2011). A most comprehensive overview of feminist critique, methodology, and intervention in computing science is provided by Corinna Bath (Bath 2012).

In her analysis of *De Digitale Stad*, the digital city project of Amsterdam, Els Rommes (Rommes 2002) employs the concept of gender scripts in technology production. She takes up Madeline Akrich's notion of technological scripts (Akrich 1992) and broadens it by defining gender as a fundamental ordering and structuring category of digital technology. Akrich, in *The Description of Technical Objects*, points out how the social and the technical, or culture and technology production, engage in a co-constructive dialog. She writes: "The configuration of technical objects defines a certain partitioning of the physical and social world, attributes roles to certain types of human and non-human actors while excluding others, authorizes certain types of relationship between these different actors and so on, in such a way that these objects play an integral part in the construction of a culture (in the anthropological sense of the term) at the same time as constituting necessary mediators in all the relationships that we engage in with the 'real world'" (Akrich 1992, p. 205). Thus, the term "script" means that technical objects contain stories and define actors. Following this, narrative elements and choices that are made as part of the design and construction process materialize in the form of hard- and software and thereby determine possibilities of action. The notion of scripting enables the examination of different levels of technological production, from anticipated usage and design engineering to end users. Furthermore, the gender scripting approach serves to reflect on how epistemological assumptions and their gendered coding shape the ways that technology is built and its output is realized. Its focus is on tracing design engineering processes of technology, rather than on merely analyzing completed products or phenomena. The approach followed in this book is inspired by this gender scripting approach. My analysis comprises the reading of the embodied agent interface construction plans and of papers that describe the design engineering tasks. I also include articles from relevant areas of expertise, such as psychology and cognitive science. Additionally, I examine the embodied agent in action through conference visits and visits to research labs.

What is obvious, from the very beginning, is that the anthropomorphizing of the interface brings the human further into the logic of engineering than with earlier human-computer interaction scenarios. In order to build a Virtual Human, one must first assume that a human consists of parts – visible and invisible – that can be identified, described, and rebuilt. In the case of social robots or embodied agents, one must believe that the parts of a human – if not all of them, then at least the crucial ones – are computable in the end. In other words, one must assume that what is crucial about a human can be abstracted from the human body and translated into the basic principles of computing.

The embodied interface agent is a special kind of technological object. Its background in artificial intelligence, and its character as intermediary between human and machine, puts it at the intersection of powerful dichotomies like "nature and culture" or "life and death". Given its hybrid character, the agent can be understood as a cyborg, which, according to Donna Haraway, entails – like any technology – being simultaneously "myth and tool, representation and device" (Hables Gray 1995, Introduction). The design engineering process of these artifacts necessarily engages a web of cultural, technological, and scientific theories and practices. Accounting for some of the major threads that hold this fabric together, and elaborating upon their gendered connotations, is the main focus of this book. Heidi Schelhowe has indicated that technology construction is always accompanied by normative settings and that these "norms are, however, not debatable, for as long as they appear inherently technological"[14].

My aim is therefore to contribute to the transdisciplinary dialog between computing, cultural studies, and gender studies. I chose an anthropormorphic computational artifact as my research object partly because I figured that it would serve as a site of transfer between these disciplines. For audiences of gender studies and cultural studies, the embodied agent provides an interesting phenomenon, one that is accessible through its graphic surface. At first glance, it looks like a film image, and it thus allows for the introduction of computing principles to a wider audience.

---

14 "Wertsetzungen jedoch nicht diskutierbar sind, solange sie als technologische Eigengesetzlichkeiten auftreten" (Schelhowe 1997, p. 187).
(All translations by Anna Panagiotou and Claude Draude, unless otherwise noted. Original language versions of translated quotes are listed in footnotes.)

For computer science or informatics, the Virtual Human provides an obvious means of addressing social categories to an even greater degree than is already enabled by human-machine communication (Schelhowe 2005). As I have stated above, one further goal of this book is to address gendered coding at the more abstract levels of the computational artifact.

C.P. Snow famously spoke about the natural sciences and the humanities as *Two Cultures* (Snow 1959). Gender studies, or cultural studies, and applied computer science certainly are two separate areas of expertise. Establishing a dialog between them poses a challenge on both sides. By no means are gender studies and applied computer science closed fields – at least not in the sense of having a canonical body of knowledge and methods. Nonetheless, they do – in a very general and simple sense – follow different paradigms, and this complicates communication: Applied computer science constructs, whereas gender studies deconstructs or serves as a reflexive science. As will become clearer in the course of this book, applied computer science, in order to build reliable artifacts, needs to formalize, generalize, and make certain normative choices during the development process. Cultural studies and gender studies question concepts of normativity and generalized assumptions. Gender studies set out as a transdisciplinary project crossing traditional fields of knowledge. The discipline deals with epistemological discourses; it highlights the social construction of knowledge and questions the history of science. The design engineering processes of Virtual Humans mostly draw on areas of knowledge from psychology and sociology that provide positivist, quantifiable results – knowledge that is readily adaptable to computing (Cassell 2000a; Trogemann 2003). From a gender studies perspective, such a strong positivist program holds problematic implications: *Nature* does not speak for itself, it is a term that reflects a site of ongoing re-negotiations that are structured through concepts of gender and gender interdependencies such as ethnicity, social positioning, sexual orientation, et al. (Orland, Scheich 1995). The same is true for the term human. On the other hand, the humanities lack the appeal and power brought about by the creation of technological objects. In its daily practices, a constructive science such as computing is inescapably confronted with soft- and hardware material and therefore has very specific problems to solve – problems that go beyond text production (Schelhowe 2005). Social robotics or virtual agents hold the potential to provide the public with artifacts that are very convincing once they function properly and start populating virtual worlds or mixed-reality environments. Furthermore, software shapes how humans can perform specific tasks. Technological choices that have been made during the design process are not visible or accessible in the end product with which the human user is usually confronted.

Within cultural studies, considerable effort has already been made to address virtual/technological forms of embodiment and the broad field of techno- and life sciences in general (Featherstone, Burrows 1995; Hables Gray 1995). Similarly, there are excellent works in feminist studies of science and technology, as well as in media studies, that are explicitly concerned with gender issues (Bath 2002; Deuber-Mankowsky 2001; Balsamo 1995) and/or with concepts of ethnicity and western culture as a paradigm of technological culture (Hillis 1996; Eglash 1995). My book seeks to contribute to this body of work by analyzing some of the threads that are constitutive for the new interface technology. I seek to follow these threads, beyond the surface, into the construction plans and personality models that inform the building of the artifact.

The first chapter of this book explains the emergence of embodied interface agents against the background of the history of the human-computer interaction. The development of the interface throughout the decades is here characterized as moving away from abstract, expert-oriented modes of communicating with the machine. Instead, more graphic solutions were realized in order to address a broader spectrum of users. As I will explain, the Virtual Human stands at the end of this process of (re)sensualization. As is reflected in the term "human-computer interaction", interface design is presumably about bridging the gap between human and machine. The anthropomorphic form of the Virtual Human is presented as a solution addressing a wider audience of computer users. And, because Virtual Humans look like humans, they serve as a means for computing technology to blend more easily into everyday surroundings. Yet, as Justine Cassell et al. (2001) prominently state, the embodied agent is *More than just a pretty face*. The new functionality, or "the spark of life", that agent technology brings to the interface is discussed at the end of this chapter.

The second chapter provides theoretical groundwork and introduces the main discursive threads that I follow. Human and machine, of course, are by no means pre-discursive entities. The question of how the boundaries between them are established – and thus of how objects and entities come into existence – lies at the core of this book. Interface design is characterized as a contested zone where different concepts, beliefs, and scientific findings meet. Throughout the years, metaphors and paradigms have shifted, and this has resulted in different interface solutions. The computer, because it is a semiotic machine, poses particular challenges for the design engineering process. Accordingly, the material-semiotic transformations that have to take place on and off the interface are of particular interest – especially in regard to the symbolic gender order. In the case of the Virtual Human, the computer screen – at least on the level of concept – almost literally serves as a mirror. In this chapter, the background of this mirroring function is reconsidered. The role of the computer screen as interface is discussed in dialog with psychoanalytic theory. Here, the doppelgänger character of the interface agent is of interest: with the computer it becomes possible to produce a *Second Self* (Turkle 1984).

In Chapter 3, embodiment, emotion, and visual relations are discussed as major topics that shape the embodied interface agent technology. Embodiment and emotion, in particular, have been reported by feminist critics as missing from the field of traditional artificial intelligence research (Adam 1998). In my analysis, for reasons of manageability, scope, and focus, I do not elaborate upon the making of the visual body of the agent. Instead, emotion and gaze are understood to be linked to the human form of embodiment, as well as to the symbolic order of the two genders. This chapter consists of the reading of construction plans of gaze and emotion models that are used in the field. Such an approach enables reconsideration of what happens when formerly excluded human traits become realized in computing and encounter the basic principles of the semiotic machine. The anthropomorphic embodiment contributes to the naturalization of the artifact. Emotions serve as a means of animation and gaze reconstructs the visual relations between human and machine as interactive: the computational object can now look back. All three aspects are employed to foster ease of use by moving technology closer to the human. They contribute to the artifact's autonomous status by facilitating a passing of the artifact's object status to a controlled subject status.

The passing of this new subject as human (or at least as a close resemblance thereof) is the goal of the research field of embodied interface agent design. The Virtual Human gives the impression of a partner, a *machine friend*, which helps and assists the human user. The acceptance of the artifact by the human is crucial for this special kind of relationship. Hence, trust and believability are key issues that are explicitly addressed in research (Ruttkay 2004). The other side of this relationship, however, has less positive connotations: fear and threat are also tied to artificial beings. Science fiction narratives demonstrate how not only utopian, but also dystopian, themes are closely interwoven with technology. Research papers, or talks given at artificial intelligence conferences, often use examples from science fiction to illustrate future prospects – and when they do, they leave the threatening aspects aside. In concluding Chapter 4, the borderline between human and machine is discussed. The Turing Test, as founding myth of artificial intelligence research, is reread against the background of its gendered coding and in terms of its implications for the research field of the Virtual Human. Although it is not actively intended within the field, Virtual Humans hold a threshold position between life and death and respond to fantasies of inorganic reproduction and transcendence. One concept that addresses matters of life-likeness and acceptance of the artifact in artificial intelligence research is the notion of the *Uncanny Valley* (Mori 1970). Like the Turing Test, the Uncanny Valley deals with the question of trusting technology, or the idea of feeling at home and at ease with it. This book concludes with a discussion of how the varying degrees of anthropomorphizing interlink this feeling of trust with the symbolic order of gender.

1. The Interface

1.1. Reconsidering the Interface

In her introduction to *The Art of Human-Computer Interface Design*, a collected volume of essays, Brenda Laurel asks a basic yet central question: "What's an interface?" (Laurel 1990b, p. xi). In computing science, the term "interface" usually stands for devices and technical solutions that define the manner in which humans interact with computers.

There are, however, different meanings of the word. A web entry sums up the uses of the term depending on context:

> "INTERFACE
> The point of interconnection between two entities. 'Public relation firms often serve as the interface between a company and the press.'
> - (computing) The point of interconnection between two systems or subsystems. 'The data is sent over the air interface to the remote system.'
> - (computing) The connection between a user and a machine. 'The options are selected via the user interface.'
> - (chemistry, physics) A thin layer or boundary between two different substances or two phases of a single substance. For example, if water and oil are mixed together, they tend to separate, and at equilibrium they are in two different strata with an oil-water interface in between. The surface of a lake is a water-air interface.
> - (computing) In object-oriented programming, a piece of code defining a set of operations that other code must implement."[15]

Taking a step back, the transfer of the word "interface", from its original meaning to computing, is interesting. The fourth definition, which relates to chemistry, describes this origin. Here, interface means "phase boundary" – a boundary between different aggregate states of a substance or a medium. These are distinct from each other precisely because they do not intermix. The substances or different systems can only exchange through an interface. The interface describes in what way they face[16] each other in order to communicate: "Moreover, the word means 'intermediate layer': for both boxes involved, it is irrelevant how each respectively treats

---
15 See: *http://en.wiktionary.org/wiki/interface*, checked on 21/08/2013
16 Note the meaning in Latin: inter = between, and facies = appearance, form, figure, visage.

messages internally, and therefore how it manages to produce answers. The delineation of boundaries is integral to itself, and the black boxes need only to know the side facing them in order to ensure communication."[17]

Therefore, the original meaning stresses the surface character, while the differences between the substances are emphasized by their characterization as black boxes. These black boxes can be distinct in their set-up or differ in their internal information and communication procedures. What counts is the interface's ability to translate or transport relevant information. Historian Hans Dieter Hellige points out that the term interface was later transferred to physics and then to electrical engineering (Hellige 2008, p. 11). Subsequently, interface came to name the conceptual space in which the computer and the human interact. To begin with, the usage of the term describes a clear separation between two entities who are then in need of intermediation. The human and the computer might as well be black boxes with their internal communication structures differing decidedly. But, as long as their output is being moderated and mediated accordingly, differences in their internal structure do not matter.

Already in the 1960s, prominent figures of technological development such as Douglas Engelbart and Josef Licklider argued against this image of black boxes. Both Engelbart and Licklider stressed the coupling of human and machine over their separation. Rather than a scenario in which two black boxes meet – with the human on one side and the computer on the other – they emphasize the formation of a new, sociotechnical space that changes (or at least has effects on) both entities. Human and computer are linked in a cybernetic feedback loop. According to this concept, human-computer interaction is a much more symbiotic, synergistic, and interlinked process than is indicated by the term interface. Licklider, for example, coined the term "man-computer intermedium" in order to grasp this process (Hellige 2008, p. 14). Others, like Frederick P. Brooks in 1965, put an emphasis on the "architecture of input-output system" and suggested that this process be understood in terms of an interaction space (quoted in Hellige 2008, p. 12). In the 1970s and 1980s, however, the term "user interface" prevailed[18]. What is of interest is the question of why this happened. Why do certain conceptualizations of human-computer interaction have more impact than others?

---

17 "Daneben bedeutet das Wort 'Zwischenschicht': Für die beiden beteiligten Boxes ist es ohne Belang, wie die jeweils andere intern mit den Botschaften umgeht, und wie die Antworten darauf zustande kommen. Die Beschreibung der Grenze ist Teil ihrer selbst, und die Black Boxes brauchen nur die ihnen zugewandte Seite zu kennen, um die Kommunikation zu gewährleisten." See: *http://de.wikipedia.org/wiki/Interface*, checked on 21/08/2013
18 For an excellent, detailed discussion, see Hellige (2008).

1.1. Reconsidering the Interface

Lasse Scherffig finds the answer in Western cultural history. He links the idea of two separate entities that collide at the interface to a modernist conception of the world. In particular, he stresses the Cartesian idea of the human subject:

> "In its most classical view human and computer meet at the interface. The computer in this view is more or less the Turing machine. The human in this view is the Cartesian subject. Between both there is a gap [Norman, 1986, p. 31]. On one side there is mind, on the other there is the physical world. In between there is a translator. For Descartes, mind-body interaction took place at the pineal gland [Beckermann, 1999, p. 50]. Today human computer interaction takes place at the interface. [...] The German term for interface is 'Schnittstelle', which literally translates to 'location of the cut'." (Scherffig 2005, pp. 33–34)

Henceforth, the distinct Cartesian separation of mind and body finds its counterpart in the concepts and realizations of the "Schnittstelle"[19]. Scherffig states that the gap even finds expression in the hyphen that divides, and at the same time links, human-computer interaction. The role of the interface is to connect these previously "cut apart" pieces – if it succeeds, then a functioning (communication) system is formed. What is of major interest for this analysis is how the bridging of this gap – the interface – gains importance and, with the embodied agent/Virtual Human, finally receives a life of its own (at least in concept).

In her analysis, according to which the computer is described as *Das Medium aus der Maschine*, or a medium that derives from the machine, Heidi Schelhowe describes how the conception of the computer – and accordingly of the interface – has changed throughout the years. In the early days of computing, which she exemplifies with Konrad Zuse's Z3, the interface was not at all conceived as a medium. Instead, the computer was to be handled like a machine. Its working principle of signal processing was rather accessible while the machine was manipulated through punch cards (Schelhowe 1997, p. 153). In this first generation of knobs, dials, and front panels, there was hardly any intermediation between human and machine. *What you touched was what you got*. The handling of the machine mirrored the modes by which one operated it.

An important shift took place, in 1961, with the Compatible Time-Sharing System (CTSS) at MIT. The basic innovation of time-sharing operating systems was that they let several users share one mainframe computer. The users – which is to say, in this case, the programmers – operated through teletypewriter machines. Because of this, the CTSS encouraged communication among users. It introduced

---

19 "The German term 'Schnittstelle', meaning interface, posits explicitly, according to DIN 44300, that it refers 'to a transition of the booundaries between two entities of the same kind'." ("Der deutsche Begriff 'Schnittstelle' postuliert ausdrücklich gemäß DIN 44300, dass es sich hierbei um einen 'Übergang an der Grenze zwischen zwei gleichartigen Einheiten handelt.'") (Hellige 2008 p. 13)

the communication aspect and thereby marked the beginning of human-computer *communication*. Fernando J. Corbató, Marjorie Merwin Daggett, and Robert C. Daley describe the need for time-sharing. Furthermore, they state that it introduced a whole set of new challenges to the field:

> "Thus, what is desired is to drastically increase the rate of interaction between the programmer and the computer without large economic loss and also to make each interaction more meaningful by extensive and complex system programming to assist in the man-computer communication. To solve these interaction problems we would like to have a computer made simultaneously available to many users in a manner somewhat like a telephone exchange. Each user would be able to use a console at his own pace and without concern for the activity of others using the system. This console could as a minimum be merely a typewriter but more ideally would contain an incrementally modifiable self-sustaining display." (Corbató et al. 1962)

Not only does time-sharing advance the role of communication, it also contributes to a distancing of the user from the machine's working mode. Schelhowe, however, stresses that at this point it is merely the sensual experience of handling a machine which recedes; the computer is still understood as a machine that computes (Schelhowe 1997, p. 154f). In order for many users to have access to one machine, the display monitor gains importance. An increased capacity of abstraction and imagination is demanded from the human, who must now converse with the machine through type-pad and screen, as interface, rather than through pushing buttons on a machine. The semiotic character[20] of the computer begins to manifest itself at the interface. Signs and symbols start mediating the interaction process between human and machine.

Time-sharing does not emphasize a strict separation between human and machine. On the contrary, the programmer is considered to be part of the system. Licklider's claims that human and computer are entangled in a cybernetic feedback loop is more obvious at this early stage. Furthermore, in the conversation paradigm of the command-line interface, programmer and computer are connected through typewritten input. For this, the human has to learn a specific language in order to handle the machine. Just as in a dialog, these commands are not represented on the screen but have to be memorized by the human. Unlike a human-to-human dialog, the used language is highly formalized and has to be precise in order to work. Particularly telling here is the term "*command*", an expression invoking the military. Interestingly, with the command-line interface, it is the commander who has to learn the language of the subordinate. To rule the computer, its logic and symbolic manipulation have to be followed exactly (Hofmann 1997, p. 73). The socio-

---

20   See Chapter 2.2.

1.1. Reconsidering the Interface

cultural setting of the technology is framed by the language and metaphors that are used, and such language and metaphors manifest themselves in technological implementations.

As mentioned above, Licklider, in particular, stresses the symbiotic character of this type of interaction. While interacting, user and computer follow different tasks: the human defines goals, makes plans, and evaluates; the machine takes over routine work and thus frees the user from presumably tiring tasks. The question of how the interface is conceptualized then becomes a question of how these assignments of tasks are distributed, organized, and represented (Schelhowe 1997, p. 156). Interestingly, this attribution of roles enhances the gap between human and machine through the way in which certain human traits are sourced out to the machine. This attribution grants the creative, decision-making, emotional part to the human and the precise, calculating, routine – and assumingly more boring – part to the computer. At this early point, a dichotomy becomes established. On one hand, there are things that are not – or that are not as readily – computable, such as creativity and emotions. On the other hand, there remain the more rule-oriented and computable routine tasks. Read against the background of the Cartesian split, rule-orientation is attributed to the computer, whereas creativity and emotions are viewed as inherently human. Logic and reason appear more easily transferable to the computer due to their roots in mathematics[21]. Simultaneously, they seem more abstractable from the human body. Emotion, the senses, and creativity, in contrast, are more tied to matter/materiality and considered inherently uncomputable – at least in these early stages[22]. The embodied agent/Virtual Human interface, which seems to challenge these dichotomies, will develop a later phase.

In order to understand the course of human-computer interaction, it should be noted that this early stage of time-sharing already constitutes the trajectory that this course will later follow: "From the user's standpoint, how they interact with the computer is an issue surpassingly more important than what the computer is built from" (Walker 1990, p. 439).

The idea of a "self-sustaining display", which Corbató et al. envisioned, proves to become more and more extrapolated throughout the course of human-computer interaction. The popular, widespread graphical user interface (GUI) and new developments like touchpad technologies come very close to this idea.

---

21 For a further discussion of this, see „Die Herschaft der Regel. Zur Grundlagengeschichte des Computers," by sociologist Bettina Heintz (1993). The author recontexualizes the field of mathematics by pointing out its social and historical situatedness. Thus, the computing machine apperas as product of modernity – that is, a machine defined by distinctively modern traits like rationality, mechaninzation, and economization.

22 Chapter 3.1.

Throughout the history of human-computer interaction, the technology changes along with the anticipated user groups and the designers. Or, more accurately, the dichotomy between users and designers itself is a product of this history. Roughly speaking, until the 1970s the programmers were the ones who handled computers. With a wider distribution of computers, however, the term "user" comes to refer to someone who is not a computer expert – that is, to a person who uses, but does not design, the technology (Hofmann 1997, p. 71). Jeanette Hofmann analyzes the establishment of this new distinction between experts and non-experts. Giving examples of word processing software and hardware solutions, she reconstructs how technology results from the "Nutzerbilder", or images of users, that are anticipated by the software designers. She finds that: "Behind every programming draft there is a more or less explicitly designed 'script', which includes the characteristics of the user, as well as their actions"[23].

These "user scripts" are gendered in a complex way. Hofmann describes common images in terms of "the eternal beginner (female)"[24], " the technical expert (female)"[25], and "the casual writer (male)"[26]. In the 1980s, word processing software typically addressed typists and secretaries – work positions that are mostly occupied by women. Depending on the anticipated user that was imagined, the soft- and hardware offered rather predetermined and static technical solutions. For example, some programs start with the idea that the "the user is a beginner" and will remain so, either because this user cannot become or does not want to become capable of handling technology that is more complex. But there are also interfaces where the technology is more open and adjustable, and these follow the idea that "the user will eventually become an expert".

Interestingly, the graphical user interface realized by the Xerox Star computer, in 1981[27], took a man, who is a manager, as user model. It introduced a desktop metaphor that catered to a person who usually did not do the typing and was too busy to remember all the complex and precise commands of other interfaces: "Graphical objects that reproduce the world of the office, are understood as concessions of the software designer to the, presumed to be weak, memories of

---

23 "Hinter jedem Programmentwurf steht ein mehr oder minder explizit formuliertes 'Script', das Eigenschaften der Nutzer sowie ihrer Tätigkeiten umfaßt." (Hofmann 1997, p. 74)
24 "Die ewige Anfängerin" (ibid., p. 75)
25 "Die technische Expertin" (ibid., p. 78)
26 "Der Gelegenheitsschreiber" (ibid., p. 85)
27 "Augment", by Doug Engelbart, can be seen as a predecessor. (ibid., p. 93)

their audience. Also, the estrangement (based on that of men) in relation to the world of digital text processing ought to be reduced with this."[28].

This "knowledge worker" is pictured as someone who conceptualizes and builds texts. In contrast to the secretary, who is understood as a mere typist, it is with the knowledge worker that writing becomes a creative process. The gendered division of labor in the workplace thus finds its counterpart in interface technologies (Hofmann 1997, p. 91f).

It is with the graphical user interface, then, that the interaction scenario changes from one defined in terms of expert users, such as the experienced typist or the programmer, to one defined in terms of the knowledge worker – and, subsequently, of the "everyday user", who should not be bothered with the working mode of the machine. It should be noted that this comprises a shift from handling the computer through precise, abstract language to handling it through more graphical, representational – and, later, even embodied or tangible – interaction scenarios.

1.2. Human-Computer Interface: Bridging the Gap – Establishing the Gap

The artist J. L. Andruszkiewicz states: "All human interaction with computers takes place at an interface. An unusual characteristic of the computer interface is, as it allows some interactions between the user and the system, it also prevents others; this is the case no matter on what system level the user is accessing the computer" (Andruszkiewicz 2009a). The role of the interface is one of intermediation. And it materializes certain possibilities of agency while neglecting others.

According to its developers, the embodied interface agent/Virtual Human is considered a post-GUI solution that will make computing technology not only accessible – easy for all to use – but also more adaptable to post-desktop environments (Cassell 2000a). Given embodied agent research's focus on the human, the technological mirroring of human cognitive abilities, behavior and appearance becomes important. For human-computer interaction, standard works, such as *User Centered System Design* (Norman, Draper 1986), make it their goal to map the multifaceted field by concentrating on the human. This perspective on the human is drawn from cognitive science.

---

[28] "Graphische Objekte, die die Bürowelt nachbilden, sind als Entgegenkommen der Softwaredesigner an das als schwach unterstellte Gedächtnis ihrer Adressaten zu verstehen. Auch das (Männern nachempfundene) Fremdheitsgefühl gegenüber der digitalen Textverarbeitungswelt sollte auf diese Weise vermindert werden." (ibid., p. 86)

Below, I provide a short review of this highly influential approach. The concept of human agency and cognitive ability that is here established is one that reoccurs within the design of sociable or embodied agents. The work of Norman and colleagues (ibid.) demonstrates how human agency becomes reformulated against the background of computer science. Two fields of knowledge, cognitive science and computing, co-construct a new field: cognitive engineering (Norman 1987, p. 326).

Donald A. Norman, a prominent figure in the field of human-computer interaction, is renowned for a special interest in usability issues. He was originally trained in electrical engineering and later became a professor of cognitive psychology as well as of computer science. Stressing the importance of usability engineering, he proposes user-centered design for all areas of construction. His interests cover a wide range of topics, including technology and society, emotions and design, interaction, and education[29]. Although his body of work is vast, it is Norman's concept of agency that is of particular interest for the analysis of the embodied agent interface. In *The Design of Everyday Things* (Norman 1988), he describes human agency as an "action cycle". His aim, partly inspired by the observation of everyday events, is to extrapolate a structure of human action[30]. According to Norman, a person, in order to perform a task, undertakes "seven stages of action". These span from the constant re-evaluation of the status quo (or of "the world") to the human's articulation of its interests (or its "goals and intentions"). The action plan is thus divided into "stages of execution" and "stages of evaluation", with "goals" playing an important role. They actually form the first stage.

---

29 See Donald Norman's website: *http://www.jnd.org/*, checked on 10/06/2013.
30 Norman 1988, p.45f

1.2. Human-Computer Interface: Bridging the Gap – Establishing the Gap

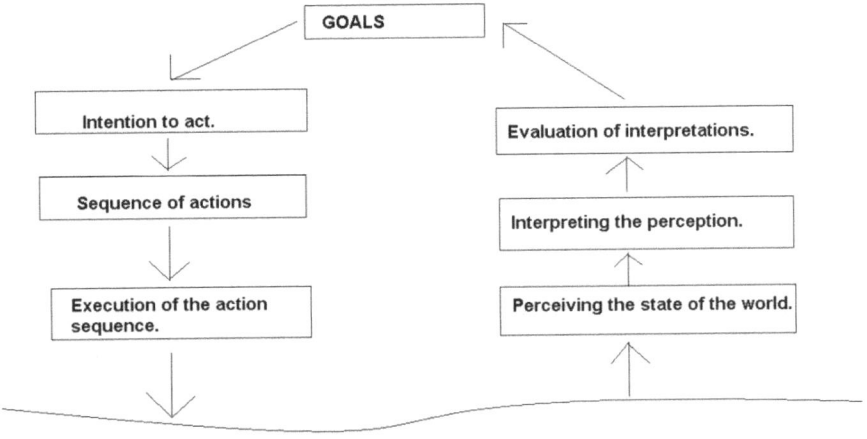

Fig. 4 Seven Stages of Action
(Source: Norman, 1988, p.45)

The terms "execution" and "evaluation" are important, for this is where interruptions or irritations in the flow may occur: execution refers to the realization, in action, of a person's intentions; evaluation refers to how well a person perceives and adjusts to "the world". Norman transfers this concept to the use of technical systems. He formulates a theory that specifies the gaps, or "gulfs", that exist between user and system. These must be bridged in order to reach a functioning state of interaction. It is in the article, *Direct Manipulation Interfaces*, which Norman co-authored with cognitive scientists Edwin L. Hutchins and James D. Hollan, that this concept is extrapolated (Norman 1986)[31]. The notion of "gulfs" is used to address the discrepancy between system and user, as well as the need for interface design to take this discrepancy into account. The "Gulf of Execution" and the "Gulf of Evaluation" are presented in the figure below.

---

[31] Since the article was published two years earlier, it is likely that the concept of human agency co-developed with the more technical usage, which is probably why it was so successfully received within the computer science community.

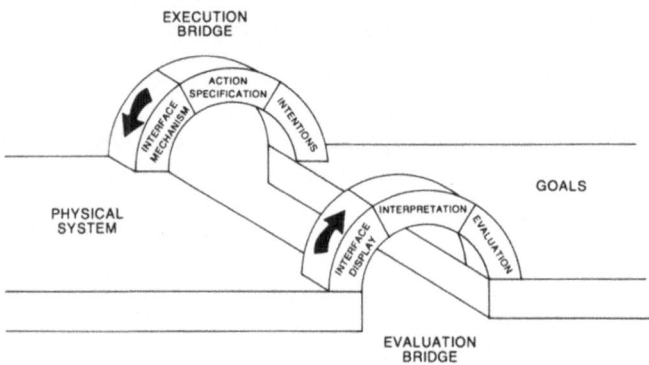

FIGURE 3.2. Bridging the Gulfs of Execution and Evaluation. The Gulf of *Execution* is bridged from the psychology side by the user's formation of intentions relevant to the system and the determination of an action sequence. It is bridged from the system side when the designer of the system builds the input characteristics of the interface. The Gulf of *Evaluation* is bridged from the psychology side by the user's perception of the system state and the interpretation placed on that perception, which is then evaluated by comparing it with the original goals and intentions. It is bridged from the system side when the designer builds the output characteristics of the interface.

Fig. 5 Gulfs of Interaction
(Source: Norman, 1986, p. 40)

The basic concept is that the user has certain goals that she or he wants to achieve by using the system, while the system needs to process this information and provide relevant output. The "Gulf of Execution" emerges in between the user's goals or intentions and the interaction possibilities that the system provides. The "Gulf of Evaluation" describes the challenge of assessing the state of the system. The better the interface manages to transmit this state to the user, the easier the interaction becomes. This transmission, however, must match the expectations of the user. Furthermore, the interface must represent an action or set of actions that will lead users to their desired goal and meet their intentions.

The design of the interface should acknowledge that the Gulf of Execution, as well as the Gulf of Evaluation, need to be overcome. This overcoming is pursued by a matching process: "The Gulf of Execution is bridged by making the commands and mechanisms of the system match the thoughts and goals of the user as much as possible" (Hutchins et al. 1986, p. 95). In this model, bridging the Gulf of Execution means that the user must form intentions, specify action sequences, execute actions, and select the right interface mechanisms. The Gulf of Evaluation then describes the challenge of assessing the state of the system according to how well the interface supports the discovery and interpretation of the system state. When the gulfs are successfully overcome, this leads "to the qualitative feeling that we are directly engaged with control of the objects – not with the programs, not with the computer, but with the semantic objects of our goals and intentions" (ibid.). In this view, the most successful interface is one that does not get noticed. Ideally, the system mirrors the user's intentions – the closer the interaction comes to realizing this goal, the more functional it is said to be.

As the Figure 5 shows, Norman's model makes a cut between user and system, but it also establishes connections between them. The original meaning of the term interface – taken from chemistry and describing a contact and a boundary surface – recedes, while the gap between user and system is highlighted. Nevertheless, the situation is ambivalent: on one side, there is the establishment of the gap between human and machine; on the other, it is possible to overcome this gap by adequate design. Looked at more closely, the concept also demonstrates that the user and the system are interwoven in an environment that is defined by a shared sequence of interaction possibilities. Here, some kind of convergence or leveling, regarding how action or agency is defined, needs to take place. Or, put differently, a concept is needed that describes human action in very close relation to the interaction possibilities that are realizable with a computer. Norman coins the term "cognitive engineering" for the emergence of what, according to him, should result from a transdisciplinary dialog between cognitive psychology and applied computer science. He writes:

> "Why cognitive engineering? Why a new term? After all there exist several terms used to describe the applied side of psychology: ergonomics, human factors, and engineering psychology. I believe a new term is needed because a new approach is needed. More than just psychology is required. More than psychology coupled with engineering." (Norman 1987, p. 326)

Norman stresses the challenge of a productive exchange between two diverse fields of knowledge. His concept has had a great impact on the field of human-computer interaction. Furthermore, this way of conceptualizing and modeling agency is prominent in artificial intelligence research and consequently recurs within architectures of embodied interface agents[32]. From a critical perspective, the success of cognitive engineering points to the fact that this approach to human cognition shares a basic logic with the cycle of information-processing, which is marked by input, process, output, and storage activities, as depicted in the following figure.

---

32 See Chapter 3.1.2.

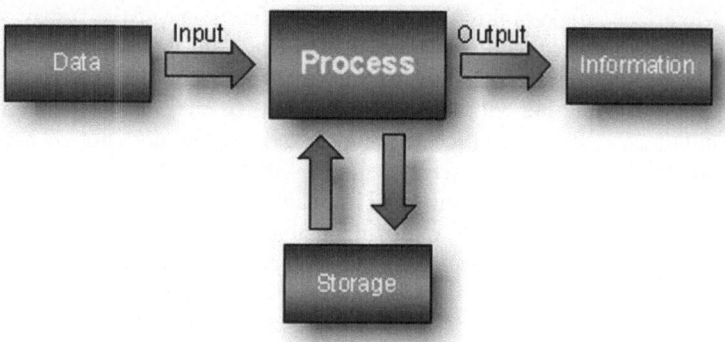

Fig. 6 Information Processing Cycle
(Source: *http://ilearnict.blogspot.de/2010/07/information-procesing-cycle.html*, checked on 6/7/2014)

Cognitive engineering defines human capacity as the ability to act by using a model of plans, intentions, and goal-orientation. The concept draws, *inter alia*, on the GOMS model, which stands for Goals, Operators, Methods, and Selection (Norman 1987, p. 328; Card et al. 1983). The GOMS model provides a theoretical framework for representing the computer user's state of mind and possible forms of action. Various specifications exist that are used for developing and evaluating (John 2003). Simply put, the user's goals have to be identified, and sub-goals, as smaller units, need to be established. Together with operators, which are the actions the system interface performs, these form the methods. If there is effectively more than one method that the human can choose in order to reach the goal, then the selection rules apply. GOMS has proven to be especially successful when the user is already familiar with the system and when he or she has a specific task to fulfill. Norman's concept is based upon the belief that human agency is a primarily cognitive process that starts with "some goal in mind". Following this, "this goal defines the final state to be satisfied. Before it can lead to actions it must be transformed into more specific intentions, into specific action sequences that bridge the gap between what one would like to do (one's intentions) and the specific capabilities of the system (the allowable physical actions)" (Norman 1987, p. 328). This theory of human agency is entangled with the logic of the cybernetic feedback loop, as another illustration of the seven stages of action shows:

1.2. Human-Computer Interface: Bridging the Gap – Establishing the Gap

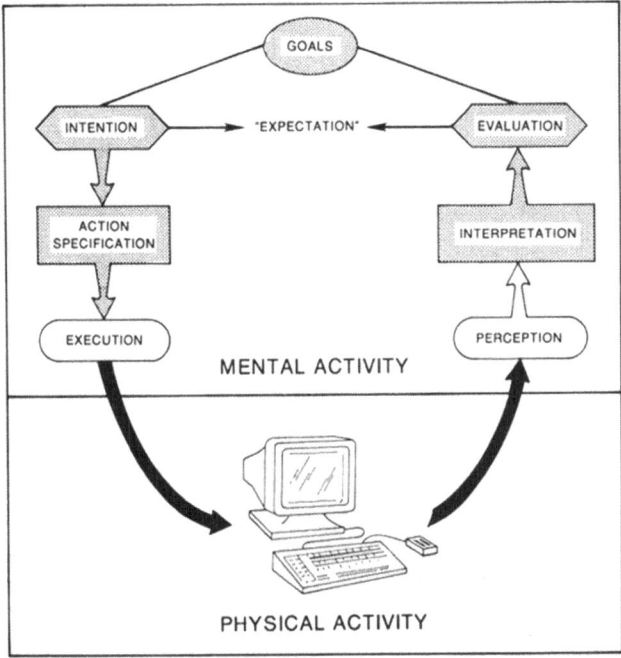

FIGURE 3.3. Seven stages of user activities involved in the performance of a task. The primary, central stage is the establishment of the goal. Then, to carry out an action requires three stages: forming the intention, specifying the action sequence, and executing the action. To assess the effect of the action also requires three stages, each in some sense complementary to the three stages of carrying out the action: perceiving the system state, interpreting the state, and evaluating the interpreted state with respect to the original goals and intentions.

Fig. 7 Seven Stages of Action II
(Source: Hutchins et al., 1986, p. 96)

Additionally, Norman writes elsewhere:

"This speaks of goals, intentions, and the internal specification of actions. The actual production of an action is only half the story, however. The other half involves the feedback loop: the perception, interpretation, and evaluation of the results of the action. This led me to postulate seven stages of action:

- forming the goal;
- forming the intention;
- specifying an action;

- executing the action;
- perceiving the system state;
- interpreting the system state;
- evaluating the outcome." (Norman 1987, p. 329)

Cognitive engineering provides a way of conceiving the entire concept of interaction. To begin with, the human user and technological artifact are separate entities, but Norman's theory of agency has the consequence of making them form a network. Conceptually, human agency and machine agency are brought to the same level. Or, put differently, human agency is reformulated in dialog with the input-processing-output model of the machine. Furthermore, Figure 7 shows a split between mental and physical activity, which invokes the Cartesian divide between mind and body.

This model of human-computer interaction has received both praise and critique – depending on the reviewer's perspective on human agency – for its information-processing approach. In the compendium, *Interfacing Thought*, John B. Black, Dana S. Kay, and Elliot M. Soloway state that "almost all of human behavior can be characterized in terms of goals and plans. In particular, most of what people do is devise plans of action and perform them in order to bring about some desired state of the world – that is, to accomplish a goal. Consequently, much of human knowledge about how to operate in the world is stored in memory in form of plan and goal knowledge representations" (Black et al. 1987, p. 36). This formalized (and rather simplified) way of conceiving human action is regarded by others as unrealistic. In the very same compendium, John Whiteside and Dennis Wixon "suggest, as a possibility, an alternative assumption: Users do not start with goals at all; rather they are always already acting in a situation, thrown to it as it were, unreflectively and unanalytically. What would theories, models, and systems based on such assumptions look like?" (Whiteside, Wixon 1987, p. 360)

The "goals and plans model" of human agency demonstrates the transfer of knowledge from one area to another. It can be described as a process of transformation resulting in new methods and practices, which finally inform the building of artifacts. Most prominently, it is Lucy Suchman who questions the goal and planning model. She criticizes the traditional view of human-computer interaction, in which the computer and the human are two separate entities that need to come together. According to Suchman, this separation – far from being a given fact – is an effect produced within the field of technology design. Suchman follows actor-network theory – which manifests itself in the statement that "we have never been modern" (Latour 2002) – in the sense that she regards all dichotomies that structure and stabilize Western culture as effects of material-semiotic practices. Dichotomies do not pre-exist as such. Suchman finds that this "clearly implies a very different understanding of the 'human-machine interface'. 'The interface' on the one hand becomes the name for a category of contingently enacted 'cuts' occurring always within sociomaterial practices, that effect 'persons' and 'machines' as distinct entities, and that in turn enable particular forms of subject/object intra-actions. At the same time, the singularity of 'the interface' explodes into a multiplicity of more and less closely aligned, dynamically configured moments of encounter between other sociomaterial configurations, objectified as persons and machines" (Suchman 2005).

This is to say that the theory of human agency depicted within the planning model follows a tradition of Western logic that favors abstract, analytical, and – most importantly – disembodied thinking (Suchman 1987, p. viii). In *Plans and Situated Actions. The Problem of Human-Machine Communication*, Suchman analyzes artificial intelligence models of agency and contrasts them with a notion of "situated action". She argues "that all activity, even the most analytic, is fundamentally concrete and embodied", and that actions are therefore always "situated actions [...], actions taken in the context of particular, concrete circumstances" (ibid.). In the preface to her book, Suchman refers to an ethnographic description of different modes of sea navigation, one whereby the Trukese navigator is contrasted with the European navigator. The European navigator follows – at least in concept – a strict planning model. The Truk's mode of navigation, on the other hand, is described as a goal-oriented action – one that is situated and that adapts to the environment using all the relevant information found along the way. Suchman's intention is not to romanticize the Trukese way of navigation, but rather to challenge the universal validity of the European approach. And it is, in fact, "the view of action exemplified by the European navigator [that] is now being reified in the design of intelligent machines" (Suchman 1987, p. ix).

In the cognitive engineering approach, for example, the human is not specified as – nor does it even appear as – a diversified concept. Norman's model addresses the fact that the interface presents to the user certain possibilities for interaction while neglecting others. This model is rooted in Western culture and presents a perspective that is based upon a modern, positivist world view. Like the GOMS model, it is considered more fitting for the representation of smaller, limited worlds and straightforward scenarios. Acting in a world that is defined by changing, unclear states, where actions often have an unpredictable outcome, is not covered by this concept. It does not picture users with non-intentional behavior or cases where people make unorthodox use of the technical system. The ability to act flexibly and the fact that action is situated in a specific local and cultural setting do not enter the focus of this particular approach. Furthermore, the logic of cognitive engineering does not consider emotions and embodiment as crucial for the cognitive process. Feminist critics of science have been particularly active in reporting, from early on, the absence of these topics from the field of artificial intelligence research (Adam 1998; Balsamo 1996).

Over the years, these issues have not only been on the agenda of (feminist) techno science critics, they have also entered the field of human-artifact interaction and computing in general. Newer concepts like "embodied cognition" mark a turn toward embodiment in parts of artificial intelligence. The manner in which concepts like emotion and embodiment are realized against the background of computer science is of major interest for the analysis of the Virtual Human interface[33].

1.3. The Embodied Agent Interface

1.3.1. Interface Metaphors

A concept of the interface based on gaps, along with the plan-oriented model of human agency, is linked not only to Donald Norman and his colleagues. It is also pervasive throughout the history of human-computer interaction[34]. Over the years, the bridging of the gap between human and computer has taken on different forms of representation, depending on differences in technical possibilities and sociocultural context. Regarding human-computer interaction, the main question for Hutchins et al. is which metaphor to follow:

> "There are two major metaphors for the nature of human-computer interaction, a conversation metaphor and a model world metaphor. In a system built on the conversation metaphor, the interface is a language medium in which the user and system have a conversation about an assumed, but not explicitly represented world. In this case, the interface is an implied intermediary between the user and the world about which things are said. In a system built on the model world metaphor, the interface is itself a world where the user can act, and that changes state in response to user actions. The world of interest is explicitly represented and there is no intermediary between user and world. Appropriate use of the model world metaphor can create the sensation in the user of acting upon the objects of the task domain themselves."
> (Hutchins et al. 1986, p. 94)

Ideally, this effect is achieved by rebuilding – at least to some degree – everyday environments, which occurs, for instance, when the desktop metaphor is used in

---

33 See Chapter 3.
34 This comes as no surprise, given Western culture's intellectual history of dichotomous structure and the modernist worldview (Fausto-Sterling 2002).

order to mirror a person's workplace environment. Accordingly, the computer users find themselves acting within a mirror-world. This world is very limited as a matter of course, but it refers to day-to-day experiences of how to deal with certain tasks through physical action, rather than through linguistic input alone. In the command-line interface, the user has to learn the computer's language, employing a specific syntax that is opposed to everyday language. Wolfgang Coy stresses that, since its establishment in the 1980s, the GUI has been predicted to be nearing its end, but that this prediction has not yet come true. This is despite the not-so-fitting metaphor of the screen as desktop, which nevertheless gives the user more support than any other realization thus far (Coy 2008, p. 315).

Graphic user interfaces follow the approach of "direct manipulation" (Shneidermann 1982; Hutchins et al. 1986), which, as the term implies, ideally leads to a scenario in which users feel directly in touch with the task they want to accomplish. According to Ben Shneidermann, the distinctively new qualities of direct manipulation are: "(1) Continuous representation of the object of interest. (2) Physical actions or labelled button presses instead of complex syntax. (3) Rapid incremental reversible operations whose impact on the object of interest is immediately visible" (Shneidermann 1982, p. 251).

Thus, when the interaction is successful, the object and its representation coincide in the user's experience. Direct manipulation interconnects human and machine very closely – at least on a phenomenological level. A sense of close interconnection and direct manipulation is established when the user's finger circulates on the touchpad of a laptop computer and the arrow symbol on the screen circulates simultaneously. Or, as I write a text with word processing software, the words appear directly on screen. To reach this effect, a further distancing from the basic working mode of the computer is pursued. The interconnection between the computer's own working and the user's side of the interface ought to be as unnoticeable as possible. While the command-line interface constantly reminds the user that she has to speak the language of the machine, direct manipulation presents an interface that aims at making the fact of the user's interaction with the machine drift into the background. This experience is qualitatively different from the knobs and dials of early computing machinery (although it does reintroduce interaction with the computer through touch, or at least through "drag and drop").

Today's experience of computer usage comes very close to the notion of the "invisible computer" (Nadin 1996) in so far as computational principles recede and the computer becomes, in experience, the interface (Schelhowe 1997, p. 148). This trend continues and is extrapolated with tablet computers, touchscreen technology, mobile computing, tangibles, and the "Internet of things". The command-line's conversation metaphor addresses the user's abstract language skills and cognitive abilities. The wording used to interact with the computer does not necessarily reflect the user's everyday language. The world metaphor brings objects and symbols to the screen. It creates the interface as a semi-physical space with windows to open and close, with objects in the background and in drawers, and with waste in a paper bin. Following this, the graphical user interface anticipates embodied interaction concepts[35]. In physical space we can move and interact with the whole body. Objects want to be touched, dragged, and dropped. We take a book from a shelf; we do not talk to the book about it. Again, this brings attention to the media artifact itself, such that awareness of interaction with the computer recedes. We could say – though at risk of oversimplification and dependence on suspicious dichotomies – that the conversation metaphor addresses the realm of the mind, whereas the world metaphor addresses the materiality of everyday environments and eventually brings the whole body into the interaction.

In his discourse analysis of interface concepts throughout history, Jörg Pflüger elaborates three basic phases of interaction with the computer: conversation, manipulation, and delegation (Pflüger 2004, p. 368). These three phases consist of Norman's conversation metaphor, the model world metaphor (as in direct manipulation), and as the model of delegation (which Pflüger introduces). This last phase, although inherent to the computer's history of taking over or substituting for human abilities (Nake 1992), gains major importance with the increase of storage and distribution power, as well as with the spread of information and communication technologies.

The shifting of metaphors also means that different senses are addressed. Issues of visibility and of what is represented on the screen vary with different interface scenarios. While direct manipulation privileges the gaze and puts an emphasis on visual relations, the conversation metaphor focuses on dialog, abstraction, and precise language skills. In this sense, direct manipulation works under the "order of the gaze" (Pflüger 2004, p. 386). Heidi Schelhowe stresses that language presumes a distance from the world of objects, whereas direct manipulation seeks to establish closeness – as with the aforementioned merging of object and representation – through immediate physical action (Schelhowe 1997, p. 166).

The effects and the success of graphical user interfaces demonstrate the convincing character of the phenomenon of direct manipulation. Even young children, who are not able to type, can interact with the touch technology of devices like smart phones or tablets. Still, what is problematic with the "world metaphor",

---

35 Of course, all interaction is embodied. I do not want to impose a false dichotomy between command-line interface as disembodied and graphical user interface as a gateway to embodied interaction. But the concept of non-verbal interaction, or multimodal interaction with a computer, nonetheless introduces a new level of what interaction in computing contains.

from an epistemological perspective, is the fact that objects do not speak for themselves. Their meaning also has to be learned in sociocultural settings, and so the meaning will vary in accordance with the variation of these settings. The emphasis on "ease of use" within the discussion that accompanies the world metaphor thus runs the risk of losing sight of the complexity, the aboutness, and the error rate of the world. Everyday surroundings and communications are, for the most part, pictured as well-functioning, easily understandable, comfortable, and universally accessible.

1.3.2. New Functionality, New Look:
The Embodied Agent Interface

From the constructor's point of view, embodied interface agents are designed to serve various purposes. Though they "are just one way of thinking about a different kind of relationship between humans and computers – it is really all about multimodal interfaces"[36], they are presented as the most "natural" way of making computer technology accessible and manageable for non-expert users. Human-human interaction is taken as a model for human-computer interaction. Since humans are experts in communicating daily through use of their whole body, a technological mirroring of their appearance and agency is pursued. Ideally, an embodied interface agent is thought of and designed as a human-like machine alter ego. Furthermore, the agent serves – depending on its area of application – as the human user's delegate, extension/substitute, and/or autonomous counterpart. In 1998, Helmut Prendinger listed various scenarios:

> "Life-like characters are used
> – as (virtual) tutors and trainers in interactive learning environments [...]
> – as presenters and sales persona on the web and at information booths [...]
> – as actors for entertainment [...]
> – as communication partners in therapy [...]
> – as personal representatives in online communities and guidance systems [...] and
> – as information experts enhancing conventional web search engines [...]"
> (Prendinger, Ishizuka 1998, p. 10)

---

36 This remark was made by Thomas Rist, of the German Institute of Artificial Intelligenz (DFKI), Saarbrücken, at the AAMAS conference, *http:www.aamas05.nl*, checked on 20/12/2013, Utrecht, July 2005. Multimodal interfaces may comprise any device in which the interation with a computational system goes beyond that of the keyboard/mouse interaction.

An aspiration for ease of use is only one characteristic of the new interface. The virtual helper, due to its character as an agent, also promises new functionality.

One major reason for the construction and employment of agents is linked to the development of information and communication technology. As Brenda Laurel puts it: "Few of us would hire an agent to push the buttons on our calculator; most of us would hire an agent to scan 5,000 pieces of junk mail" (Laurel 1990a, p. 357). Accordingly, new information and communication structures call for new interface solutions that reach beyond the desktop metaphor. Already in 1998, Terry Winograd stated that with the increasing use of the Internet, the phenomenological and semantic aspects of the computer's mediation will outstrip the technological aspects of the device (Winograd 1998, p. 152).

Pattie Maes, who works at MIT's Media Laboratory and was an early agent advocate, points out that:

> "The Internet is part of the motivation for agents – it's going to be impossible, if it isn't already, for people to deal with the complexity of the online world. I'm convinced that the only solution is to have agents that help us to manage the complexity of information. I don't think designing better interfaces is going to do it. There will be so many different things going on, so much new information and software becoming available, we will need agents that are our alter egos; they will know what we are interested in, and monitor databases and parts of networks."
> (quoted in Meek 1995)

The rise of the Internet, as well as the need to model increasingly complex real world scenarios, explains the boost of popularity that agent technology has experienced since the mid-1980s[37]. The scenario of the "embodied interface agent" became popular at a time when computing technology became both more pervasive and more accessible. The agent is presented as the "user's little helper" in times of information overflow and complex data structures. Human time is valuable. Thus, in a new form of time-sharing, routine tasks get delegated to the agent (Pflüger 2004, p. 394). The direct manipulation interface is non-obtrusive. It is conceived as a passive environment waiting for human input. In contrast, agent technology introduces pro-activeness to the interface. Part of the new functionality is that the agent "knows" when to interact with the user – for example, by giving reminders of important dates or notifying the user when a task is completed. With the command-line interface, the formal conversation between human and machine is not represented on the screen – it has a fleeting character (ibid.). Moreover, the anthropomorphic agent presents the possibility of conversing with a computer that has been cast into an actual embodied form. Following the phases of conversation,

---

[37] Agent technology is a relatively young research area, dating back to the 1970s, but basic research started in the 1980s (Reif 2001).

manipulation, and delegation, the embodied agent interface demonstrates a new phase of negotiation. The agent and the human now interact in a hybrid interspace, one that follows the model of human-human interaction and that is marked by conversation and social processes of renegotiation (Magnenat-Thalmann 2004, p. 2).

The idea of a personal agent, however, is not a new one. The history of human-computer interaction is not linear, it is instead characterized by overlapping or parallel developments, by sudden cuts, and by dead-end technological developments. In the 1950s, John McCarthy favored the idea of a "soft robot" – a software equivalent to a robot moving through physical space (Kay 1984). Oliver Selfridge[38], who also worked at the MIT at the time, coined the term "agent" a couple of years later in order to describe a software program that functions like a little worker inside the grand machinery.

Following this, agents provide a fitting idea for an application that is capable of roaming[39] the World Wide Web. The embodied agent comes into play as a form of materializing the concept of the abstract agent – a form that the human user can address more easily. It is an agent with a familiar face. Since they directly address the users, embodied interface agents, like social robots, provide the field of agent technologies with an example that is much easier (than more abstract or hidden applications) to grasp. They visualize, as a new form of interface, a change in the paradigm of computing (Wooldridge 2008). According to agent technology experts, agents provide a new metaphor, as well as new corresponding techniques, that co-evolve with computational systems.

In 1997, Oliver Selfridge wrote that "the concept of an intermediary that would act as an agent doing things you wanted done, still thrives today. Still, I am dreaming of agents that can understand and interpret high level goals and purposes. What is important? What is correct? What should be done? I want an agent to remind me, 'hey boss but yesterday you said...' or 'Professor, you want me to lie to the IRS...' or 'But, honey that's wrong....'" (Selfridge 1997). In Selfridge's vision, the agent uses natural language as input and output, just like the Librarian in the novel *Snow Crash*, where the interface agent is envisioned as fully embodied. In the novel the interface actually consists of a mixed-media world, where the agent is "fully fleshed out" (Laurel 1990a, p. 357):

---

38 In 1968, Robert Taylor and J.C.R. Licklider suggested the development of an Email-client agent named – in honor of Selfridge – as OLIVER (Pflüger 2004, p. 394).
39 Cp. Alan Turing's considerations on Intelligent Machinery. In 1948, he reflects on a machine that would "imitate any small part of a man [...] In order that the machine should have a chance of finding things out for itself it should be allowed to roam the countryside, and the danger to the ordinary citizen would be serious. [...] Thus although this method is probably the 'sure' way of producing a thinking machine it seems to be altogether too slow and impracticable." (Turing 1948, p. 9)

"A man walks into the office. The Librarian demon looks like a pleasant, fiftyish, silver-haired, bearded man with bright blue eyes, wearing a V-neck sweater over a work shirt, with a coarsely woven, tweedy-looking wool tie. The tie is loosened, the sleeves pushed up. Even though he's just a piece of software, he has reason to be cheerful; he can move through the nearly infinite stacks of information in the Library with the agility of a spider dancing across a vast web of cross-references." (Stephenson 1992, p. 107)

The narration of the Librarian sums up characteristics that are central to the "embodied agent as interface concept", or to its deployment in a hybrid interaction space: ease of use; autonomous, intelligent sorting and presenting of information; pleasant appearance and trustworthy behavior. The scenario is an augmented reality world, a concept that reaches far beyond the desktop metaphor (Cassell 2000a; Krämer, Bente 2002). After the conversation metaphor, where human and computer are engaged in dialog, and direct manipulation, where the computer serves as a task-oriented tool in a media environment, the agent metaphor serves as a solution that integrates and supersedes both concepts (Pflüger 2008, p. 323). Furthermore, the agent metaphor fits the development of human-computer interaction as it moves beyond the personal computer. Hans Dieter Hellige describes a paradigmatic shift away from the GUI and toward the point of "smart interfaces". Now, it is not only that the interface is equated with the computer, it is also that, ultimately, the whole world may serve as interface. The working modes of the machine, or the computational principles, become more and more inaccessible – often losing any sense of transparency – for the average user. Hellige describes the "total interface":

> "Through the ultimate equipment of computers with software intelligence, the 'total interface' or 'intelligent interface' is said to overcome the current disparity between people and computers, and eventually enable a 'conversation' amongst almost equivalent intelligence levels. Whereas with the 'concept of dialogue' the computer must always wait first for a highly specific input from the user, and return the feedback visually, the actively intelligent interfaces now can continuously capture all speech utterances, gestures, facial expressions, emotions, bodily movements, as well as bodily conditions and environmental conditions, interpret them and react proactively. The user is, therefore, no longer chained to the PC and its monitor, since now the human body itself and 'real world objects' serve as 'the total UI'."[40]

---

40 "Das 'totale Interface' bzw. das 'intelligente Interface' soll durch die Ausstattung des Computers mit Programm-Intelligenz endgültig die bestehende, ja inzwischen noch verschärfte Disparität zwischen Mensch und Computer aufheben und am Ende eine 'Konversation' auf annähernd gleichem Intelligenzniveau ermöglichen. Während beim 'concept of dialogue' der Computer immer erst auf die äußerst schmalbandigen Eingaben des Users warten muss und die Ergebnisse visuell rückkoppelt, erfassen die aktiven intelligenten Interfaces nun permanent alle sprachlichen Äußerungen, Gestik, Mimik, Emotionen, Körperbewegungen sowie Zustände des Körpers und der

1.3. The Embodied Agent Interface

At least on the level of concept, this means that the demarcation line between human and machine dissolves. Their relation becomes intimate. Anything, from the everyday surroundings of the home to the human body, may serve as interface. Whereas "graphical interfaces still separate the real world of the users from the virtual world of computation, PSAs[41] would set out a more natural way to move back and forth across this boundary'"[42]. Embodied agent technology demonstrates an interface solution that seeks to completely transgress the idea of the interface. Thus, as the quote by Hellige suggests, agent technology is treated as an act of liberation. Future scenarios picture, on one hand, secretive, intelligent everyday objects and, on the other, an anthropomorphic interface agent that guides users in a technologically mediated world marked by vast information and storage facilities and by an always available worldwide connectivity.

Prospectively, the embodied interface agent combines the good looks and smooth movements of an avatar with the functionality of agents[43]. The tendency to anthropomorphize inanimate machinery (or animals) is not a new move (Papapetros 2012; Schott 2011). In computer science, however, there have been strict adversaries of stressing this idea (Dijkstra 1989; Weizenbaum 1984). Enhancing the tendency to animate or anthropomorphize by means of design has been considered problematic. Others, though still critical, emphasize that the character of the computer inherently promotes anthropomorphic metaphors (Nake 2000, p. 175; Petri 1983). Brenda Laurel states:

> "All of the computer-based personae that weave through popular culture have one thing in common: they mediate a relationship between the labyrinthine precision of computers and the fuzzy complexity of man. Why is this tendency to personify interfaces so natural as to be virtually universal in our collective vision of the future? (Laurel 1990a, p. 355)

Following this, the fact that computers have agency and implement specific actions and formal behaviors contributes to their anthropomorphization. With the embodied agent interface, and in line with artificial intelligence's research agenda, this trait is actively pursued further.

Umgebung, interpretieren sie und reagieren proaktiv. Der Benutzer ist hierbei nicht mehr an den PC und seinen Bildschirm gekettet, denn nun dienen der menschliche Körper selber und 'real world objects' als 'the total UI'." (Hellige 2008, p. 69)

41 Personal Service Assistants is an alternate term for Virtual Humans or Embodied Conversational Agents.

42 "graphische Interfaces nach wie vor die reale Welt des Nutzers von der virtuellen Welt der Berechnung trennen, würden PSAs einen natürlichen Weg darstellen, ‚to move back and forth across this boundary'" (Pflüger 2008, p. 370)

43 Actually, an interface agent may consist of several sub-agents or sub-systems, depending on the definition and the technology.

1.3.3. The Spark of Life

According to Brenda Laurel, "an interface agent can be defined as a character, enacted by the computer, who acts on behalf of the user in a virtual (computer-based) environment" (Laurel 1990a, p. 356)[44]. There exist a variety of terms relating to this research area of human-computer interaction. Avatar, personal service assistant, embodied conversational agent, Virtual Human – all of these comprise virtual forms of embodiment. Although the concepts and technologies are actually gradient, the strict distinction that is made in the field of research between avatars and agents is noteworthy. Avatars are mostly seen as graphical user representations – as "dead bodies" or mere "puppets" – whereas agents are considered intelligent entities displaying personality, emotion, and social behavior (AAMAS CFP 2002). The precise point at which, and the manner in which, the artifact is considered to be animated is of importance. The avatar needs the power of the user to come to life, whereas the agent is considered lifelike by itself. Or, as Justine Cassell puts it, embodied interface agents are *More than just a pretty face* (Cassell et al. 2001). She gives an account of the transition from manually steered "pretty faces" to autonomous agents:

> "I built the very first embodied conversational agent as NSF visiting faculty at the University of Pennsylvania, in the 'Center for Human Modeling and Simulation'[45]. [...] Previously professional animators manually synthesized conversational behaviors for animated figures based on their intuitions, and they "hard wired" facial expressions and gestures. Although the intuitions of such animation artists are excellent, and hard-wiring is a satisfactory approach to regular animation, their approach cannot be extended to the generation of these behaviors in systems running independently of a human designer. My work introduced the first rule-governed, autonomous generation of verbal and non-verbal conversational behaviors in animated characters. Secondly, previous conversational interfaces or dialogue systems concentrated on the content of the conversation -- the statements and questions that advance the discourse. My work introduced for the first time a conversational agent capable of generating and understanding both those propositional components and synchronized interactional components such as back-channel speech, gestures and facial expressions." [46]

This shift from inanimate objects to animate artifacts becomes clearer by reconsidering the development of agent technologies. Although software agents usually are not "fleshed out" (Laurel 1990a, p. 357) in the manner of the Librarian in Stephenson's novel, they share, as a basic theme, an important shift in conceptualizing the way humans interact with computer technology (Wooldridge 2008;

---

44 See also Brennan (1991).
45 See: *http://www.cis.upenn.edu/~hms/home.html*, checked on 20/12/2013.
46 See: *http://web.media.mit.edu/~justine/research.html*, checked on 25/07/2013.

Reif 2001). Agents add a spark of life to the digital embodiment that is not realized with the avatar.

Interestingly, the fictional characterization of a daemon in *Snow Crash* (Stephenson 1992) matches the description of software agent technology. A software agent is considered to function as an autonomous, pro-active system. Decision-making is based on internal states, context-awareness, situated action – the exhibition of goal-directed behavior – and the ability to interact and cooperate with others. Consequently, all of these are considered to be important traits (Wooldridge 1997). Embodied agents, when serving as an interface solution, address users directly and are designed to be human-like in behavior and appearance (Cassell 2000a). The tendency to anthropomorphize the artifact, however, is inherent even to the most abstract or "hidden" agent applications.

To begin with, agents provide a new concept as well as new corresponding techniques for the development of computational systems, where "agents provide designers and developers with a way of structuring an application around autonomous, communicative components, and lead to the construction of software tools and infrastructure to support the design metaphor" (Luck et al. 2005b, p. 7). Agent technologies are considered suitable for the development of complex, open, and dynamic systems. They seem fitting for the modeling of "real world problems" and are thus said to result in applications that are capable of dealing with changes in the "state of the world" around them; whatever is characterized as "world" here is thereby integrated to be perceivable:

> "As we all know, but seem not to have fully understood (at least in the way physicists have), the world is complex and dynamic, a place where chaos is the norm, not the exception. We also know that computational systems have practical limitations, which limit the information they can access and the computations they can perform. Conventional software systems are designed for static worlds with perfect knowledge – we are instead interested in environments that are dynamic and uncertain (or chaotic), and where the computational system only has a local view of the world (i.e., has limited access to information) and is resource bounded (i.e., has finite computational resources). These constraints have certain fundamental implications for the design of the underlying computational architecture." (Bratman 1987)

From this perspective, the agent metaphor appears like a technology that is derived from co-evolution with today's globalized, multi-structured, complex world. It provides a technological metaphor that matches an epistemological stance that differs from the stance of modernist approaches. The use of agents presents itself as being closer to postmodernism or poststructuralism[47]: partialized perspective, localized and situated knowledge, regard for changing viewpoints, decentralization,

---

47 See the works of Michel Foucault, Jean-François Lyotard, Hélène Cixous, and Judith Butler.

and communication are all on the agenda. The embodied interface agent and the abstract system component have a different – yet ultimately similar – obligation: they assist the human in a place where the overload of available information and the complexity of data structures leads to an experience of chaos and excessive demands. The Librarian helps to sort through and manage information, while the agent allows the programmer to build and maintain an adequate computational system. In both cases, the human is able to delegate tasks and the artifact acts on behalf of the user or programmer. What is certain is that computer technology always functions as a kind of "Stellvertretertechnologie" (*substitute or delegate technology*) for specific human abilities[48].

However, with the agent metaphor, the power of computer artifacts to interact is emphasized and gains a new quality. The idea is that programmers using agent technology do not build a functioning, but still somewhat passive, object; what they instead initiate is an entity that is responsive in the most comprehensive way. Borrowing its epistemological stance from artificial intelligence research, agent technology thus attributes liveliness to the computer.

This paradigmatic shift becomes even clearer when contrasted with the method of object-orientation. The latter also works with a concept of software entities that obtain a certain internal state and are able – to some degree – to act upon this state (and even to interact through the passing of messages)[49]. Objects, however, do not occur as a technological analogy to the human. In *Intelligent Agents*, Michael Wooldridge summarizes that agents, in contrast to objects, have a higher level of autonomy, for they "decide for themselves whether or not to perform an action on request from another agent". In order to illustrate this, Wooldridge interestingly quotes the slogan, "objects do it for free; agents do it for money", which enhances the perception of agents as smart little workers or helpers (Wooldridge 1999, p. 35f). Probably unintentionally, this introduction of the agent into the monetary order simultaneously introduces a sexual innuendo (Braun 2012).

Furthermore, agents are said to be "capable of flexible (reactive, pro-active, social) behavior, whereas the standard object model has nothing to say about such types of behavior" (Wooldridge 1999, p. 35f). Apparently, significant boundaries are drawn here: animate agents / inanimate objects; proactive agents / passive objects. The agents obtain a subject status, whereas objects stay true to their name.

Since more and more areas of the "complex and dynamic real world" find themselves pervaded by computing technology, it comes as no surprise that approaches mirroring this unpredictable state of the complexity of the real world are favored, and that matching metaphors and subsequent technologies are developed.

---

48 Frieder Nake describes the history of information technology as the "mechanisation of mental labour" ("Maschinisierung von Kopfarbeit"), see Nake (1992).
49 For a feminist analysis of object-orientation, see Crutzen (2003).

Along these lines, we can say that agents are software programs that work, according to their internal structure, independently from further human input. They gather and process information, and they may "travel" across platforms or stay as local agents on their system's platform. Agents execute tasks autonomously as well as in collaboration with other agents (Luck et al. 2005a). This collaborative execution of tasks, which entails the design of multi-agent systems (MAS), is one of many challenges. When it comes to coordinating diverse agents and their interaction, the notion of the agent's *social ability* is established. The picture thus painted is no longer one of precise computing machinery, which operates like clockwork, it instead becomes one of a social society with intelligent behavioral units. This society is characterized by reasonable decisions that are made according to the internal structure of the agent in coordination with the agent's sense of its environment and the behavior of other agents. In multi-agent systems, the "components act more and more like 'individuals' that deserve attributes like autonomous, rational, intelligent, and so forth rather than just as 'parts'" (Weiss 1999, p. 7). Once again, what is noteworthy is the transition from machine-like parts to personification and individuality.

Certainly, transfers between the meanings of the social and the technical are not a one-way process. According to Jörg Pflüger, the concept of social interaction becomes autonomous and pervasive regardless of whether it is characterized as human-human, human-artifact, or artifact-artifact:

> "To date, we have only encountered agents in interdependence with their users, that is, as interface-agents. Here, the archetypes of an interactive negotiation between expectations and outcomes, delegation and cooperation are accommodated. The agent paradigm, though, generalises the concept of interactivity and detracts it from the coupling of human and machine. The concept of the interaction, developed in the 'interspace', is incorporated into the world of the program and distilled by modules into fundamental operation procedures. Agents ought to communicate with their own kind in similar ways as they do with their users: they ought to interact with one another, debate and cooperate."[50]

A complete leveling of human and non-human actors is a significant epistemological move. When it comes to realizing multiagent systems, however, sociality means applying strict norms and rules that constrain the behavior of the agent

---

50 "Bislang sind uns Agenten nur in Interdependenz mit ihren Usern begegnet, also als Interface-Agenten. Hier hausen die Urbilder einer interaktiven Aushandlung von Erwartungen und Leistungen, von Delegation und Kooperation. Das Agentenparadigma verallgemeinert jedoch die Idee der Interaktivität und entzieht sie der Kopplung von Mensch und Maschine. Das im 'Interspace' gewonnene Konzept der Interaktion wird in die Programmwelt eingemeindet und zur fundamentalen Operationsweise von Modulen erklärt. Agenten sollen mit ihresgleichen in ähnlicher Weise verkehren wie mit ihren Usern: sie sollen miteinander interagieren, verhandeln und kooperieren." (Pflüger 2004, p. 397)

(Boella et al. 2005; van der Hoek, Wiebe et al. 2005). Still, on the level of concept, human and machine agency basically become the same. We could say that, with the transference Pflüger describes, a vitalistic spark derived from the human gets added to the machine. Consequently, the artifact appears animated in a way that was not formerly realized. The anthropomorphizing effect shows itself, *inter alia*, in the language used. The shift from object to subject status is much more prevalent when it comes to the case of the embodied interface agent. This move may be considered as forming a new intimacy between human and machine. And, with this, Licklider's aforementioned vision of a "man-computer symbiosis" comes to mind.

Throughout the history of human-computer interaction, this symbiosis is of ongoing significance, although it progresses in a way not anticipated by Licklider. He and his colleagues suggested a further development of the conversation metaphor and proposed natural language interfaces as a solution. The conversation metaphor puts humans in dialog with the machine – and it is the term dialog that is misleading. Any "conversation" with a computer has a formal character. Susanne Maaß characterizes the computer as a "virtual communication partner with formal communication behavior"[51]. She stresses, furthermore, the virtual nature of the realization of the human-computer interface:

> "From the moment on, in which the user initiates a dialog with the computer system, a special image of the machine is offered to him on the basis of his user identification, and a special virtual machine is made available to him. This machine is virtual insofar as the user has no connection to the actual internal machine processes, but only perceives the abstract functions that the system realizes for him."[52]

In the conversation metaphor, the representation on the screen is rather lean and minimalist. With direct manipulation, the intermediary process between human and machine becomes substantial for the design of the interface. In contrast to the command-line interface, the users do not need to memorize the interaction possibilities. A new layer evolves from the space created between human and machine and presents interaction possibilities right on the screen. A quite paradoxical situation thus occurs: on one hand, the interface as an intermediary between user and artifact is significant in its materiality when it comes to design and construction;

---

51 "virtuellen Kommunikationspartner mit formalem Kommunikationsverhalten" (Maaß 1984, p. 8)
52 "Von dem Moment an, in dem der Benutzer einen Dialog mit dem Computersystem beginnt, wird ihm aufgrund seiner Benutzeridentifikation ein spezielles Bild der Maschine geboten und eine spezielle virtuelle Maschine zugänglich gemacht. Virtuell ist diese Maschine insofern, als der Benutzer losgelöst von den tatsächlichen internen Maschinenabläufen nur die abstrakteren Funktionen wahrnimmt, die das System für ihn realisiert." (Maaß 1984, p. 31)

1.3. The Embodied Agent Interface

on the other, the best interface is considered to be the one that is not felt as such by the user. As Yuang Zong and colleagues write:

> "In a sense, an interface is a necessary evil. The ideal user interface would let us perform our tasks without being aware of the interface as the intermediary. The longevity and ubiquity of the now two decades old graphical user interface should not mislead us into thinking that it is an ideal interface. Among many possible Post-GUI interfaces, multimodal interface is supposed to be the most potential one. Multimodal interface uses the character agent as the middle layer between between user and computer, interacting with user and controlling the device." (Zong et al. 2000)

This can be read, following Christina von Braun, as symptomatic for the historico-cultural development of Western society's relationship with technology, whereby "culture as a state of nature" is established. In this sense, the most successful technologies are those technologies that become naturalized in experience. Von Braun states "that simulation technologies aim consistently at making the technology itself invisible. As nature is revealed to the eyes of science, technology shows evidence of exactly the opposite: it veils itself from the eyes of the users, in order to become perceived as a natural state"[53].

Against this background, the embodied agent presents a special, almost inherently logical, interface solution. It is, or it aims to be, human in form and expression: an interface solution inspired by human nature in order to shield the user from having to deal with the technological character of the computing machine. And, with regard to the conversation metaphor and the model world metaphor, the embodied agent can be viewed as a scenario that realizes both of them. Ideally, the human can talk to it without having to learn specific commands, and it acts on the human's behalf in a computer-generated or augmented environment. Just like the fictitious Librarian in Stephenson's novel, the embodied agent can take the books off their virtual shelves for the user and, more generally, help with information retrieval and organization (Berners-Lee et al. 2001). The incommensurability of the conversation metaphor and the model world metaphor, however, has been questioned at an earlier point in the development of human-computer interaction. Already in 1990, psychologist Susan E. Brennan found that the opposition between the two metaphors is a false one. For her, human-human communication, just as it is the credo of embodied interface agent research, is the model after which

---

[53] "dass Simulationsstechnologien immer wieder darauf abzielen, die Technik selbst unsichtbar zu machen. Entschleiert sich die Natur vor den Augen der Wissenschaft, so läßt sich für die Technologie genau das Gegenteil diagnostizieren: Sie verschleiert sich vor den Augen des Benutzers, um als Naturzustand wahrgenommen zu werden" (Braun 2001, p. 103)

human-computer communication should be designed. Thus, a combination of metaphors and corresponding technologies is required:

> "[R]eal conversations actually fulfill many of the criteria for direct manipulation. For example, two people talking to each other continuously represent the things of mutual interest within their separate mental models. They can refer to anything that's within their common ground, and they can do this with less effort than it takes to point to a screen with a mouse. As they talk, they introduce new material to each other, relate it to old, coordinate their attention, and negotiate their understanding, step by step. When they understand each other, they end up behaving as if they shared a single mental model – a virtual workspace containing entities available for inspection and manipulation by both." (Brennan 1990, p. 393)

Still, for human-computer interaction, it makes a difference not just which models the users have in mind, but also what is represented and supported by the interface. It is remarkable that, within the field of human-computer interaction, the human and the humane have gained increasing importance. Furthermore, it is important to take note of what counts as human and what does not. For the most part, human is used as synonymous with nature and natural (as in easy or effortless) communication. Human/nature is set in contrast to the abstract, formal, precise, and disembodied world of the computer. Agents provide a metaphor that challenges this border. The embodied interface agent emerges as a means to *heal* the split in human-computer interaction by providing a gestalt that dresses up technology as nature.

2. Reflections

2.1. Mirrors and Windows: Amplifying the Imaginary

2.1.1. The Changing Role of the Screen

The history of the human-computer interface demonstrates how the screen or display becomes increasingly important for the interaction. Already in 1995, Deborah Lupton writes: "I am face-to-face with my computer for far longer than I look into any human face" (Lupton 1995, p. 97). This is a rather extreme statement. Yet, depending on a person's area of work or leisure activities, it may even be true for a larger number of people today. Humans watch the computer screen for feedback. The surface changes while typing on the keyboard or while dragging around symbols using the mouse or touchpad. Lupton states that the screen is an interaction point, but that it also forms a barrier to underlying technological principles: "Despite this dependency, many people who use their PC almost every day have very little knowledge of how they work, of what lies behind the bland, blue screen. Thus trust and dependency are combined with mystique" (Lupton 1995, p. 98).

The computer display obtains a mediating character. It serves as an entry surface to the content stored on the computer and to the programs by which this content can be accessed and altered. At the same time, it provides feedback about the content and relevant information on states of the machine. Furthermore, the display forms a window, or even allows for various windows/perspectives into the world that information and communication technology provide. It facilitates exchange with others. This happens even more so with the rise of mobile technology and the use of social media. The display, with its oscillating character, can be viewed as a gateway, a counterpart, a workspace.

From early on, Microsoft named its operating system and user interface "Windows". With this, the corporation turned what was "the common description of GUIs at that point of time", which was "windowing systems", into a brand name (Hanson 2010). Its logo resembles four windows, where each has a different color but the background is the same. The name Windows was meant to show that this new system encourages multiple views into the world[54].

The later development of smart mobile computers is a culmination of the earlier attempt to create a *Medium out of the Machine*[55]. The computational character of these appliances becomes almost unoticeable by focusing on the screen or display, which is the main input device for the human. Most prominently, the Apple iPad brings the role of the screen to such an extreme that the character of the machine is completely superimposed by the display. A multitouch display lets the user interact with the machine. In Apple's promotional video, the multitouch display through which the user interacts with the machine is presented as a skin; the "display comes to life" (Ive 2010). Stretching this point, the human skin makes contact with the machine "skin", which even provides physical feedback through vibration[56].

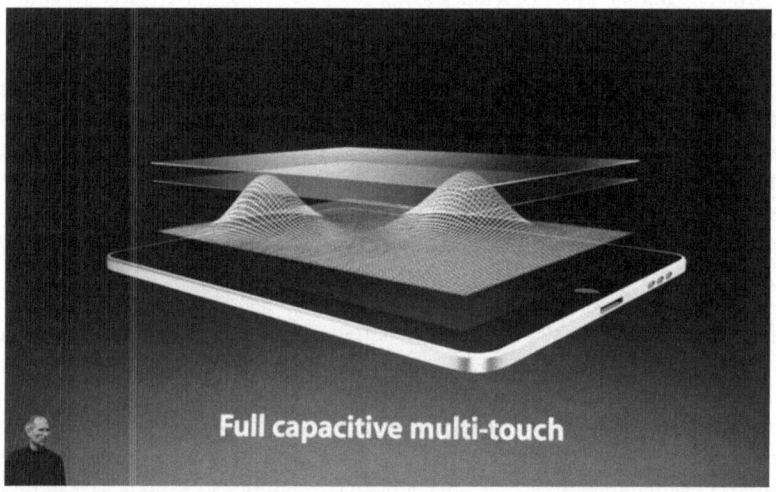

Fig. 8 iPad Multi-touch
(Source: Still taken from Steve Job's Apple iPad presentation, January 27th, 2010 - http://www.gizmodo.com, checked on 12/1/2014)

---

54 "When I joined Microsoft as Vice President of Corporate Communications, I came from the cosmetics / skin care industry where perception (branding) was far more important than reality." (Hanson 2010)
55 Medium aus der Maschine (Schelhowe 1997)
56 Skin-as-interface would be an interesting point for further analysis, for example, by rereading touch technologies against the background of psychoanalyst Didier Anzieu's *The Skin Ego (Das Haut-Ich)* (1991).

What Apple exemplifies with the iPad is the strengthening of two qualities of technology: it enhances the magic or mystic powers of the device[57]; and, relatedly, the device represents a gateway to a mixed media world that was not previously realizable. Abstract data and information patterns become something substantial, with the effect that: "It just feels right to hold the internet in your hands as you surf it. [...] And if you see something just tab it. It's completely natural, you don't even have to think about it" (Forstall 2010).

The iPad is a magic box that is experienced as containing the world, or at least as giving access to or augmenting the world. With this interface, the world of information becomes tangible. While the drag and drop navigation of the direct manipulation interface allowed the pointer device to get in the way, the human can now touch the symbols/objects directly. On a phenomenological level, looking at an object and touching it coincide in this experience. The iPad, as well as other mobile devices, point at a reconfiguration of the human-computer interface and, furthermore, at a change in the cultural use of computers in general. This change is perceived as something to be embraced:

> "That is what is important about the Apple's new mobile computer. It shows that computers have – must be – an invisible platform, one that shifts its appearance to give people the tools to complete the tasks they want to accomplish, whatever these are. To enjoy and create content. To play. To communicate. To work. By being invisible and letting the applications do the work in the most simple way possible, the power of the computer will, at last, be available for everyone. No previous knowledge required. From a 3-year-old baby to your 90-year-old grandma, people will be able to just do things." (Diaz 2010)

Again, ease of use and a design that presumably works for everybody means that the technological character of the computer recedes and the media objects are in the foreground. The ideal of computer usage is to provide a non-disruptive, "natural experience" – one that is unnoticeable as such in everyday life. Technology now includes people that are perceived as non-technological, such as the given example of a baby or a grandmother. This interface scenario presents itself as closer to the human, as sensual, already embodied, and tangible. It is far from the abstract communication mode of the command-line interface. Here again, the split between mind and body – or the overcoming of this split – becomes evident. Interestingly, with the broadening of the anticipated user group, it also becomes clear that some humans have been situated further away from abstract modes than others have been.

---

57 "It's true, when something exceeds your ability to understand how it works, it sort of becomes magical. And that's exactly what the iPad is." (Ive 2010)

2.1.2. Entering a Mathematical Wonderland

The idea that the computer screen serves as a window into another world – a world where it will eventually be possible to experience data and telecommunication with the whole human body – is not a new one in computing science.

In the 1960s, Ivan E. Sutherland, a prominent figure in the development of computer graphics (among other areas), saw the power of computing technology to visualize and *bring to life* forms of knowledge that otherwise would stay abstract[58]. Illustrating the potential power of the computer screen, Sutherland draws on the example of the living-room mirror in Lewis Carroll's famous novel *Through the Looking-Glass and What Alice Found There* (Carroll 1992b).

The idea of the computer "display as a looking-glass" (Nake 2004) can be traced back to the early years of graphic data processing and representation. Ivan E. Sutherland – whose dissertation thesis, *Sketchpad: A man-machine graphical communication system* (Sutherland 2003 (1965)), has been highly influential[59] in the field of human-computer interaction and has triggered the concepts of graphical user interfaces and direct manipulation as well as the technology of Virtual Reality – stresses that "a display connected to a digital computer gives us a chance to gain familiarity with concepts not realizable in the physical world. It is a looking glass into a mathematical wonderland" (Sutherland 1965, p. 506).

Following this, the graphic computer display does not simply aim at representing states of the world, it opens up the possibility to create a new world. It provides a window into worlds that were formerly impossible and it simultaneously creates these worlds. A mirroring and superseding of the given world is also implied. Sutherland's mathematical wonderland is not one of clear separation between the virtual and the real, it puts a claim on physical reality. He writes:

> "The ultimate display would, of course, be a room within which the computer can control the existence of matter. A chair displayed in such a room would be good enough to sit in. Handcuffs displayed in such a room would be confining, and a bullet displayed in such a room would be fatal. With appropriate programming such a display could literally be the Wonderland into which Alice walked." (Sutherland 1965, p. 508)

---

58 This aspect certainly has gained major importance. There have emerged, for example, from the practices of techno- and life sciences, new forms of representation and even material semiotic objects in co-construction with computing technology. For a critical review on knowledge and visualization see, Heintz; Benz (2001).

59 In the preface to the 2003 Cambridge electronic edition of Sutherland's thesis, the editors, Alan Blackwell and Kerry Roddin, state that the impact of his work lies more in the ideas than in the rather limited distribution of the actual executable program (Sutherland 2003 (1965)).

2.1. Mirrors and Windows: Amplifying the Imaginary

Ivan E. Sutherland is not alone with his reference. The story of Alice, or at least of her character, is quite often cited in computing. This reference to the figure of Alice in computer science[60] mostly serves to illustrate a form of embodiment that functions as a vessel for holding and translating abstract ideas[61].

---

60 And not just there: German telecommunication company Hansenet (now sold to Telefonicá) markets their products via *Alice*, who is impersonated by the young model Vanessa Hessler. In the Hansenet description, technology and model superimpose: "Alice stands for the following values, which reflect the brand and corporate philosophy and thereby determine these specifics:
Alice is uncomplicated
Alice stands for need-based solutions and simple to use technology. Alice is open and accessible. Everything about Alice is easily comprehensible, compact and clear.
Alice is decent
Alice is open and honest. Alice has no tricks up her sleeve. Alice is focused on customers and their needs and is reliable towards customers as well as partners.
Alice is lively
Alice is engaged in all that she does, is always surprised in the best sense and is herself surprising. Alice is young, fresh and energetic.
Alice is beautiful
Alice nurtures pleasant relationships, internally with colleagues as well as externally with customers, partners and suppliers. Alice has, therefore, a sensitive and agreeable appearance.
With Alice, it is possible to convey a sense of life through emotional values and simultaneously to become synonymous with the most modern communication products. With Alice, everyone can make more of their lives — through more communication, encounters and experiences."
("Alice steht für folgende Werte, die die Philosophie der Marke und des Unternehmens widerspiegeln und dabei auch das Besondere ermitteln:
Alice ist unkompliziert
Alice steht für bedarfsgerechte Lösungen und Technik, die einfach zu nutzen ist. Alice ist offen und zugänglich. Alles von Alice ist leicht nachvollziehbar, kompakt und übersichtlich.
Alice ist fair
Alice ist offen und ehrlich. Es gibt keine Tricks bei Alice. Alice orientiert sich am Kunden und seinen Bedürfnissen und ist verlässlich. Gegenüber Kunden ebenso wie Partnern.
Alice ist lebendig
Alice ist in allem, was sie tut, engagiert, überrascht immer wieder im besten Sinne und ist überraschend anders. Alice ist jung, frisch und energetisch.
Alice ist schön
Alice pflegt eine angenehme Verbindung - Intern unter Kollegen wie auch extern mit Kunden, Partnern und Lieferanten. Dabei hat Alice ein ansprechendes und angenehmes Erscheinungsbild.
Mit Alice ist es gelungen, über emotionale Werte ein Lebensgefühl zu vermitteln und gleichzeitig Synonym für modernste Kommunikationsprodukte zu sein [...] Mit Alice kann jeder mehr aus seinem Leben machen – durch mehr Kommunikation, Erfahrungen, Erleben.")
http://www.alice-dsl.de/kundencenter/export/de/unternehmen/ueber_uns/index.html, checked on 03/09/2012.

61 See, for example, the Alice programming environment by Duke University, http://www.cs.duke.edu/csed/alice/aliceInSchools/, checked on 30/04/2013, or the Alice-System,

A closer look at the narrative provides insight into what makes the figure of Alice so interesting, especially when it comes to human-computer interaction and to the interface, the ideas of interspace, and the concepts of virtual reality technologies in general.

Like the *Chronicles of Narnia* (Lewis, Baynes 2000) and other classic tales, Alice's adventures are stories of passage and transition, of overcoming a threshold or barrier where the protagonist leaves the known world behind and arrives in a fantasy world or parallel universe.

In *Through the Looking-Glass and What Alice Found There,* which is the sequel to *Alice's Adventures in Wonderland,* Lewis Carroll tells a story in which Alice arrives once more in a world that at first seems similar to the human world she is used to but that, after the entrance scene, becomes completely different. In this sequel, however, she is no longer playing outside of the house (as she was in the first novel). Alice now chats with her cat Kitty in the living room. As she sees herself and the room reflected in the mirror above the fireplace, she begins to think about the world presented in this image.

Alice continues to wonder about the substance of the things she notices in the mirror:

> "I'll tell you all my ideas about Looking-glass House. First, there's the room you can see through the glass – that's just the same as our drawing-room, only the things go the other way. I can see all of it when I get upon a chair – all but the bit just behind the fire-place. Oh! I do so wish I could see that bit! I want so much to know whether they've a fire in the winter: you never can tell, you know, unless our fire smokes, and then smoke comes up in that room too – but that may only be pretence, just to make it look as if they had a fire..." (Carroll 1992b, p. 112)

The fire "may only be pretence": it may look like a fire, but it still might not have the ability to heat the room. Alice wonders about it, but she cannot be sure. Thus, looking at the world in the mirror is not enough; in order to find out more about the quality of things on the other side, she has to take further steps. Consequently, Alice wants to be inside of the image, not just staring at it. Moreover, she suspects that the wonderland reaches further than the glimpse she catches. The world in the looking-glass might even expand beyond the current aperture. Accordingly, she comes to think of the mirror as a gateway and imagines finding a way of getting through.

---

which is "an ontology based e-commerce project which aims to support online users in the task of shopping" (Domingue et al. 2002, p. 335).

2.1. Mirrors and Windows: Amplifying the Imaginary

Fig. 9 Alice Entering the Looking-glass
(Source: Illustration by Sir John Tenniel - *http://en.wikipedia.org/wiki/Through_the_Looking-Glass#mediaviewer/File:Aliceroom3.jpg*, checked on 2/14/2014)

> "How nice it would be if we could only get through into Looking-glass House! I'm sure it's got, oh! such beautiful things in it! Let's pretend there's a way of getting through into it somehow [...] Let's pretend the glass has got soft like gauze, so that we can get through..." (Carroll 1992b, p. 113)

The mirror serves as a device to get through to the other side, as well as to provoke the existence of this alternate world in the first place. At first glance, it simply doubles the family's living room. But without this doubling effect, Alice would not wonder about the location and character of the living room and the world beyond. Alice mistrusts the simple representation of her known environment by the mirror. She thinks there might be more going on – a diffraction allowing for something new to happen, a change in perspective that could alter the course of the following events[62].

As noted above, in contrast to the earlier novel, where Alice follows the white rabbit and falls through a hole in the earth, this new transit from the everyday world to the wonderland does not take place outside. It is winter, not summer or spring, and Alice plays inside the house and enjoys the warmth of the fire. The gateway provides passage from natural surroundings to technology. The mirror, which serves as the interactive device, is human-made and belongs to the cultural

---

62 Cp. Karen Barad's continuation of Donna Haraway's concept of diffraction (Barad 2003, p. 803).

sphere. Notably, Alice does not look outside the windows into the garden. Her gaze concentrates on the interior of the house.

And, with the looking-glass, Alice really does find a technology that contains stories and that defines actors and objects. A co-construction of device, narrative, and identity takes place. As she will find out, the mirror has not simply duplicated her familiar environment. It has gotten soft and now introduces her to a fairy-tale, where seemingly dead matters come to life and the natural order of things – the world of physical laws – no longer applies. Instead, she is able to literally touch a different kind of reality. She finds surprises everywhere:

> "They don't keep this room so tidy as the other, Alice thought to herself, as she noticed several of the chessmen down in the hearth among the cinders: but in another moment, with a little 'Oh!' of surprise, she was down on her hands and knees watching them. The chessmen were walking about, two and two!" (Carroll 1992b, p. 113)

The second novel puts Alice even closer to Sutherland's notion of the mathematical wonderland that the computer may provide. Lewis Carroll was the pseudonym that Charles Lutwidge Dogson, a mathematician and tutor at Oxford, used for his art work. His interest in logic and geometry, as well as his studies in classics, are reflected in his writings[63]. Whereas *Alice's Adventures in Wonderland* centers around a deck of cards, *Alice Through the Looking-Glass* takes place on a chessboard with fields marking the squares. Many of the characters in the book are animals or chess pieces. Alice herself is a white pawn, and eventually – upon reaching the eighth square – becomes queen (Beer 2012, p. 139).

---

63 See: *http://www-history.mcs.st-and.ac.uk/Biographies/Dodgson.html*, checked on 30/04/2013.

2.1. Mirrors and Windows: Amplifying the Imaginary 63

White Pawn (Alice) to play, and win in eleven moves.

	PAGE		
1. Alice meets R. Q.	140	1. R. Q. to K. R.'s 4th	
2. Alice through Q.'s 3rd *(by railway)* .. to Q.'s 4th *(Tweedledum and Tweedledee)*	147	2. W. Q. to Q. B.'s 4th *(after shawl)*	
		3. W. Q. to Q. B.'s 5th *(becomes sheep)*	
3. Alice meets W. Q. *(with shawl)*	149 168	4. W. Q. to K. B.'s 8th *(leaves egg on shelf)*	
4. Alice to Q.'s 5th *(shop, river, shop)*	173	5. W. Q. to Q. B.'s 8th *(flying from R. Kt.)*	
5. Alice to Q.'s 6th *(Humpty Dumpty)*	179		
6. Alice to Q.'s 7th *(forest)*	200	6. R. Kt. to K.'s 2nd (ch.)	
7. W. Kt. takes R. Kt	202	7. W. Kt. to K. B.'s 5th	
8. Alice to Q.'s 8th *(coronation)*	213	8. R. Q. to K.'s sq. *(examination)*	
9. Alice becomes Queen	220	9. Queens castle	
10. Alice castles *(feast)*	223	10. W. Q. to Q. R.'s 6th *(soup)*	
11. Alice takes R.Q. & wins	230		

Fig. 10 Alice as a White Pawn
(Source: *http://ebooks.adelaide.edu.au/c/carroll/lewis/looking/images/chess.png*, checked on 14/2/2014)

The rule-orientation and formalized mode of the game of chess, which is fitting for mathematics and computing[64], finds its counterpart in the inversion of the mirror world. Here, rules of time and space run differently. As Gilian Beer writes:

---

[64] It is no coincidence that artificial intelligence research's most popular and successful project is IBM's Deep Blue chess computer, which beat the world chess champion in 1997. See *http://www-03.ibm.com/ibm/history/ibm100/us/en/icons/deepblue/*, checked on 30/04/2013.

> "The combination of the flat chessboard and the curved perspective of the mirror, suggests the still dubious insight that time and space can become curved. Especially in Alice Through the Looking Glass, Alice realises that our way of living in time is actually not absolutely without an alternative: a dumber arrangement is imaginable. The White Queen remembers: '[…] we had such a thunderstorm last Tuesday—I mean one of the last set of Tuesdays, you know.'
>
> 'In our country,' Alice interjected, 'there's only one day at a time.' To this, the Black Queen replied, 'That's a poor thin way of doing things. Now here, we mostly have days and nights two or three at a time, and sometimes in the winter we take as many as five nights together - for warmth, you know.'"[65]

This alternate conception of time and space shows that the pushing and transcending of boundaries not only marks the entry point into the wonderland, where the materiality of the mirror itself transforms, but also serves as the major theme of the story. Alice, throughout her journey, can never be quite certain what will happen next. Her body changes and she must constantly adapt to new environments. The task of distinguishing between "real reality" and "virtual reality", together with issues of identity's de- and reconstruction, are on the agenda.

The citation of Alice in computer science usually leaves the more confusing aspects of the story aside and focuses on the successful journey into the beyond as it is made through use of the mirror as an interface. With the mirror, Alice finds a world that is already on display, while the surface also holds the promise that she might experience more of this world if she "could only get through". When she finally does manage to get through, the mirror has turned into a reflective window. The narrative of Alice spans between the two meanings that accompany the concept of "utopia" or "eutopia". Utopia, in its Greek origin, means "no place", whereas the English homophone eutopia means "good place"[66].

With the mirror as interface, this "not possible world", the no-place, becomes possible. For Alice, this means excitement and freedom from adult supervision. Just because Alice is able to reach beyond the mirror, it does not mean that everybody else can do so as well. Others might be able to see her, but not "get to her":

---

[65] "Die Kombination aus flachem Schachbrett und der gekrümmten Optik des Spiegels legt die noch dubiose Erkenntnis nahe, dass Zeit und Raum geknüllt werden können. Besonders in Alice hinter den Spiegeln wird sich Alice bewusst, dass unsere Art in der Zeit zu leben, eigentlich und nicht unbedingt ohne Alternative ist: Eine dümmere Regelung ist vorstellbar. Die weiße Königin erinnert sich: '[...] das war aber mal ein Gewitter letzten Dienstag - einen aus der Schar Dienstage, meine ich natürlich.'
'Bei uns zu Haus', warf Alice ein, 'haben wir immer nur einen Tag auf einmal." Darauf sagte die Schwarze Königin: 'Ein kümmerliches, unsolides Verfahren. Wir hier nehmen immer zwei oder drei Nächte auf einmal und im Winter manchmal bis zu fünf - wegen der Kälte, versteht sich.'"
(Beer 2012, p. 142)

[66] See: *http://www.etymonline.com/index.php?term=utopia* , checked on 10/08/2014.

2.1. Mirrors and Windows: Amplifying the Imaginary 65

> "In another moment Alice was through the glass, and had jumped lightly down into the Looking-glass room. The very first thing she did was to look whether there was a fire in the fireplace, and she was quite pleased to find that there was a real one, blazing away as brightly as the one she had left behind. 'So I shall be as warm here as I was in the old room,' thought Alice: 'warmer, in fact, because there'll be no one here to scold me away from the fire. Oh, what fun it'll be, when they see me through the glass in here, and can't get at me!'" (Carroll 1992b, p. 113)

The story of Alice interweaves technology and the imaginary. And with Alice, issues of identity construction, gender coding, and representation are brought into the picture.

Teresa de Lauretis writes: "Lewis Carroll's Alice is hardly a feminist heroine; and the well-known biographical fact of the author's erotic interest in the seven year old girl for whom the book was written would suffice to discourage a sentimental reading of the character" (Lauretis 2000, p. 2). This condemnation of Carroll as a pedophile has recently become a matter of discussion (Woolf 2010), and the allegations made against him have been put into their Victorian context of romantic idealization of children and popular child photography (Rowbotham, Stevenson 2003).

However the person of Lewis Carroll is perceived, what is certain is that the placing of Alice as an allegory for technology – the woman as medium – is not unproblematic and that this does not happen by coincidence[67]. The appearance of the Alice character as an allegory for technology is in line with the dialectical role of representations of women in the history of culture in general (Bovenschen 1995). Christina von Braun and Gaby Dietze point out the core of a paradox of Western civilization:

> "Every 'advance', every innovation in the sense of a mature approach to immaturity, was accompanied by an alteration of the symbolic gender roles, which means by a change in the function that was assigned to the gendered I in the new social order."[68]

---

67 For the role of woman, women, and representation see also Teresa de Lauretis, e.g. on Lacan and Lévi-Strauss she writes: "The semiotician is puzzled. First, sexual difference is supposed to be a meaning-effect produced in representation; then, paradoxically, it turns out to be the very support of representation. [...] To say that woman is a sign (Lévi-Strauss) or the phallus (Lacan) is to equate woman with representation; but to say that woman is an object of exchange (Lévi-Strauss) or that she is the real, or Truth (Lacan), implies that her sexual difference is a value founded in nature, that it preexists or exceeds symbolization and culture." (Lauretis 2000, p. 24)

68 "Jeder 'Fortschritt', jede Neuerung im Sinne einer mündigen Annäherung an die Unmündigkeit, wurde von einer Veränderung der symbolischen Geschlechterrollen begleitet, d.h. von einem Wandel der Funktion, die dem geschlechtlichen Ich in der neuen gesellschaftlichen Ordnung zugewiesen wurde." (Braun, Dietze 1999, p. 13)

In the story, the fictional Alice, who travels through the mirror, is a substitute for the real Alice Liddell, for whom the story was originally written. The real Alice finds a doppelgänger in the fictional Alice. Furthermore, it is not quite clear if the fictional Alice experiences her adventures awake or if these adventures belong to a fictional universe in which she has been placed by her dreams – in any case, only the doppelgänger is able to pass through the mirror. Just like the Virtual Human/embodied interface agent, the fictional Alice can do this precisely because she has been written, coded, scripted. This points to the fact that computers are, at essence, semiotic machines.

2.1.3. Mirrors and Identities

At the international art exhibition Documenta 11[69], artist Ken Lum built a *Mirror Maze with 12 Signs of Depression*. For the installation, Lum took the mirror maze aesthetics found in amusement parks and linked them to mainstream views on depression. The most common sentences he discovered were sand-blasted onto the mirrors.

The mirror maze plays with refraction, structures of gaze, and identity deconstruction. Walking through the maze, visitors are confronted with their reflections. They encounter other visitors and the passing images of these visitors – as well as of themselves – in the mirrors. Furthermore, the mirror maze structure reflects and replicates itself. This creates a vast visual space that is simultaneously confined by the physical existence of the mirrors. As a visitor, your gaze reaches much farther than your movements are able to reach. Regarding this work, which is inspired by a depiction of depression[70], Lum states that "you cannot get through, where you see yourself". In the maze, when you see yourself, you are in front of the glass of the mirror, looking at your reflection. This bears similarities to Alice standing in front of the looking-glass. What is noteworthy, however, is that Alice breaks with the metaphor for depression. She actually moves through her own reflection. Once she has passed through the looking-glass, she undergoes many transformations of self and identity.

In contrast to both the standard description of depression and the famous mirror story of Narcissus, Alice is neither stuck with her image nor bound to death (whether through drowning or otherwise). Interestingly, Alice does not seem to be preoccupied with herself in the first place. She is more interested in the space

---

69 Kassel, Germany, 2002.
70 "I RUN AROUND IN A CIRCLE, CANNOT FIND AN ESCAPE ROUTE AND SEE ONLY MYSELF." See *http://www.spiegelart.de/en/testimonials.html*, checked on 10/10/2012.

2.1. Mirrors and Windows: Amplifying the Imaginary

beyond the mirror, in excitement, play, and possible adventures. She herself functions as a liminal creature. Her young age probably adds to this functioning: she is at a point where she has learned enough in order to use the mirror properly – and to not get scared, confused, distorted, or captivated by it, as does Narcissus – but she still believes in magic, too.

There are different versions of the Narcissus myth. In the most classic one, Ovid tells of how Narcissus, after having rejected the love of Ameinias, becomes cursed and falls in love with his reflection, which appears in the water. Upon realizing the unsatisfiable character of his love, Narcissus beats himself and bleeds to death. From this blood springs the narcissus flower (Brooks, Ovid 2010, part 3.337). In a variation of this, Narcissus stays at the waterside, unable to move, and wastes away[71]. Also interesting is the role of Echo, a nymph that falls in love with, and is then rejected by, Narcissus. Echo also receives a curse – one that initially leaves her with only the ability to repeat the last words said by somebody else. Subsequently, she moves into a cage, loses her body, and consists merely of her voice[72].

In his analysis of the Narcissus myth and the function of mirrors, Thomas Macho finds that Narcissus, by staring at the image, foresees his own death (Macho 2002). Even when he is still alive, he wants to become immaterial like the image. Narcissus thus becomes an allegory for the longing of transcendence promised by a disembodied existence. In contrast to the human body, the image will never fade and never perish. This theme – which is found, for example, in *The Picture of Dorian Gray* (Wilde 1993) – is what the avatar, in both its technological and religious form, depicts[73].

In the Greek reading (Pausanias et al. 191835, part 9.31.7-8), Pausanias follows Ovid's story line. Additionally, he tells a version in which Narcissus sees, in the water's reflection, his deceased twin sister with whom he was in love. Another version reports that Narcissus falls in love with the image and drowns by attempting to merge with the illusion. In a variation of this version, divine intervention causes a leaf to fall into the water, crimp the surface, and distort the image. This distortion destroys the beautiful image of Narcissus and, upon finding himself ugly, he drowns himself. After his death he transforms into a narcissus flower.

In 1912, artist Claude Cahun, whose work involved extrapolating images of herself, wrote:

---

[71] See: *http://www.theoi.com/Heros/Narkissos.html*, checked on 30/04/2013.
[72] "One day the nymph Echo saw him, driving frightened deer into his nets, she of the echoing voice, who cannot be silent when others have spoken, nor learn how to speak first herself. Echo still had a body then and was not merely a voice." (Ovid, Book III, pp. 339-401)
[73] See Chapter 3.1.2.

"The myth of Narcissus is everywhere. It haunts us. It has never ceased to inspire the things that make life perfect since the fateful day when that wave without wrinkles was captured. For the invention of polished metal derives from a clear narcissian etymology. Bronze – silver – glass: our mirrors are almost perfect. We still suffer from their vertical position; yet it's more comfortable than lying flat on your stomach on the lawn. Lazy people stretched out on their shadow admire themselves in the sky. But the slightest irritation wrenches them from their indolence, with the sound of broken glass the reflection shatters. Now would be the moment to fix the image in time as it is in space, to seize completed movements – surprise oneself from behind. 'Mirror', 'fix', these are words that have no place here. In fact what troubles Narcissus the voyeur most is insufficiency, when his own gaze is interrupted." (Cahun 2007, p. 21)

Among other aspects, Cahun points not only to the special quality of the water mirror, but also to its position in space. The technologization of the mirror produces "almost perfect mirrors" that, with their change from the horizontal to the vertical, fix the position in space. Photography, then, "fixes the mirror in time". Virtual forms of embodiment can be read as taking this one step further, and this is especially the case with avatars: as delegates of humans, they produce mirror images. Just like films, these virtual forms are animated.

Taking a step back, and reading these scenarios of mirrors, reflections, and identity against the background of user and artifact, it can be understood that Alice and Narcissus describe quite different scenarios. Alice's journey, though confusing, is successful. The interaction of Narcissus, the water, and his reflection, however, does not end well. The optical illusion of the mirroring device – its potential to diffract, but also to establish recognition or wholeness and thereby to heal the split – works differently for Alice and Narcissus.

But why does Alice escape harm? One possible explanation is that this is due to her place in the gender order. Femininity has a history of being defined by absence, fractions, and/or male projections. This might be one of the reasons why Alice's identity is not as threatened – she already serves as a reflection.

Adding to this, the Alice narration takes place at a different point in history. Klaus Theweleit remarks that Narcissus misuses the new medium. In reference to McLuhan, he stresses that any mirror is an extension of the eye and furthermore a technology of self-extension. Narcissus is not able to integrate the reflection in the water into his concept of himself. He separates it from himself and falls in love with this other: "He becomes an 'operating part' of his extension, he no longer turns his eyes away from it, he becomes a closed system"[74]. And in the end the system fails.

---

[74] "er wird zum 'bedienenden Teil' seiner Ausweitung, er wendet den Blick nicht mehr von ihr, er wird zum geschlossenen System" (Theweleit 1986, p. 369)

2.1. Mirrors and Windows: Amplifying the Imaginary

What is noteworthy is that the water mirror installs a quality, the animation of the image, that will later – with moving images and, of course, with computing technology – play an important role:

> "The mirror image, in which Narcissus saw himself, possessed a different quality than a mirror normally offers to the gaze. Water reflects not just one's own gestures, but also mixes in its waves an additional movement, that occasionally can have an uncanny effect. The reflected face appears sometimes 'to submerge', sometimes 'to emerge' — it shivers here and there and hides in the similarly quavering landscape reflecting itself in the water. The image in the water feigns a life of its own."[75]

The reflected self is thus moved by an external source. Thomas Macho links the history of looking-glasses, from Archimedes' concave mirror to modern mirrors, to the role of looking and self-conception. In this sense, the gaze must be understood as a process defined by cultural history. With respect to the embodied agent interface, the most interesting point to be drawn from this concerns the difference between pre-modern and modern mirrors. Pre-modern mirrors were used as tools – the reflection of the self in the mirror was not of interest. Adding to this disinterest in the mirror's capacity to self-reflect were the material conditions of pre-modernity and, of course, the idea of "Sehstrahlung". This prevailing concept of the ancient world regarded looking as a process in which a ray of light from the human eye scans the environment by literally touching the object. What a person sees is derived from this activity. The "Sehstrahl", or optic ray, was conceived like an entity, as an extension of the human body, but also as a physical object in the modern sense:

> "The optic ray is construed as a kind of extension of the soul, one that is associated with light and fire, and touches, so to speak, objects from a distance. The theory relies on an involuntary equivalence with physical contact, as if it were the action of a sensitive psycho-podium originating from the pupils. It follows therefore, that the optic ray in our culture is, in the strictest sense, an inconceivable entity. It has spatial qualities, is more or less fiery, reproduces itself in a linear fashion and is diverted by obstacles — all characteristics, which for us in the modern era apply to a physical object. Yet, it is in itself endowed with sensibility, a sensibility moreover, which acts beyond the body — which likewise turns it into a physical object, that,

---

75 "Das Spiegelbild, in dem sich Narzissos gesehen hat, besaß eine andere Qualität als normalerweise ein Spiegel zur Ansicht gibt. Denn Wasser reflektiert nicht nur die eigenen Bewegungen, sondern mischt mit seinen Wellen eine zusätzliche Bewegung hinein, die zuweilen gespenstisch wirken kann. Das reflektierte Gesicht scheint `mal abzutauchen, `mal aufzutauchen – zittert hin und her und versteckt sich in der ebenfalls zittrig bewegten Landschaft, die sich im Wasser spiegelt. Das Bild im Wasser gaukelt ein Eigenleben vor." (Rumpf 1999)

furthermore, conforms to nothing of what we have learnt to recognize as the anatomy and physiology of our own body."[76]

In this sense, touch and gaze coincided – or, at least, they were not as separated as they are today. Given the emergence of new interface technologies, such as the touch-surface of tablets and eye-tracking technologies, it becomes necessary to ask: Do these technologies bring about a kind of renaissance of the pre-modern means of organizing the relation between touch and gaze?

Pre-modern mirrors that corresponded with the "Sehstrahl" theory were made of brass and other polished metals. These did not have the smooth surface of the later looking-glasses. Although mirrors were first made of glass during the 14th century, in Venice, the turning point for mirror design occurred in the second half of the 17th century, in France, when Bernard Perrot applied for a patent on the rolling of bigger glass panels. From this point on, it became possible to manufacture larger mirrors that could reflect the whole body. These were used for interior design. This move marks an intersection between the construction of technology and alteration in cultural concepts. As Macho shows, the pre-modern mirrors meant transformation, fraction, and distortion – "transformation magic"[77] – whereas the new mirrors facilitate duplication, representation, and similarity – "duplication magic"[78]. Unsurprisingly, the narrations change as well: with the epoch of Romanticism, the motif of the doppelgänger emerges and replaces the scenarios of transformation (ibid.). Macho writes: "The monsters of the 'Metamorphoses' (from werewolves to sirens) were later replaced by the 'doppelgangers' of romanticism"[79]. Actually, *replaced* might not be the accurate term, since monsters, of course, continue to occur. What alters, more precisely, is the mode of transformation and the character of their hybridity[80]. The theme of the

---

76 "Der Sehstrahl wird als eine Art Auswuchs der Seele aufgefaßt, der mit dem Licht und dem Feuer verwandt ist und die Dinge sozusagen auf Distanz betastet. Die Theorie beruht auf einem unwillkürlichen Vergleich mit der Berührung, so als ob es sich um ein sensitives, aus der Pupille austretendes Psychopodium handelte. Daraus folgt, daß der Sehstrahl eine in unserer Kultur im strengen Sinne undenkbare Entität ist. Er ist räumlich, mehr oder weniger feurig, pflanzt sich geradlinig fort und wird von einem Hindernis abgelenkt - all dies Charakteristika, die für uns Moderne für ein physikalisches Objekt gelten. Und doch ist er aus sich heraus mit Sensibilität begabt, mit einer Sensibilität also, die sich außerhalb des Körpers betätigt - was ihn zugleich zu einem psychischen Objekt macht, welches aber zudem und darüber hinaus in nichts dem entspricht, was uns Anatomie und Physiologie von unserem Körper zu denken gelehrt haben." (Simon 1992, p. 232, quoted in Macho (2002)).
77 "eine Magie der Verwandlung" (Macho 2002, p. 16)
78 "eine Magie der Verdopplung" (Macho 2002, p. 16)
79 "Die Ungeheuer der 'Metamorphosen' (von den Werwölfen bis zu den Sirenen) wurden folgerichtig von den 'Doppelgängern' der Romantik abgelöst" (Macho 2002, p. 16)
80 See, for example, Kittler (1997) on writing and the double.

doppelgänger, obvious with every mirror technology, reoccurs with the Virtual Human.

In folk-psychology, the story of Narcissus is mostly cited as a warning case against vanity, self-obsession, and egoism. But, according to the history of mirrors, both Alice and Narcissus have to be seen as children of their respective times, which provide them with different media devices and, concomitantly, with different concepts of self and identity.

The Lacanian mirror stage establishes a link between the image/imago and the development of the ego (this is marked by the imaginary phase). In *The Mirror Stage as Formative of the Function of the I*, Jaques Lacan describes how the young child – still dependent, without adult language and limited in motor abilities – experiences its existence, which until this point the child assumed to be fragmented, as unified in the reflection of the mirror. It is the mirror that provides the child with the sensation of being whole, which is achieved through visualization in the form of a body. As Lacan makes clear, this stage functions through distance, or exteriority – and in doing so it alters proportions, which in effect is a means of denaturalization:

> "The fact is that the total form of the body by which the subject anticipates in a mirage the maturation of his power is given to him only as *Gestalt*, that is to say, in an exteriority in which this form is certainly more constituent than constituted, but in which it appears to him above all in a contrasting size *(un relief de stature)* that fixes it and in a symmetry that inverts it, in contrast with the turbulent movements that the subject feels are animating him." (Lacan 1977, p. 2)

The visual relation establishes boundaries and defines identities. For Lacan, the visual relation is conceived as the gaze that becomes self-conscious and that sets humans apart from animals. The gaze defines the relation between the "Innenwelt" (inner world) and the "Umwelt" (outer world), as well as the relation between the self and the other (ibid., p. 4). The mirror is an apparatus that creates a double of the child, and it is through this mirror that the child secures a concept of self that would otherwise be unrealizable. Lacan writes:

> "We have only to understand the mirror stage, as an identification, in the full sense that analysis gives to the term: namely, the transformation that takes place in the subject when he assumes an image – whose predestination to this phase-effect is sufficiently indicated by the use, in analytic theory, of the ancient term imago." (Lacan 1977, p. 2)

This "Gestalt" ("figuration") produces "formative effects in the organism" (ibid.). Lacan stresses the process-like character of identity building. One does not *have* a self, one *becomes* a self. It is an on-going performance. But this formative effect also introduces the realm of dis/illusion (techniques) (Deuber-Mankowsky 2007). It introduces doubt: with the mirror comes the possibility to conceive as well as to misconceive[81]. What follows from this is that the mirror stage is a process of learned misrecognition, a process that is actively supported by the parent – which in Lacan's picture is the mother – who reassures the child in front of the mirror ("yes, that is you"). The mirror stage introduces a split and produces an ambivalent situation: with the double in the mirror, the "I" becomes experiential – something that is looked at, as well as felt. The double, of course, is not really a double self – it is *I* and it is *not-I*. For Lacan, the self is an illusion[82].

In *Psychoanalytic Feminism*, Emily Zakin describes this early stage of self-formation as narcissistic and inherently aggressive. She writes:

> "Lacan's account of the mirror stage establishes the ego as fundamentally imaginary, formed through the infant's specular captivation with the unitary form presented in images of itself which it assumes as its own through identification. This perceptual image of coherent bodily contours and boundaries is at odds with the infant's motor incapacity and the "turbulent movements" or fragmented drives that animate its own body and processes. The ego, with its illusion of self-mastery and containment, is formed through misrecognition, an anticipatory identification with an idealized, stable, self-enclosed, citadel of self. This identification with an image of oneself sets up the ego as rivalrous, narcissistic, and aggressive. While the act of misrecognition becomes the basis for a sense of self or for self-consciousness, it is also an act of alienation, exclusion, or self-division; by erecting an imaginary ideal, representing oneself

---

81 Cp. "to recognize myself – to misconceive" – "me connaître – méconnaître", Lacan (1977, p. 6).
82 Cp. also Klaus Theweleit on Narcissus and the mirror-stage: "What is Narcissus narcotized by? By the image, that also numbs the small images, when they see someone in the mirror but they do not know that it is themselves they see. Does the image ever show 'themselves'? This is an open question. They learn to connect to themselves the, initially strange, object in the mirror; in the course of the I-development they say, 'This is I' (to that which they initially, quite correctly, had recognised as distinct from themselves, as *foreign*). The moving image in the mirror is then actually outside of someone's own body; it cannot simply be 'I'; not as image in any case. 'I' is a composite of the parts of the person that look out and the ones that are being looked at. Thus, 'I' is something that, in the moment of specific perceptions, *emerges from two*, from a 'me' and an 'other', as Lacan says."
("Wovon ist Narziß narkotisiert? Vom Bild, das auch die kleinen Bilder betäubt, wenn sie jemanden im Spiegel sehen, von dem sie noch nicht wissen, es sind sie selber. Zeigt das Bild jemals 'sie selber'? Das ist eine offene Frage. Sie lernen, das Objekt im Spiegel, das zunächst fremd ist, sich zuzuziehen; im Vorgang der Ich-Bildung sagen sie 'Das bin Ich' (zu dem, was sie zunächst - ganz richtig - als unterschieden von sich, als *fremd* erkannt haben). Das sich bewegende Bild im Spiegel ist ja tatsächlich außerhalb des eigenen Körpers; kann also nicht einfach 'Ich' sein; als Bild jedenfalls nicht. 'Ich' ist eine Zusammensetzung aus dem blickenden und aus dem angeblickten Teil der Person. 'Ich' ist also etwas, das, im Moment bestimmter Wahrnehmungen, *aus Zweien wird*, aus 'mir' und einem 'andern', wie Lacan sagt.") (Theweleit 1986, p. 357)

2.1. Mirrors and Windows: Amplifying the Imaginary 73

in a perfected image, the self is also split and rendered unconscious to itself, cut off from the multiplicity of dispersed drives." (Zakin 2011)

To understand the relevance of the mirror stage for the cases of Alice and Narcissus, and for the embodied interface agent scenario, the larger psychoanalytic background of the birth of the psychic self has to be kept in mind. To sum up very roughly[83]: Lacan specifies three phases[84] (the Real, the Imaginary, and the Symbolic) that form an irresolvable triad marked by the different levels of need, demand, and desire. Most important for my analysis of the machinic doppelgänger is the idea that the development of the self, of the I, emerges as a distancing from an assumed original sense of unity and wholeness, which is first threatened by birth. At an early stage, however, the infant does not have a sense of separation and reflection, of *I* and *other*; there are only needs that want to be fulfilled. The image or imago in the mirror is always an "ideal ego", one the child (and later adult) will never be able to fully achieve. It is a wholesome, stable, compact version of self and therefore always "other". This image serves as compensation of the always already lost experience of original unity. The Imaginary then can be described as the phase in which the child projects its ideas of "self" onto the mirror image. Judith Butler, in reference to Lacan, states: "The body in the mirror does not represent a body that is, as it were, before the mirror: the mirror, even as it is instigated by that unrepresentable body 'before' the mirror, produces that body as its delirious effect – a delirium, by the way, which we are compelled to live" (Butler 1993, p. 126).

Autonomy, or becoming a self, thus comes at the price of losing the original unity and the feeling of belonging and security. The child loses the absolute world of the Real, but gains the formation of the I, the ability to abstract and differentiate. The entry into the world of language, which plays an important role in Lacanian theory, completes the entry in the Symbolic ordering system. This is the psychic place where the child should be able to integrate the *other* in the mirror and establish a concept of self-identity. With the Symbolic, the child overcomes the dualistic split of other/self that the occurrence of the mirror stage, as part of the Imaginary, describes. This is a very interesting and very modern concept of the human self. Identity formation is reached through a dissociative process that begins by identifying oneself with the other in the mirror, and then proceeds by integrating this other. The concept of self is thus established through what is not-self, and specifically by means of a technical device. Mary Klages, however, stresses: "This is not the same as a binary opposition, where 'self' = what is not 'other', and 'other' = what

---

[83] This brief account does not do justice to the complexity of Lacanian theory, as I single out aspects that are of importance for the course of this analysis.
[84] Cp. Freud's stages of psychosexual development (Freud 2010).

is not 'self'. Rather, 'self' IS 'other', in Lacan's view; the idea of the self, that inner being we designate by 'I', is based on an image, an other" (Klages 2001).

The entrance into the Symbolic order means entering the big Other (which Lacan distinguishes from "the other" through capitalized spelling) of language and discourse. Becoming a subject, or forming an intelligible identity, means obeying the rules and laws that language provides. This stage is constituted by the "Law of the Father". The original (presumed) unity of the child with the mother is lost in order to become a subject that can speak. Feminist critics of Lacan have pointed out this strong gendering of the identity system[85]. As I have stated above, Lacan provides a denaturalized (and therefore non-biologically essentialist) concept of the gender order, but the patriarchal system is still persistent in form of the "Law of the Father"[86].

Mary Klages writes about the big Other, which is defined by the "Law or the Name of the Father":

> "The Other (capital O) is a structural position in the Symbolic order. It is the place that everyone is trying to get to, to merge with, in order to get rid of the separation between 'self' and 'other'. It is, in Derrida's sense, the CENTER of the system, of the Symbolic and/or of language itself. As such, the Other is the thing to which every element relates. But, as the center, the Other (again, not a person but a position) can't be merged with. Nothing can be in the center with the Other, even though everything in the system (people, e.g.) wants to be. So the position of the Other creates and sustains a never-ending LACK, which Lacan calls DESIRE. Desire is the desire to be the Other. By definition, desire can never be fulfilled: it's not desire for some object (which would be need) or desire for love or another person's recognition of oneself (which would be demand), but desire to be the center of the system, the center of the Symbolic, the center of language itself." (Klages 2001)

Now Alice, within the narrative of *Alice Through the Looking-Glass*, not only sees herself in the mirror, as "the other" that she has integrated into her concept of self. She also – and in contrast to Narcissus – manages to pass through this "learned misrecognition" and emerges at the other side. Because she is able to do this – which within the given ordering system (and, of course, within reality) is impossible – Alice suddenly finds herself at the center, "the Other". And here, at the center of language itself, the most peculiar things happen to her.

Wordplay, dislocation, and mathematical riddles are important parts of Carroll's work. When the White King faints, for example, Alice needs to throw ink

---

85 For a summary, see Zakin (2011) and Klages (2001).
86 "Nonetheless, while Lacan centers human experience not on the supposed biological fixity of anatomical distinctions, but on a representational economy, the phallus retains its associations with masculinity and remains the focal point of sexual identity." (Zakin 2011)

2.1. Mirrors and Windows: Amplifying the Imaginary

over him in order to revive him – and in doing so she finds a book in a foreign language, which, of course, happens to consist of mirror writing:

> "There was a book lying near Alice on the table, and while she sat watching the White King (for she was still a little anxious about him, and had the ink all ready to throw over him, in case he fainted again), she turned over the leaves, to find some part that she could read, '– for it's all in some language I don't know,' she said to herself.
> It was like this:
>
> YKCOWREBBAJ
>
> sevot yhtils eht dna ,gillirb sawT`
> ;ebaw eht ni elbmig dna eryg diD`
> ,sevogorob eht erew ysmim llA
> .ebargtuo shtar emom eht dnA
>
> She puzzled over this for some time, but at last a bright thought struck her. `Why, it's a Looking-glass book, of course! And if I hold it up to a glass, the words will all go the right way again." (Carroll 1992b, pp. 116–117)

Accordingly, in her book *Alice Doesn't*, Teresa de Lauretis places Alice in the world of discourse and semiotics. The actual Alice Liddell is an inspiration for the fictional Alice, whose identities, adventures, and new environments are produced by words. In the "Looking-glass" house, the actual constraints of Alice's former embodied reality are no longer binding – there's freedom in writing and storytelling. Alice experiences a shattering of her identity and her environment, which is brought upon her through semiotic de- and reconstruction and is mediated through the mirror interface:

> "The Looking-Glass world which the brave and sensible Alice enters, refusing to be caught up in her own reflection on the mantelpiece, is not a place of symmetrical reversal, of antimatter, or a mirror-image inversion of the one she comes from. It is the world of discourse and of asymmetry, whose arbitrary rules work to displace the subject, Alice, from any possibility of naturalistic identification." (Lauretis 2000, p. 2)

For de Lauretis, the identity de- and reconstruction is not triggered by the power of the mirror as a visual device of doubling and inversion as such. Instead she stresses the constructive power of the semiotic and locates Alice at the heart of language. With the story, the real Alice gets rewritten. Expressed in computer terminology, she is coded differently and runs a new program. The Virtual Human expresses human traits against the background of computer technology. Notably, it is a figuration that is built to mediate between the physical world of the human user and the world of technology. As a metaphor, but as an actual technology as well, the embodied agent can reach through the screen (or be projected out of it) on behalf of the user. Against the background of the suggested reading of *Alice Through the Looking-Glass*, the technology might transport an even bigger promise: namely, that the embodied agent is able, on behalf of the user, to reach where humans cannot and to merge with "the Other", right at the center of language.

2.2. "The so-called mirror is always already coded."

When I first started researching mirrors and computers, I found a post in an online discussion forum asking about how to turn the computer screen into a mirror. Literally, the post said. The person asking already had tried to scan a mirror, and now the question was whether there existed some kind of silver shiny background available for download[87]. Of course, there were a lot of answers mocking the inquirer, but there were also serious answers, like: "No. The image on a computer screen comes from a bunch of tiny little lights. What you are asking would require changing the physical properties of the display. Maybe we'll have technology like that one day, but not now." Or: "An image of a mirror will not reflect. The mirror uses highly polished metal and high quality glass to achieve this. You cannot reproduce this with a light-produced image on a computer screen."[88]

Especially this last one, "an image of a mirror will not reflect", is highly interesting because it points at the material basis, the working modes and the possibilities, of the technology. The quote also touches on issues of representation and reproduction, of copy and original, which lie at the core of the embodied agent discourse.

Apart from the technical possibilities, the computer also serves as a mirror for societal or individual changes. Sherry Turkle, who has done extensive studies on computers and concepts of self, writes: "We search for ways to see ourselves. The computer is a new mirror, the first psychological machine. Beyond its nature as an analytical engine lies its second nature as an evocative object" (Turkle 1984, p. 306). Throughout the construction processes, as well as in the reflections that the technology produces, the concept of what it means to be human becomes reformulated (Meyer-Drawe 1996). For Turkle, the computer is "the test object for

---

87 "Hi. Does anyone know if it's possible to use a background that would essentially turn my computer monitor into a mirror? Scanning a mirror doesn't work." *http://ca.answers.yahoo.com/question/index;_ylt=AszNCcDSztwp2kvHUGO5HRh6QBV.;_ylv=3?qid=20091204185236AAgu5GC*, checked on 03/09/2013

88 See: *http://ca.answers.yahoo.com/question/index;_ylt=AszNCcDSztwp2kvHUGO5HRh6QBV.;_ylv=3?qid=20091204185236AAgu5GC*, checked on 03/09/2013

postmodernism, [...] which enables us to contemplate mental life that exists apart from bodies. [...] The computer is an evocative object that causes old boundaries to be renegotiated" (Turkle 1995, p. 22). In a way, this is what fiction does, too. As I have stated earlier, the fictional Alice is able to go where Alice Liddell cannot go. The Alice who has been turned into language can transgress the limits of the real world's laws of physics – that is, at least to a certain degree, for the power of discourse is still at play.

The analogy of the computer screen and the looking-glass is not a coincidence. The computer display, like the mirror in Alice's living room, is a special kind of artifact. It may serve as a window and/or reflective tool – or even as a means for self-introspection. As Turkle makes clear, this character of the computer reaches beyond the screen. The computer as a whole is an interesting object. In reconsidering Jaques Lacan's concept of the mirror stage, software artist J.L. Andruszkiewicz brings the role of the user, or the formation of the user-self, into correspondence with the interface technology. He finds that "the computer is simultaneously a reflective and transparent machine. Transparent because it is not just about the screen and the gaze of the user, the nature of the interface goes beyond, behind the screen". And in the interaction space it all comes together, like it or not, consciously or unconsciously: "the computer's reflective nature becomes apparent because the user cannot avoid reflecting on their relation to the screen" (Andruszkiewicz 2009b). For a successful interaction, users have to react to what is happening on the screen, and their subsequent input then changes the screen. Again, computer and human form a network. They are entangled in a cybernetic feedback loop.

My analysis focuses on how humanness can be, or is sought to be, expressed against the background of computing technology. From this, a couple of central questions arise. The naïve-sounding forum post about turning the screen into a mirror kept me wondering about what kind of mirrors computers actually produce. What further possibilities does this technology offer? And how do the basic working principles determine the output?

In *Inner Workings*, John Cayley reflects on the role of code and representations in new media poetics and asks: "Is such a complex surface still a mirror?" Further on, he states:

"The so-called mirror is always already coded. The signs we read on and within its surface are themselves objects of code, produced by and informed by code. What they mean depends on the codes running at the times they were received, recorded, transmitted; depends on how they were, at one or many specific times, symbolically manipulated." (Cayley 2003)

This points to a central question, namely that of how anything can become an object that can be processed by a computer. Or, put differently, what qualities do computational objects need to possess or consist of? And, furthermore, what does this mean regarding the design of interfaces and the embodied interface agent?

2.2.1. The Interface as a Place of Sign/Signal Mediating

Computers are *Semiotic Machines* (Nadin 2007). The material world as such cannot be processed by computers, hence, there need to be modes of translation or transference. Frieder Nake states that unless something is expressed as a sign, it cannot find entry into the computational world:

> "Without the world becoming a sign, we do not get a hold of it. And without the world becoming sign, we cannot process it with a computer. In the sign, the world appears to us simultaneously as an object of knowledge and one of information processing. No wonder, that artificial intelligence emerged from this, the world constantly leads to signs. Furthermore, we need to attribute to signs the power to create the world, and foremost this is true for the computational signs."[89]

Nake emphasizes the circulating and relational character of the sign that is derived from the world but that also has formative effects, and thus always draws upon the world. For this process, Nake coined the poetic term "Zeichenhaut" – meaning that all matters must grow a skin consisting of signs (Nake 1993b, p. 168). The use of the term "Haut", or "skin", is noteworthy, for it makes a connection between the sign and the body.

For computer usage, semioticization – the growing of a skin made of signs – alone is not sufficient. Due to the character of the computer as a symbolic system or machine (Andersen 1990; Krämer 1988; Simon 1982 (1969)), further steps of abstraction and transformation need to take place, namely formalization and the building of algorithms (Nake 1993b, p. 168). Formalization means standardization. In order to achieve standardization, individual contexts, subjective viewpoints, and local stories are neglected (or at least put into a more general form). As Sybille Krämer puts it: "We understand the idea of for-

---

89 "Ohne daß die Welt zum Zeichen wird, haben wir sie bekanntlich nicht. Und ohne daß Welt zum Zeichen wird, können wir sie mit einem Computer nicht bearbeiten. Im Zeichen erscheint uns Welt gleichzeitig als Gegenstand der Erkenntnis und der informationstechnischen Bearbeitung. Kein Wunder, daß der Gedanke an künstliche Intelligenz sich entzündete, Welt führt ständig zu Zeichen. Wir müssen den Zeichen, den computertragenden schon gleich ganz, aber auch die Kraft zubilligen, Welt erst zu erschaffen." (Nake 1993b, p. 165)

2.2. "The so-called mirror is always already coded."

malization, when we can explain why we cannot tell any stories with formal descriptions"[90].
Through generalization, knowledge becomes exchangeable in an operational way. For the computer, the standardized knowledge then needs to become computable (Nake 1993b, p. 169). This is the process of constructing algorithms[91].
Each of these steps can be viewed as reductive. Computers do not process material objects as other machines might do, they process semiotic representations – descriptions of objects, bodies, environments, etc. The sign is stripped from the context and becomes computable. But, as Nake stresses, reduction is only one way of characterizing abstraction. Simultaneously, a kind of doubling effect takes place inherent to the procedure of semioticization (Nake 1993b, p. 169). Here, the constructive character of language, as pointed out above by Nake, becomes viable. With the co-constructive technologies of life- and techno sciences, new material-semiotic objects emerge. Donna Haraway points out the epistemological move made throughout the history of artificial intelligence research. She describes this move as one in which "organisms and machines alike were repositioned on the same ontological level, where attention was riveted on semiosis, or the process by which something functioned as a sign" (Haraway 1997, p. 128). Artificial intelligence research is centered around "the translation of the world into a problem of coding" (Haraway 1991a, p. 164). Or, put differently, knowledge about the world has to be made available in form of the "algorithmic sign" (Nake 2001, p. 4). Consequently, the thus reformulated knowledge recirculates in the world in the form of artifacts, simulations, or adapted knowledge.
Today, computer usage mostly means accessing the computer through graphical user interfaces. For most users, the dragging and dropping of objects across the computer screen is so familiar that they do not think twice about it. Still, the ability to use a graphical user interface is the product of learned experience. For the most part, the symbols on the screen consist of computerized abstractions of objects from a real world environment to which humans can attribute meaning. As Sybille Krämer writes: "The operations with signs take the place of operations

---

90 "Wir verstehen die Idee der Formalisierung, wenn wir erklären können, warum wir mit formalen Beschreibungen keine Geschichten erzählen können" (Krämer 1988, p. 1)
91 Cp. Sybille Krämer on simulation: "Computer-generated simulations emerge at the intersection of four developmental lines of contemporary sciences: mathematisation, modeling, visualization and digitalisation (computerisation)." ("Computergenerierte Simulationen entstehen im Kreuzungspunkt von vier Entwicklungstendenzen neuzeitlicher Wissenschaft: der *Mathematisierung, Modellierung, Visualisierung* und *Digitalisierung (Computerisierung)*.") (Krämer 2011, p. 308)

with the things themselves, and this is not just temporary, but lasting"[92]. And this process continues further than this.

From a technical perspective, the users already reach through the looking-glass. Nake, in reference to Bôdker (1990), states that people do not operate *on* the screen, but that they have to access the objects they want to alter *through* the screen:

> "Whereas, in the story, Carroll's Alice passes through the mirror into a world of which, through some heightened imagination, we can fully accept that it is the world, of which we become aware by looking at the glass of the mirror — Bôdker, in contrast, calls attention to the fact that the users of software do not operate on the glass surface of the interface, but rather that through this surface they grab onto things, which they intend to deal with."[93]

This reaching beyond the surface, beyond the image, also manifests itself with the Virtual Human, which should not just look human, but also act human.

The basic working principle on the side of the computer is signal processing. It is this principle of operating on just two states, due to the electro-physical basis, that marks the distinctiveness[94] of the computer (Schinzel 2004, p. 34). Nake describes signals as being ultimately stripped of context and meaning: "Signals are initially far from any meaning. They are what remains of the sign, when I entrust it to a machine"[95].

Following the development of interface solutions throughout the years, the crucial question seems to have been whether to "move the system closer to the user" or to "move the user closer to the system" (Norman, Draper 1986, p. 43). Simply put: from a semiotic point of view, the question is whether the signs of/on the interface are organized in a way that the user experiences them as being further away from or closer to the computational basis. The computational basis in this discourse is set as abstract and difficult to understand. It presents a sphere for experts, not the everyday user – and this is precisely because signal-processing appears to be context-free and disembodied. According to new media theorist Lev Manovich, "an electronic signal does not have a singular identity – a particular

---

92 "Die Operationen mit Zeichen treten an die Stelle der Operationen mit den Sachen selbst und dies nicht nur temporär, sondern auf Dauer." (Krämer 2011, p. 310)
93 "Dringt Carrolls Alice in der Erzählung durch den Spiegel hindurch in eine Welt ein, von der wir bei etwas gesteigerter Fantasie durchaus annehmen können, daß sie es sei, derer wir beim Blick in das Glas des Spiegels gewärtig werden – so macht Bôdker darauf aufmerksam, daß die Benutzerinnen von Software nicht auf der Glasoberfläche des Interface operieren, sondern vielmehr durch diese hindurch auf Gegenstände zugreifen, die sie zu bearbeiten vorhaben." (Nake 2004, p. 340)
94 This distinctiveness of discrete signals, too, must first be produced.
95 "Signale sind zunächst fern jeder Bedeutung. Sie sind das, was vom Zeichen übrigbleibt, wenn ich es einer Maschine anvertraue" (Nake 1993b, p. 166)

2.2. "The so-called mirror is always already coded."

state qualitatively different from all other possible states. [...] In contrast to a material object, the electronic signal is essentially mutable" (Manovich 2001, p. 132).

The signal, strictly speaking, is not a sign but a state that is changeable. Its variability increases the further away it is set from the material world. Humans, however, cannot grasp this state without attributing meaning to it, which in itself is a semiotic process. Consequently, 0 and 1 stand for this basic working principle of the computer[96].

From this perspective, the interface can be seen as the result of a process of sign mediation or transformation. According to Peter B. Andersen, "the discipline that is most easy to relate to a semiotic viewpoint is human-computer interaction (HCI) research, since it concerns itself with the system parts that are interpreted by users and are therefore used as signs" (Andersen 1990, p. 4).

Further on, Andersen specifies the actors in the interface scenario by defining the system processes, the computer based-sign and, of course, the role of the interface:

> "System processes: all possible computer processes allowed by the system structure.
>
> Computer-based sign: a sign whose expression plane is manifested in the processes changing the substance of the input and output media of the computer [...]
>
> Interface: a collection of computer-based signs, viz. all parts of system processes that are seen or heard, used and interpreted by a community of users.
>
> The important thing in this description of interface is that it denotes a relation between the perceptible parts of a computer system and its users. The system processes are substances that can be turned into expressions of computer-based signs in an interpretative process that simultaneously establishes their content." (Andersen 1990, p. 129)

Andersen stresses the relational character of the computer sign and the importance of the computer user. Interface design, in this sense, has to be aware of the co-constructive as well as the co-interpretative character of the interaction process.

As Nake states, the "algorithmic sign" is a special one – it gets interpreted simultaneously by the computer and by the user (Nake 2001, p. 4). The computer and the human participate in an on-going process of sign/signal exchange and interpretation/processing. In current interface scenarios, the computer screen plays an important role. The sign or symbol on the screen is to be interpreted by the user. Likewise, the user manipulates computational objects following the executive character of the algorithmic sign. Nake refers, once more, to *Alice Through the Looking-Glass*:

---

[96] See Plant (1997) for a cyberfeminist reconstruction of this mode.

"We have seen that the monitor's surface, the display as a looking-glass, is the place where signs, which signify, and things, which are being signified, can be manipulated at a stroke, yes, the place even, where signs that signify tools, automata and processes can be pushed, which then are put into motion, and just like the seemingly dead things in Alice's Looking-Glass House do, they can roam about. Informatics has, to put it all together, to do with signs, with signs of a new kind: with signs that are both calculated and calculating."[97]

Interface design, in this sense, means organizing the process of sign mediation in a way that the interpretative activity of the user corresponds with the functioning principle of the computer. This double-nature is the challenge software designers have to face (Nake 2001, p. 5). The computer's language in this picture appears to be precise, rule-oriented, and non-ambiguous – and the human's language appears as the opposite. For the human, a sign is relational and complex; for the computer, the signal is a state[98]. Thus, to build a manageable model the designer/programmer needs to single out certain features of an environment. The determinate character of the computer's basis limits the possibilities as well as the modes of representation.

Ivan E. Sutherland's sketchpad (Sutherland 2003 (1965)) became so renowned, among other reasons, because with it Sutherland faced, at an early point, the challenge of mediating between the abstract processes of the computer and the interpretative capacities of users who were not programmers. The power of abstraction, according to Nake, means a process of de-sensualizing (Nake 1993b, p. 173). Sutherland was looking for a way to close the gap between the rule-oriented mode of the machine and the everyday world of the user. It is here that the aforementioned "doubling effect" – the constructive effect of semiotics – enters the picture. As mentioned earlier, with the desktop metaphor, contemporary graphical user interfaces try to simulate office workplace environments. The interface is the place where a re-sensualizing of abstract movements is located. Hence, the process of sign intermediation itself is mainly characterized by a two-way translation:

---

97 "Wir haben gesehen, daß die Bildschirmoberfläche, the display as a looking-glass, der Ort ist, wo Zeichen, die bezeichnen, und Dinge, die bezeichnet werden, in einem Zug manipuliert werden können, ja, der Ort gar, wo Zeichen angestoßen werden, die Werkzeuge, Automaten und Prozesse bezeichnen, welche auch sogleich in Bewegung geraten und ganz so, wie die scheinbar toten Dinge in Alices Spiegelhaus, ihr Wesen treiben. Die Informatik hat, sagen wir es nur in einem, mit Zeichen zu tun, mit Zeichen einer neuen Art: mit Zeichen, die sowohl kalkuliert wie kalkulierend sind." (Nake 2004, p. 361)

98 "Is the sign ontologically closely connected to appearance, as a relation it always points beyond itself and is important only in connection with other signs, thus, in a computer only the total of the co-existing repertoire counts and the syntactical structuredness leading back to the substrate of signs." ("Ist das Zeichen ontologisch eng mit dem Schein verbunden, weist es als Relation immer über sich hinaus und ist belangvoll stets nur in Verbindung mit anderen Zeichen, so zählt im Computer nur das ganz auf Repertoire-Zugehörigkeit und syntaktische Strukturiertheit zurückgeführte Zeichensubstrat.") (Nake 1993a, pp. 12–13)

2.2. "The so-called mirror is always already coded."

> "The things and procedures that, after being reduced to computable signal conglomerates, dissapear within the computer and that have thus become inaccessible to our senses, are now covered by visual signs and are drawn to the display via these images in a new way."[99]

With the Virtual Human/embodied agent interface, Nake's term "Zeichenhaut" becomes remarkably literal. Virtual Humans stand for the ultimate endeavor to close the gap between user and system. They are designed to bring back the sensual dimension by providing an embodiment for the abstract and formalized algorithmic sign. In the reflection of the new mirror computer, the construction of Virtual Humans sets out for a believable "doubling effect" of the human user. Reviewing the described semiotic approach of interface design, however, the term doubling proves to be misleading. This is because doubling implies a mirroring of the world, whereas this book seeks to provide analysis of how such mirroring is always a process of de- and reconstructing (Rolf 2003). In other words, "the so-called mirror is always already coded" (Cayley 2003). In her article on the role of computer simulation in science, Sybille Krämer elaborates upon the special character of this coded mirror in contrast to the regular looking-glass, turning once more to the role of the semiotic:

> "'Virtual' is a concept of optics and refers to images formed of deceptive light waves. Mirror images are virtual objects, insofar as they deceive the viewer, suggesting that the reflected objects are located behind the mirror's surface: mirroring does not simply create a second object, but rather a second location for an object, so that completely new observation perspectives arise: objects can now be contemplated from behind and from in front or we can see ourselves with the eyes of another. Besides, mirror images are depictions without the status of a sign. That is because mirror images have – unlike artificial worlds of signs – no autonomy, but are causally (and precisely not semiotic) linked to the reflected object: thus, they cannot be fixed or altered as autonomous objects can, unless through manipulations of the reflected things themselves. Let us imagine as a thought experiment a mirror, which – unlike regular mirrors – possesses three properties: the world of the mirror receives the status of an independent semiotic representation; in this, time can be implemented and can also be made dynamic; and finally the observer does not simply remain external, but can become a participant in the reflected world. That we have designated the computer as a 'virtualization machine', then means in the horizon of our mirror metaphor: the computer is an interactive mirror of a dynamic world of symbols."[100]

---

99 "Die Gegenstände und Abläufe, die auf berechenbare Signal-Konglomerate reduziert, im Rechner verschwunden und dabei unseren Sinnen unzugänglich geworden waren, werden nun mit einer Hülle aus visuellen Zeichen umgeben und an diesen Bildern in neuer Form auf den Bildschirm gezogen." (Nake 1993b, pp. 174–175)

100 ",Virtuell' ist ein Begriff der Optik und bezieht sich auf lichtwellentäuschende Bilder. Spiegelbilder sind virtuelle Objekte, insofern sie dem Betrachter vortäuschen, dass sich die gespiegelten Objekte hinter der Spiegelfläche befinden: es wird durch Spiegelung also nicht einfach ein zweites

Users today mostly operate on the "surface shine"[101] of the symbols of light on the screen. According to Sherry Turkle, the way human-computer interaction has evolved may be described in terms of an overall shift "from a culture of calculation toward a culture of simulation" (Turkle 1995, p. 23), in which "we have learned to take things at interface value" (ibid., p. 19). Sybille Krämer also elaborates upon this trait when she talks about simulation: "Through the imitation of symptoms, the manifestation of something is suggested, something that is actually not present 'behind' or 'under' these symptoms. A surface-like behavior does not correspond to any analogous deep structure"[102]. As I have stated earlier, the embodied interface agent design seeks to simulate humanness on all levels of the application. Nevertheless, the basic computing principles show through when interacting with the machine. This may appear in the form of limitation, such as when the screen design promises something that cannot be maintained within the interaction, or in the form of possibility, such as when the appearance of a media object can be

---

Objekt, vielmehr ein zweiter Ort für ein Objekt geschaffen, so dass ganz neue Beobachtungsperspektiven entstehen: Objekte können nun von hinten und vorne betrachtet werden oder wir können uns selbst mit den Augen der anderen sehen. Allerdings sind Spiegelbilder Abbilder ohne Zeichenstatus. Denn Spiegelbilder haben – anders als artifizielle Zeichenwelten - keine Autonomie, sondern sind kausal (und eben nicht semiotisch) verknüpft mit dem gespiegelten Objekt: Sie können also nicht als autonome Objekte fixiert oder verändert werden – es sei denn durch Manipulationen an den gespiegelten Dingen selbst. Stellen wir uns wie in einem Gedankenexperiment einen Spiegel vor, der – abweichend von gewöhnlichen Spiegeln - drei Eigenschaften besitzt: Die Spiegelwelt bekommt den Status einer eigenständigen semiotischen Repräsentation; in sie kann Zeit implementiert, sie kann also dynamisiert werden; und schließlich bleibt der Betrachter nicht einfach externer Beobachter, sondern kann zum Teilnehmer der gespiegelten Welt werden. Dass wir den Computer als eine ‚Virtualisierungsmaschine' bezeichnet haben, bedeutet dann im Horizont unserer Spiegelmetapher: Der Computer ist ein interaktiver Spiegel dynamisierter Symbolwelten." (Krämer 2011, p. 313)

101 "Oberflächenglanz" (Pias 2000, p. 231)

102 "Durch die Imitation von Symptomen wird dabei die Erscheinungsform von etwas suggeriert, das ‚hinter' oder ‚unter' dieser Erscheinung gar nicht vorhanden ist. Einem Oberflächenverhalten korrespondiert keine entsprechende Tiefenstruktur" (Krämer 2011, p. 305).

Cp. ibid.: "Only because we are symbol-producing beings, who in dealing with themselves and their environment create an intermediate world made up of signs, it is that these semiotic intermediate worlds can bear traits that claim similarity to reality. Discovering similarities relies on judgement. Whether a similarity is used for a fraudulent or a truthful purpose does not change the fact that the simulation always remains tied to knowledge. Indeed – and this is crucial for the following thoughts – this knowledge refers firstly to the knowledge of the behavior of a system's surface." ("Nur, weil wir symbolproduzierende Wesen sind, die in der Auseinandersetzung mit sich selbst und ihrer Umwelt eine aus Zeichen gewirkte Zwischenwelt erschaffen, können solchen semiotischen Zwischenwelten auch Züge verliehen werden, die beanspruchen eine Ähnlichkeit zum Realen aufzuweisen. Ähnlichkeiten zu entdecken, beruht auf einem Urteil. Ob eine Ähnlichkeit nun in betrügerischer oder wahrheitssuchender Absicht genutzt wird, ändert nichts daran, dass das Simulieren stets an ein Wissen gebunden bleibt. Allerdings – und dies ist für die weiteren Überlegungen entscheidend – bezieht sich dieses Wissen zuerst einmal auf die Kenntnis des Oberflächenverhaltens eines Systems.")

changed completely with a single click. When it comes to reconstructing human appearance and behavior – as is the case with the Virtual Human research agenda, and with artificial intelligence research in general – the basic working modes of the computer provide a challenge. The model of the human has to be reconfigured against the background of the semiotic machine. The human, facing the informatic mirror, needs to pass through the provided image and into the heart of the code, or the center of the symbolic.

2.2.2. Principles of New Media Objects

In *The Language of New Media*, Lev Manovich provides a theoretic concept for the changes that accompany a world that is increasingly defined, affected, and, at least to some degree, generated by computerization (Manovich 2001). His focus is on what he calls new media objects, with an emphasis on visual media rather than on the computer as such. Like Nake's, Manovich's approach is influenced by semiotics. He asks how it is that media became "new" and finds five principles, or general tendencies (as he calls them), that differentiate new media from old (pre-computer) media objects. Nake's three steps of abstraction, as stated above, can be located here, but Manovich adds to this perspective by focusing on the media object output. The formalization and construction of algorithms, for example, is subsumed under the first principle of "Numerical Representation", and this consequently means that the new media object becomes programmable. The major advance he makes concerns the specification of the concept of digitization. In order to become digitized, objects need to undergo the two steps of sampling and quantification. "Sampling turns continuous data into *discrete* data, that is data occurring in distinct units: people, the pages of a book, pixels. Second, each sample is *quantified*, that is, it is assigned a numerical value drawn from a defined range" (Manovich 2001, p. 28).

The second step – quantification – is the significant one. "Old" media objects may contain continuous as well as discrete coding, but they are never quantified. For old media, Manovich gives the example of a motion picture film. The existence of discrete units, such as the single picture frames of the film, he traces back to modern semiotics and to the Industrial Revolution (Manovich 2001, p. 28f).

The following principles of "modularity", "automation", and "transcoding" are drawn from these first two basic modes of operation. Manovich describes modularity as "the fractal structure of new media": "Media elements, be they images, sounds, shapes, or behaviors, are represented as collections of discrete samples (pixels, polygons, vowels, characters, scripts). These elements are assembled into larger-scale objects but continue to maintain their separate identities. The objects can be combined into even larger objects – again, without losing their independence" (Manovich 2001, p. 30).

Manovich uses Macromedia Director software (the flash format, which is by now already dated) as well as the html structure of a website, or the whole World Wide Web, as examples. The success of Web 2.0 technologies and social software, such as Facebook, Twitter, or Instagram, is based on this concept of modularity.

On an obvious level, the principle of "automation" is the most relevant one for the construction of embodied agents. Manovich differentiates between "low-level" automation[103], as in the automatic correction of the red-eye effect in digital imaging, and "high-level" automation, which comprises artificial intelligence research, and with that autonomous agent technologies, whether embodied or not (Manovich 2001, p. 32f). From the principle of automation is derived the effect of experiencing something that is created without the goal-oriented help of a human. Manovich refers to projects that set out to generate semantic content in the 1970s, like works of poetry or fiction. According to Manovich, successful embodied artificial intelligence characters are now found in computer games rather than in human-computer interfaces. In contrast to Manovich's position, I have found, by reviewing material on Virtual Humans/embodied agents, that its goals differ from those that need to be attained in the design of characters in computer games. For the Virtual Human, a concept of automation needs to be applied that is closely connected to the concept of human autonomy and agency. The interaction setting also differs from that of computer games. The Virtual Human is designed to manage real world scenarios, not a story line.

"Variability", the fourth concept, is closely connected to automation as well as to modularity. Modularity is the precondition for variability and automation. It comes into play when, for example, web pages are assembled once the user accesses a site and retrieves data from the database. Some social media services allow users to employ a variation of layouts for their personal site – additional applications, like music players or slide show generators, can be easily added, and colors, scaling, typography, etc., often can be changed with just a few clicks. The popular photography application, Instagram, lets users choose different filters that give a semi-personalized look-and-feel to their pictures.

Manovich characterizes new media as matching "the postindustrial logic of 'production on demand' and 'just in time' delivery logics that were themselves made possible by the use of computers and computer networks at all stages of manufacturing and distribution" (Manovich 2001, p. 36). Throughout his analysis, he provides a sociocultural and historically embedded perspective. What is most

---

103 There is, of course, a lot more to the aspect of automation and computers. Manovich puts an emphasis on the media objects created with / by the computer.

2.2. "The so-called mirror is always already coded." 87

interesting for this book is the way he describes the core basis of the new media object and its relation to the material world, which makes it so fitting for "the postindustrial logic":

> "Because the machine is used as both showroom and factory, that is, the same computer generates and displays media – and because the media exists not as a material object but as data that can be sent through wires at the speed of light, the customized version created in response to the user's input is delivered almost immediately." (Manovich 2001, p. 37)

It is this characteristic that leads to a perception of the new media object as "liquid, mutable, variable" (ibid.). This is why (embodied) agent technology holds the promise to be omnipresent, appearing at the user interface as well as traveling the web for information. Within cyberculture, this notion of variability, as an underlying working principle of the computer, brought forward concepts of variability/interchangeability in other areas as well. This concerns concepts of the self and embodiment, in particular. Sherry Turkle finds that:

> "Dreams and beasts were the test objects for Freud and Darwin, the test objects for modernism. In the past decade, the computer has become the test object for postmodernism. The computer takes us beyond a world of dreams and beasts because it enables us to contemplate mental life that exists apart from bodies. It enables us to contemplate dreams that do not need beasts." (Turkle 1995, p. 22)

Following this, one aspect of the fascination of the computer derives from the principles Manovich describes, and implicitly from the acclaimed freedom that comes from the computer's power to abstract from the material world.

In 1990s cyberfeminist discourse, this possible distancing from embodied, real-life existence was seen as a way to deconstruct fixed, normative forms of identity (Plant 1997; Stone 1991). New online mediated forms of communication and new media art projects brought forward ideas of a post-gender playground. Of course, a simple split between the real and the virtual world, between offline and online, is – and was very soon discussed as – problematic. The often proclaimed freedom of the Internet neglects an understanding of technology that is always embedded in social contexts. It masks the embodied realities of people, the production of technology, hierarchical structures, and in- and exclusions, as well as the inequalities of distribution and access (Draude 2001). In her famous *A Cyborg Manifesto*, Donna Haraway elaborated on the paradoxical potential of techno and life sciences to simultaneously transgress and reinstate borders (Haraway 1991a). Disembodied qualities are just one part of computing. With the Virtual Human, a new form of embodiment is actively constructed. Furthermore, with ongoing computerization, abstract and non-graphic processes and products of computing are embedded in the world, and these lay claim on bodies and identities. There is a constant interchange between abstraction from the world and production of impact on the world.

The "computer as a testbed" – the effect of transference or exchange, the evocative or mirror-like nature of the computer – is what Manovich subsumes under the last, important principle of "transcoding". Transcoding – a term borrowed from computer science – is set as a meta-principle. In this sense, the computer is understood as a cultural player, with its logic affecting increasing numbers of areas. The computer, of course, always has to be regarded as a part of – and never as opposed to – the sociocultural world. Manovich coined the term transcoding to elaborate on what he calls "cultural reconceptualization". In short, this consists of the manifold, interwoven processes of translation and transfer between computer culture and culture at large. Transcoding, in particular, means that the underlying working principles of new media, which make the computer so special, will eventually transform all other spheres of knowledge and expression (Manovich 2001, p. 47)[104]. For the production of scientific knowledge, and for the realm of techno and life sciences in particular, Britta Schinzel states the impact of computer science's way of structuring, representing, and thus co-constructing knowledge:

> "The means of information technology provided by informatics, as well as their – at least implicitly brought along with informatics – formal models and algorithmic methods, are used extensively today. In both functions, algorithmic problem solving and the usage as a medium of representation, the computer is needed in all scientific fields. Informatics however does not only supply a neutral medium, it also forms scientific knowledge through its formal and technical properties, its preferred structure formations, as well as capabilities of integration and simulation."[105]

Here, transcoding describes the computer's power to favor certain forms of knowledge and knowledge construction over others.

---

104 "Computers use numerical representation and modularity so as to automate functions and offer variability within the media objects. These four traits of computer based media helps to win its broader social effect, a 'transcoding' between computer and culture, so we begin to inhabit the new forms of a computable culture." (Warner 2001)
105 "Die von der Informatik bereit gestellten informationstechnischen Mittel, sowie ihre – zumindest implizit mit ersteren transportierten – formalen Modelle und algorithmischen Methoden werden heute extensiv genutzt. In beiden Funktionen, der algorithmischen Problemlösung und der Nutzung als Repräsentationsmedium, wird der Computer für alle Wissenschaften gebraucht. Aber die Informatik stellt nicht nur ein neutrales Medium bereit, sie formt wissenschaftliches Wissen auch durch ihre formaltechnische Eigenart, ihre bevorzugten Strukturbildungen und Integrations- und Simulationsfähigkeiten." (Schinzel 2004, p. 30)

2.2. "The so-called mirror is always already coded."

Manovich mainly uses visual culture references and draws heavily on cinema as a modern cultural narrative. Conferred to the analysis of the construction of Virtual Humans, his approach helps to mark the steps that any object must undergo in order to become a new media – that is, a computerized – object. The visual appearance as well as the behavior of the interface agent is determined by these principles.

Manovich rejects the metaphor of the computer screen as merely a projective device or a device of representation. He argues rather strongly that computer generated simulation functions like a virus "which reflects who we are, while infecting us with its own alien logic" (Manovich 2000, p. 32). I have already agreed, by way of the earlier remark "that the mirror is always already coded", that the narratives that affect technological production processes do not stop at (inter)face value. In contrast to Manovich, however, I do not want to put an emphasis on the "alien logic" of the computer. Instead, I find that it is precisely because the "culture layer" and the "computer layer" (Manovich 2001, p. 46) are so closely interwoven that the computer proves to have such an pervasive impact. Furthermore, the power of the world *Through the Looking-Glass* that the computer provides is closely connected to the principles of new media – respectively the processes of abstraction from the material world and the productive power that comes with the semiotic machine. As Sherry Turkle writes, the computer *"enables us to contemplate mental life that exists apart from bodies"* (Turkle 1995, p. 22). This wish for transcendence, of which the computer is thus a manifestation, certainly is deeply rooted in Western culture. As I noted earlier, computer graphics visionary Ivan E. Sutherland stated that the computer display would eventually serve as the entry point into an Alice-like wonderland. However, he does not talk about the beings that the computer user would encounter there, and he neglects the rather deconstructive or delusional effect that the journey has on Alice's identity. Instead, the "mathematical wonderland" is pictured as a realm where the formerly invisible world of abstract concepts will become visible, and furthermore where the computer is in control over the material world. Or, put differently, the mathematical wonderland is pictured as a realm where the algorithmic sign controls the material world through the computer, which serves as a constructive, or maybe even corrective, mirror.

What makes the computer display as a looking-glass so intriguing is that it takes the film image or photograph a step further by basing them on the modes of the semiotic machine of the computer. In effect, the imagery/imaginary falls under the law of the aforementioned principles that Manovich as well as others have pointed out.

2.3. Between Science and Fiction

2.3.1. Boundary Objects

The embodied interface agent is in manifold ways a challenging object to grasp for research. It is a scenario for future human-computer interaction as well as a technology in-the-making, where a variety of prototypes already have been built. Remarkably, its design is constantly illustrated by researchers using examples from fiction. Thus, it is not only that the embodied agent has a hybrid character in concept, it is also that the way it is perceived or talked about changes with specific contexts and situations. In this sense, it can be considered a "boundary object". This was developed by Susan Leigh Star and James R. Griesemer for their study on different groups of people who contributed to the early work of the Museum of Vertebrate Zoology at the University of California in Berkeley:

> "This is an analytic concept of those scientific objects which both inhabit several intersecting social worlds [...] and satisfy the informational requirements of both of them. Boundary objects are objects which are both plastic enough to adapt to local needs and the constraints of the several parties employing them, yet robust enough to maintain a common identity across sites. They are weakly structured in common use and become strongly structured in individual-site use. These objects may be abstract or concrete. They have different meanings in different social worlds but their structure is common enough to more than one world to make them recognizable, a means of translation." (Leigh Star, Griesemer 1989, p. 393)

Although this original concept is more fitting to grasp collaborative work and can be used to analyze how people make sense of various objects and ideas that emerge within the process, it has also been used for technological artifacts in the context of work (Gal 2008). Viewing the embodied agent as a boundary object stretches the original idea even further, since this book does not provide a sociological analysis of a work flow or an organizational structure. Still, the intermediate character of the embodied agent invites the notion of boundaries and boundary crossing. The perception of the embodied agent changes, depending on whether one is a researcher in the field (and, furthermore, depending on which area), a science fiction writer, a user of the technology, or an analyst of the phenomenon of virtual embodiment. Nevertheless, the virtual mirroring of the human by way of the machine provides the common reference point. An anthropomorphic, multimodal interface is indeed "weakly structured in common use", but it has to become very specific and thus "strongly structured in individual-site use". The field of tension between those poles, the transfers and translations of the figuration and the processes of demarcation that go along with this, are of particular interest. As in a journey, they

2.3. Between Science and Fiction

form different transitional points that are marked by arriving, staying, and leaving. Anthropomorphic agents travel under various names: Embodied Conversational Agent, Personal Service Assistant, Lifelike Character (Cassell 2000a; Prendinger, Ishizuka 1998), and – perhaps most precisely – Virtual Human (Magnenat-Thalmann 2004). These artifacts form boundary objects between human and machine, between designers and users, and between science and fiction.

The embodied agent demonstrates how the demarcation line between human and non-human is constructed in an ongoing process, and how, in a productive dialog, categories such as gender and gender interdependencies entangle in a technocultural web to co-produce powerful fields of knowledge like nature, culture, self, and intelligible identity. Following this, the Virtual Human is both an abstract concept and a local practice. Embodied interface agents travel along grand Western narratives, like that of transcendence or overcoming death[106], for example, but of course they do not amount to them. Depending on the area or "community of practice" where the interface agent occurs, its character changes: in a narration, an agent may be pictured beyond any technical limits; whereas in designing an agent and eventually experiencing one as a user, the constraints of current hard- and software options and choices determine the object. One thread this analysis follows is the relation between the actual application and (some of) the narrative threads this application entails. The cultural imaginary plays a crucial role in technological design. Sociocultural anthropologist Arjun Appadurai stresses the constructive, material-semiotic character of "the imaginary", which in his view should not be underestimated:

> "The image, the imagined, the imaginary – these are all terms that direct us to something critical and new in global cultural processes: the imagination as a social practice. No longer mere fantasy (opium for the masses whose real work is somewhere else), no longer simple escape (from a world defined principally by more concrete purposes and structures), no longer elite pastime (thus not relevant to the lives of ordinary people), and no longer mere contemplation (irrelevant for new forms of desire and subjectivity), the imagination has become an organized field of social practices, a form of work (in the sense of both labor and culturally organized practice), and a form of negotiation between sites of agency (individuals) and globally defined fields of possibility. This unleashing of the imagination links the play of pastiche (in some settings) to the terror and coercion of states and their competitors. The imagination is now central to all forms of agency, is itself a social fact, and is the key component of the new global order." (Appadurai 1996, p. 31)

Appadurai defines the imaginary as a highly political field. As the intersection of science, technology, and fiction shows, this is a very crucial point to make for the Virtual Human. Moreover, the order of gender is always a symbolic order and

---

106 See Chapter 4.

never – regardless of how we define the term – a "natural" inevitability. Within the narrations that accommodate the technology, there also lies the possibility for change. This, of course, does not mean that technology is simply the material effect of the power of discourse. Rather, this point is to stress the interdependence of both fields. Technology is always embedded in a contextual setting.

This can be actively used as a design technique, as is the case, for example, with usage scenarios in participatory design or user-centered-design (Bath 2009, p. 218f). By interviewing and observing future users, knowledge can be gained about the users' work or leisure environment, typical activities, and special circumstances. Scenarios, as a method for "requirement analysis", are employed in order to turn the information into a narrative. These narratives are then presented to the users and this "enables fast feedback from the users to the designers, so that the narratives allow themselves to be easily corrected. Therefore, it is suitable as a means of requirements analysis"[107].

Adding to this, Corinna Bath stresses that scenarios also can be used as means for change:

> "Alternatively, the scenario-method can similarly be applied in order to illustrate what future technology could look like. The use of the prospective system can be represented as a narrative description of usage episodes on the basis of distinct work practices, without the actual realization of the system them or even without having determined its specification. Admittedly, the scenarios lack graphic depiction and completeness of system description."[108]

Of course, the cultural imaginary of technology, as it occurs within science fiction stories, is not a scenario design technique. Like much artificial intelligence research, the field of embodied interface agents mainly consists of basic research that does not employ user participation in early stages. However, narrations that accompany a technology do form a scenario – a grander scheme that shapes future research. Artificial intelligence, by its own research agenda, provokes questions about human nature in its contrast with computing machines. This relation revolves around terms like virtual and real, and original and copy. In the research field of anthropomorphic artifacts, these terms are linked to issues of believability,

---

107 "ermöglicht ein schnelles Feedback von den NutzerInnen an die DesignerInnen, denn die Geschichten lassen sich leicht korrigieren. Somit eignet sie sich als ein Mittel zur Anforderungsanalyse" (Bath 2009, p. 233)
108 "Die Szenarien-Methode kann jedoch andererseits ebenso eingesetzt werden, um zu veranschaulichen, wie die zukünftige Technologie aussehen könnte. Denn die Benutzung des zu entwickelnden Systems kann als erzählende Beschreibung von Benutzungs-Episoden auf der Basis der erhobenen Arbeitsabläufe dargestellt werden, ohne dass dieses bereits realisiert oder auch nur durch eine Spezifikation festgelegt worden wäre. Allerdings fehlen den Szenarien grafische Darstellung und Vollständigkeit der Systembeschreibung." (ibid.)

2.3. Between Science and Fiction

authenticity, and trust (Ruttkay 2004), which in consequence are important for a successful user-artifact interaction and the desired functioning of the application. The most important boundary seems to be the one between "the real" and "the virtual". In *Alice Through the Looking-Glass*, the boundary device is the mirror. In the case of the anthropomorphic agent, the computer screen takes this part of the boundary device. Alice turns into a collection of signs – she becomes scripture, or the semiotic version of Alice Liddell, and passes through the glass. In the case of human-computer interaction, the human falls under the law of the semiotic machine while the human's representative, the Virtual Human, passes through the screen.

Brenda Laurel, who has been a pioneer of anthropomorphic interface solutions since the early 1990s, talks about the relation between human-computer interaction and story-telling or fiction. She regards the interface as a form of theater:

"The form of a play and that of an interface are similar in a fundamental way: Both are mimetic. A mimesis is a particular kind of representation. It is a made thing, not an accidental or arbitrary one: using a pebble to represent a person is not mimetic; using a doll is. The object of mimesis (e.g., that which is intended to represent) may be a 'real' thing or a 'virtual' one. A painting, for instance, might be a mimesis of a real landscape or an imaginary one; a play may be a mimesis of events (literally a series of actions) that are taken from history or that are entirely 'made up'." (Laurel 1986, p. 70)

Laurel sets the boundary between "real" and "virtual" as "real" and "imaginary". In any case, narrations are closed systems that have an inner logic. However weird or unconventional a story may be, it needs to make sense.

The way virtual and real are used in new media culture is often not very clear or precise. In the most common sense, real reality means everyday life, the world outside the screen, while virtual reality means online worlds, forums, and communities that are accessible through the screen. This separation has always been a problematic one – not just from an epistemological point of view but in experience as well[109]. Philosopher Elena Esposito elaborates on the concept of real/virtual and the false opposition of true/untrue (authentic/non-authentic) in which the common usage places them. In contrast, she finds, virtuality has to be described as a space of alternative parallel possibilities ("Möglichkeitsraum"). As Esposito states:

"It is no coincidence that dictionaries often suggest the word 'latent' as a synonym for virtual: one or more realms of possibility beside reality, that accompany it and obstruct the distinction between true and false (and are thus indifferent in relation to this distinction) [...] This

---

109 For a summary of the interconnectedness of online and offline life, see Draude (2001).

particular relation of the virtual in regards of the separation of reality/fiction must also be considered. This is, for example, the basis of the often neglected distinction of virtuality and simulation. One speaks of possible worlds as simulated realities, and through that their specificity gets largely lost."[110]

Like Laurel, Esposito notes that these alternative spaces have their own inner logic[111]. Instead of referring to mimesis, Esposito points out the relation between simulation, virtuality, and the philosophical term of contingency. Simulation has received the role of substitution, of pretense, of as-if. But virtuality refers to an alternate world that contains real objects. As a concept, virtuality cuts the link to other realities. She writes:

> "Similar to modeling, the simulation allows to create fictional objects that 'pretend' as if they were something different than they are, yet still do so inside the semiotic paradigm. The model 'stands for' real atmospheric events. The simulation intends to reproduce some of the features of that which remains a referent as truthfully as possible.
> Virtuality in the proper sense follows a much more substantial intention; it exceeds the characteristics of the simulation and can no longer be applied to the distinction between the sign and the signified. Its goal is to make a 'concret de pensée' as an alternative dimension of reality: no fake real objects, but true virtual objects, for which the question of true reality is completely irrelevant."[112]

What is regarded as real and valid is thus a relational category within this ordering system. This important epistemological differentiation poses several problems for

---

110 "Nicht zufällig geben die Wörterbücher oft das Wort 'latent' als Synonym zu virtuell an: ein oder mehrere Möglichkeitsbereiche neben dem Realen, die es begleiten und zur Unterscheidung zwischen wahr und falsch querstehen (also ihr gegenüber gleichgültig sind) [...] Diese besondere Beziehung des Virtuellen zu der Unterscheidung Realiät/Fiktion muß also berücksichtigt werden. Das ist die Basis z.B. der oft vernachlässigten Unterscheidung von Virtualität und Simulation. Man spricht von den möglichen Welten als simulierten Realitäten, und dadurch geht ihre Spezifität weitgehend verloren." (Esposito 2003, p. 270)

111 "For the real world, as well as for the represented world it can be determined, what is respectively true or false, and both distinctions are independent from one another." ("Sowohl für die reale Welt als auch für die dargestellte Welt kann festgestellt werden, was jeweils wahr und was falsch ist, und beide Unterscheidungen sind voneinander unabhängig.") (Esposito 2003, p. 273)

112 "Die Simulation erlaubt wie die Modellierung, fiktionale Objekte zu schaffen, die 'so tun', als ob sie etwas anderes wären, doch dies innerhalb eines immer noch semiotischen Paradigmas. Das Modell 'steht für' die realen athmosphärischen Ereignisse. Die Simulation beabsichtigt, so treu wie möglich einige Eigenschaften dessen zu reproduzieren, was ein Referent bleibt.
Die Virtualität im eigentlichen Sinne verfolgt eine viel reichhaltigere Absicht; sie geht über die Eigenschaften der Simulation hinaus und kann nicht mehr auf die Unterscheidung von Zeichen und Referent bezogen werden. Ihr Zweck ist, ein 'concret de pensée' als eine alternative Realitätsdimension zu schaffen: keine falschen realen Objekte, sondern wahre virtuelle Objekte, für welche die Frage der realen Realität ganz und gar gleichgültig ist." (Esposito 2003, p. 270)

2.3. Between Science and Fiction

human-computer interaction, but it might also be viewed as a challenge. The role of the interface is, precisely as its name indicates, that of interfacing and mediating, and this involves a mixture of different levels of reality/realities. The case of the Virtual Human – who in the above ordering system is more precisely called a simulated human – forms a mixed media scenario. The embodiment of the agent needs to function in real reality. This differs from the scenario found in computer games, where users are, in most cases, immersed in an alternate virtual world.

This is the main reason why interface agents rarely appear in the form of fantasy embodiments or cartoon characters but instead strive for forms that "realistically" mirror humans. In contrast to *Alice's Adventures in in Wonderland* and *Alice Through the Looking-Glass*, the agent does not transport the human user into a fabulous land of absurdities where anything could happen. The role of the agent, furthermore, is to reside at the threshold between human and machine and to constantly move back and forth.

Still, the epistemological clarification made by Esposito provides a different outlook on computing, and especially on the design of embodied interface agents. To paraphrase Esposito, instead of designing "real false humans", the goal would be to design "real virtual humans" or rather beings, thus dismissing the idea of a human copy. At this point, research in the field of the embodied agent has in no way maxed out the "Möglichkeitsräume" ("spaces of possibilities"). Other possibilities are invited, due to the fact that computational artifacts always need to undergo a process of material-semiotic transformation. Esposito asks: "What kind of relationship exists between a real fiction and a non-present possibility?"[113] In this sense, virtual reality technology serves as space where "non-present possibilites" may come true, or where, as Sutherland states, abstract – or otherwise not experienced – concepts can be realized. The Spatial Cognition research group at the University of Bremen, Germany, for example, builds "Impossible Rooms" – spatial structures that do not abide by the laws of physics[114]. Virtual, in this sense, is not the opposite of real, but of physically not yet realized – or not realizable at all – aspects of space. In an essay on epistemological implications of new technology, Bernhard Waldenfels proposes that new technology, and virtual reality in particular, is able to question and evaluate what commonly counts as reality (Waldenfels 2003). Technology is the place where scientific visions become real, or rather, where they become experienced in a manner that extends beyond the status of thought experiments (ibid., p.224). Waldenfels emphasizes the validity of these experiments: "To the world belongs, not only what currently can be experienced,

---

[113] "Was für ein Verhältnis besteht zwischen einer realen Fiktion und einer inaktuellen Möglichkeit?" (Esposito 2003, p. 269)
[114] The "Impossible Rooms" are constructed for the Virtuesphere, see *http://www.sfbtr8.spatial-cognition.de/en/project/action/a5-actionspace/details/*, checked on 20/12/2013

but also what could potentially be experienced, that which is more or less predetermined by experience. On the basis of the potential for experience, real possibilities are distinguished from simply logical, conceptual possibilities"[115].

The embodied interface agent seeks to realize the rebuilding of a human (at least to a certain degree) for interaction purposes within the digital realm. Interestingly, the narrations that accompany the technology, while employing techno-futuristic themes, nonetheless contain traditional Western values – as is exemplified by recurring science fiction themes in artificial intelligence research.

2.3.2. Narrations

At the 2005 conference on Autonomous Agents and Multiagent Systems, in Utrecht, Netherlands, Cynthia Breazeal gave a keynote lecture about her work as a roboticist at MIT[116]. Breazeal started her talk by showing a film still from the 2001 Steven Spielberg movie, *A.I. Artificial Intelligence*.

Fig. 11 Robot Boy with Robot Teddy
(Source: Film still taken from A.I., Steven Spielberg, 2001)

---

115 "Zur Welt gehört nicht nur das aktuelle Erfahrbare, sondern auch das potentiell Erfahrbare, das in der Erfahrung mehr oder weniger vorgezeichnet ist. Aufgrund der Erfahrbarkeit unterscheiden reale Möglichkeiten sich von bloß logischen, gedachten Möglichkeiten" (Waldenfels 2003, p. 218)
116 Massachusetts Institute of Technology, Cambridge, USA

The picture shows David, a robot boy, with Teddy – an intelligent, interactive toy. To illustrate the future of artificially intelligent artifact design, Breazeal pointed at Teddy. This is a noteworthy move, particularly in so far as she did not mention the background story of the film, in which the robot boy serves as a substitute for the severely sick son of a white, upper-class heterosexual couple. By referring strictly to Teddy as a role model for future robotics, Breazeal avoids ethically controversial issues such as the cloning of humans or the threat of the Uncanny Valley[117]. With Teddy, she is still able to address human-like behavior. Although Teddy does not look human, it is an animated, intelligent, conversational artifact – one that is more like a smart child itself than a toy bear. Its design as a toy, however, stresses the character of the artifact as fun, assisting, and non-threatening.

In the opening scene of *A.I.*, Professor Hubby of Cybertronic Manufacturing proclaims that "to create an artificial being has been the dream of men since the birth of science". As in other science fiction films and novels, a future is envisioned where advanced computing technology is ubiquitous and where being human is redefined in co-evolution with the development of technology. Humans and humanoids – or, in *A.I.*, robotic androids called "mechas" – maintain a close, but asymmetric, relationship with one another: humans invent the androids in order to serve human needs, which reach from everyday household tasks to sexual pleasures. Notably, female-coded as well as lower-class areas of work are the ones being replaced by robots.

In a speech to his employees, Professor Hubby uses a woman android, Sheila, as a demonstration of current human-machine interaction, which he does not find satisfying. Although Sheila, he states, is "the perfect simulacrum of the human", she is still regarded as a mere "sensory toy with intelligent behavioral circuits". Sheila is a highly sophisticated humanoid and, for the audience, it is hardly possible to separate her from the Cybertronic staff by simply looking at her. But when Hubby, while using Sheila as an example, finally opens the front of her head in order to refer to a technical detail, the engineer-artifact relation between them becomes explicit. Professor Hubby continues by introducing a new enterprise he has in mind: "I propose that we build a robot that can love". Since Cybertronic already ships, each month, hundreds of lover robot models – robots that serve as sex workers (in the film, a male lover robot has one of the leading parts) – Hubby's audience (his employees) does not quite understand what he has in mind. Finally, he refers to a concept of love that transcends what the sensory circuits of the existing androids can comprehend. Hubby clearly distinguishes sexuality, which is linked to physical sensations of the body, from a transcendent model of pure love, which he exemplifies through a mother's care for her child[118].

---

117 See Chapter 4.1.1.
118 Cp. classical bonding theory, Bowlby ([1950] 1995).

Cybertronic's endeavor culminates in the production of the robot boy David – "the perfect child, never sick, always loving". Figure 11, the picture Breazeal used in her talk, shows David with Teddy. Still, Professor Hubby's project fails in the end. It fails not because of the artifact's inadequate appearance or behavior, but because of the human's receptivity. After the parents' biological child recovers and gets well enough, he reclaims his place in the family. The artifact itself works perfectly – it is the humans who do not hold up their place in the interaction scenario. The mother knows not only that this child is not her own flesh and blood, but also that he is not flesh and blood at all. The film stresses the validity of the material basis of life; it links the concept of humanness to the mortal, vulnerable human body, a body through whose veins flow blood – not electricity. In the course of the story, robot David goes on a journey to search for his own kind. The only one to keep it/him company is the robot Teddy. The movie *A.I.* tells a rather conservative tale about the ethics of technological reproduction and about the obstacles and losses of a high-tech world in general. The movie produces a crisis where classic modern boundaries are first threatened and then reestablished. The robot child cannot really take the place of the human child. In order to count as an intelligible child, one has to be linked to the authenticity of an organic human body.

The plot of *A.I.* demonstrates how categories like gender, heterosexual orientation, the concept of whiteness[119], and social positioning are brought into dialog with advanced scientific knowledge, and how these narratives form the contested zone of what is considered as human. The social construction of whiteness in this context is remarkable, considering the master-servant connotation the interaction concept bears.

The stepping out of human genealogy, as much as it may be desired with the creation of artificial beings, proves to be problematic in the end. As Sherry Turkle puts it:

> "A being that is not born of a mother, that does not feel the vulnerability of childhood, a being that does not know sexuality or anticipate death, this being is alien." (Turkle 1984, p. 311)

The *A.I.* film scenario provides a vision for future human-machine relationships. It touches various nodal points that are under negotiation not only in fiction but also in science. Obviously, the borderline between humans and computers is one that is not stable, but rather constantly shifting. This shifting depends on technical possibilities as well as on the scenarios that are possible to imagine. Robots and

---

119 For further references on the in/visibilty of whiteness and its relation to systematic racism see the concept of critical whiteness studies at *http://education.oxfordre.com/view/10.1093/acrefore/ 9780190264093.001.0001/acrefore-9780190264093-e-5*, checked on 30/11/2014

2.3. Between Science and Fiction

embodied agents alike bring the concept of "the human", and thus the social world, to the center of computer technology. As *A.I.* demonstrates, the desire "to create an artificial being" requires that the entirety of the human and its relationships fall under the logic of computing. According to Manovich's notion of transcoding, the film scenario shows how principles like modularity and delegation are transferred to the functioning of the nuclear family. Technology, here in form of the robot boy David, serves to reassure and stabilize this setting. Maintaining the symbolic gender order supersedes the realities of the living bodies, which are prone to illness and death.

In 2008, the US-American Defense Centers of Excellence for Psychological Health and Traumatic Brain Injury released a program call for a *Virtual Dialogue Application for Families of Deployed Service Members*. The call for a serious games application recognizes the stress military deployment puts on the family, noting young children in particular. Although technological possibilities for real-time interaction are advancing rapidly, the call looks for a technology that creates a virtual counterpart for the child:

> "Historically, families have derived comfort and support from photographs or mementos. [...] The challenge is to design an application that would allow a child to receive comfort from being able to have simple, virtual conversations with a parent who is not available 'in-person'. [...] The child should be able to have a simulated conversation with a parent about generic, everyday topics. For instance, a child may get a response from saying 'I love you', or; I miss you', or 'Good night mommy/daddy.' This is a technologically challenging application because it relies on the ability to have convincing voice-recognition, artificial intelligence, and the ability to easily and inexpensively develop a customized application tailored to a specific parent."[120]

The introductory passage about photography is remarkable. It contributes to the tone of the call, which aims at maintaining a picture of the family, almost as if the parent is not at war or in a crisis area. Even in cases where real-time communication is possible, the question is whether this interaction would not reveal too much of threatening background information. However this particular point is regarded, the technology is designed – in a manner similar to the film scenario of *A.I.* – to keep the image of the nuclear family unspoiled until the real parent comes back home.

The overlay of science and fiction scenarios is noteworthy, but not really surprising. Since advanced artificial intelligence artifacts, and especially embodied agent interfaces or social robots, are rather rarely encountered by the average

---

120 See: *http://www.dodtechmatch.com/DOD/Opportunities/SBIRView.aspx?id=OSD09-H03*, checked on 03/04/2013.

computer user, scientific talks, lectures, and articles often use science fiction stories as a reference point for demonstrating the character of the research. One fascinating aspect of science fiction is its ability to offer a place for the visualization and exaggeration of technologies that have not yet emerged in a properly scientific manner. Such technologies may develop a fictional life of their own and become part of the "imaginary public sphere" (Stone 1991, p. 1).

Technological artifacts are not developed in a blank space, they come with a history and with settings that specify them. Madeleine Akrich states that "it makes sense to say that technical objects have political strength" (Akrich 1992, p. 222). One cannot envision the artifact alone – even if it may not be explicitly stated, a fitting scenario is always needed.

In *Situating Cyberspace: The Popularisation of Virtual Reality*, Philipp Hayward refers to the presentation, in (science) fiction, of this interwoven and productive dialog between technology construction and the cultural imaginary. He makes a rather strong point by stating that, through interpretation and further development of new technology's potentials, science fiction films and novels form the grounds for their sociocultural framing, acceptance, and understanding:

> "Discussions of cyberspace have principally addressed its potential in terms of a set of applications which appear to be just beyond the technological horizon. In this sense, even when most sober and technically informed, discussions of likely social and cultural developments premised on the delivery of new technologies have followed the classic mode of (predictive) science *fiction*.
>
> And just as science fiction in general has tended to inform – or even determine – the nature, character and perceptions of subsequent science fact; so writing on cyberspace has created the conditions for a form which still principally exists in prototype.
>
> Writing ahead of actual technologies and accomplishment, virtual reality practitioners have fired the imagination of writers and the public about cyberspace much as early science fiction magazines stimulated interest in the potential of space travel." (Hayward 1993, p. 181f)

When it comes to information and communication technologies, as well as to artificial intelligence that extends beyond robotics, the cyberpunk[121] genre has played an important role.

Sandy Stone, amongst others, stresses the transgressive character of cyberpunk works, with their "massive intertextual presence not only in other literary productions of the 1980s, but in technical publications, conference topics, hardware design, and scientific and technological discourses in the large" (Stone 1991,

---

121 Cyberpunk emerged in the 1980s, first as a literary label and subsequently as a reference point for hackers, nerds, and geeks (*http://www.streettech.com/bcp/BCPtext/Glossary/gloslist.html*, checked on 20/12/2013). The genre is closely connected to the works of authors like William Gibson, Bruce Sterling, Pat Cadigan, and Neal Stephenson.

2.3. Between Science and Fiction

p. 1). Cyberpunk fiction depicts a world where virtual reality and real reality have overcome their epistemological and experiential split by merging into a sphere of mixed reality. People and objects are likewise surrounded and interpenetrated by information patterns. This captured the zeitgeist of the time with high-tech magazines like *Wired*[122] or *Mondo 2000*[123] acting as amplifiers for virtual reality practices and metaphors that envision internet technologies as providing the grounds for a digital wonderland freed from the constraints of the real world. The strong version of this vision fell into discredit as "Californian ideology" (Barbrook, Cameron 1997). Still, cyberpunk brings the aforementioned "translation of the world into a problem of coding" (Haraway 1991a, p. 164) to a head: the boundaries between the organic world and technological devices are constantly renegotiated, which leads to a multitude of interface solutions between humans and machines. In this sense, Cyberpunk serves as a conceptual playground for a prospective living with new technologies, and it has therefore sparked discussions about post- and transhumanism (Moravec 1995). The works of William Gibson, in particular, have made an impact both on the sociocultural framing of upcoming web related technologies and on their further technological development. In the novel *Neuromancer*, for example, Gibson coined the term cyberspace (Gibson 1995). Virtual reality constructors, such as Jaron Lanier, have been highly influenced by concepts elaborated in Cyberpunk (Featherstone, Burrows 1995).

An overlay of fiction narratives with existing technologies or concepts can be frequently observed. Sometimes, passages from science papers read like scenarios from science fiction. Nadia Magnenat-Thalmann, renowned for her research in Virtual Human design and construction, states:

> "The ultimate research objective is the simulation of Virtual Worlds inhabited by a Virtual Human Society, where Virtual Humans will co-operate, negotiate, make friends, communicate, group and break up, depending on their likes, moods, emotions, goals, dears, etc." (Magnenat-Thalmann 2004, p. 2)

This description sounds like an advanced version of existing online-worlds such as Second Life[124]. It also demonstrates the hybrid character of the Virtual Human/embodied interface agent, which is both a figuration and a technology.

Nadia Magnenat-Thalmann's description of an ideal virtual world reads like a version of the Metaverse, a scenario from another work of Cyberpunk. In Neal Stephenson's novel, *Snow Crash*, the world is defined by advanced ambient intelligence, pervasive computing, and virtual reality technologies (Stephenson

---

122 See: *http://www.wired.com/*, checked on 20/12/2013.
123 See: *http://hplusmagazine.com/2010/05/26/mondo-2000-history-project/*, checked on 20/12/2013.
124 See: *http://secondlife.com/*, checked on 20/12/2013.

1992)[125]. Humans "jack in and out of" the Metaverse, a computer-generated, three-dimensional world that has been created by computer hackers. The Metaverse is the global information universe and meeting point. It differs from the World Wide Web and Web 2.0 technologies in the way that it is organized like a digital mirror world with actual public and private spaces. The users move through information as if they were players in a never-ending computer game – and for this they need bodies. Or rather, they need a concept of a body that is translatable to the digital medium. They need "data body" substitutes. The human-computer interaction scenario pictured here is no longer that of a single desktop computer user sitting in front of the screen. Instead, users find themselves, depending on their various degrees of access and technological literacy, in a world where humans, robots, and agents interact. (Self-)representations, the digital bodies of users and artifacts, are called avatars. Comparable to William Gibson's definition of cyberspace in *Neuromancer*, Neal Stephenson's concept of avatars led to a popularization of the term within cyberculture. The use of this concept ranges from the labeling of simple icons in discussion forums to the naming of advanced characters in online communities or games.

In *Snow Crash*, avatars occur as user representations and as autonomous software agents – the difference is not always detectable or even necessary to detect. Software agents that represent non-users are referred to as "daemons", which is a term borrowed from the UNIX system, where daemons name programs that run in the background, performing repetitive tasks or becoming triggered into action by a particular set of circumstances. In the novel, a daemon is defined as "a robot that lives in the Metaverse. A kind of spirit that inhabits the machine, usually with some particular role to carry out" (Stephenson 1992, p. 55). Furthermore, it presents an information interface for the user, like the aforementioned Librarian – a software program that is not only able to compile and sort information autonomously, but that is also able to adapt to the user's preferences. As the interaction extends, the Librarian "learns" what is of potential interest for the specific user, an ability that is enhanced on an ongoing basis through conversations between the user and the agent. The Librarian presents a very advanced version of what e-commerce sites, such as Amazon, try to do already: learn what the user/customer likes and offer an individualized interface solution. The ideal of an interface agent as a "user's little helper" that offers non-obtrusive assistance is also depicted in William Gibson's novel *Idoru*. Here, the Music Master not only "provides musical variety", but is also there to "keep [...] company" (Gibson 1996, p. 43). Both the Librarian and the Music Master are perceived as social entities with whom the human spends time and conducts conversations. Interestingly, however, they do

---

125 In my Introduction, I mentioned the Librarian from this novel.

2.3. Between Science and Fiction

not transgress their role. They are limited to a specific application area. Most commonly, science fiction plots evolve through narration of a transgression by the non-human artifact. The tension between fear and fascination of artificial beings can also be found in research material on interface agents or social robots.

Depending on the research context, the embodied interface agent is pictured as a helper, personal assistant, friend, or user representative. Trust and believability are seen as key issues in the research field. A lack of these threatens successful user-artifact interactions and culminates, in its extreme form, in the notion of the "Uncanny Valley" effect (Mori 1970b)[126]. The embodied interface agent should be helpful, semi-intelligent, and autonomous – but only to a certain degree, as Catherine Pelachaud makes clear in a call for workshop contributions:

> "Nowadays, humanoid agents are being employed to provide information, explain pedagogical material, or sell products. But they promise even more; they can be the individualized, privileged companion of a user; they can be assisting and entertaining, and they can be emotive. By the simple fact of their human-like appearance and behavior, users tend to build up relationships with ECAs and human-like robots, just as they do with human folks. In order that the user perceives and accepts the ECA as a companion, the ECA too should maintain such a relationship. Tying and maintaining these bonds is highly related to the engagement between interactants. But engagement does not mean pervasiveness. Humanoids should not invade the user's working space, nor should they intervene at any time. Rather, they ought to gain the capability to determine when to intervene and for which reason."[127]

Brenda Laurel finds that trusting a software agent is linked to the transparency of the technology: "For most uses, an interface agent, like a dramatic character, must pass a kind of anti-Turing test in order to be effectively understood and employed by the user. We want to know that the choices and actions of our agents, whether computational or human, will not be clouded by complex and contradictory psychological variables" (Laurel 1990a, p. 363).

As with any software program, trust and believability in embodied agent research are achieved through smooth functioning and reliable implementation. With embodied agents this comprises a lot: the agent's behavior, language, emotions, and appearance should make the user comfortable and must not produce irritations (Ruttkay 2004). They should give the impression of a human, but with well defined limitations. In the Siri marketing keynote, the Apple representative stated, "Getting personal is a question of trust"[128]. Depending on whether the Virtual Human or embodied agent is designed as a salesperson, a museum guide, or a

---

126 See Chapter 4.1.
127 See: *http://www.iut.univ-paris8.fr/~pelachaud/AAMAS05*, checked on 04/01/2014.
128 Siri is an assistive application for iPhone (see Introduction). Apple Siri Introduction, 2011, see: https://www.youtube.com/watch?v=agzItTz35QQ, checked on 30/11/2014.

substitute for a family member, the level of closeness, of intimacy, with the technology changes. In any case, the role of the machine as friend(ly counterpart) is actively pursued within the field of research.

3. Realizing the Agent Interface

3.1. The Return of the Body

3.1.1. Addressing the Body

With human-computer interaction, the embodied existence of the human – that is, its situatedness in a specific time and context – obviously plays an important role. At least this should seem obvious. How – or even if – embodiment is addressed, though, varies throughout the history of the field. It changes with the specific settings, the variety of affordances, and the technical possibilities and developments. The anthropomorphic interface, with its aim to mirror the human, brings a new quality to the research field. The design goal is now a machine counterpart that resembles human bodies and behavior. As researcher Justine Cassell states:

> "Human-computer conversation has only recently become more than a metaphor. That is, just lately have designers taken the metaphor seriously enough to attempt to design computer interfaces that can hold up their end of the conversation, interfaces that have bodies and know how to use them for conversation, interfaces that realize conversational behaviors as a function of the demands of dialogue and also as a function of emotion, personality, and social convention." (Cassell 2000b, p. 2)

What is new is the active and constructive role of human embodiment. With the software agent, just as with social robotics, the reconstruction or simulation of the human becomes a topic for research. The quote by Justine Cassell points at a paradigm shift in artificial intelligence research in general: it is now prevalently understood that intelligent behavior means embodied behavior.

While it seems counter-intuitive to think of intelligence as disembodied, this has been, for a long time, the guiding principle in large parts of artificial intelligence research. This is illustrated by the fact that the term embodiment gets added to research areas in order to make its inclusion clear – as happens, for example, with embodied cognition. Stressing the term "embodiment", however, points to its former exclusion. George Lakoff and Mark Johnson, for example, when elaborating on Western culture and cognitive concepts, point out the challenges that the integration of embodiment holds for the conception of knowledge in this area (Lakoff, Johnson 1999).

At the Dagstuhl seminar in 2003, computer scientists Rolf Pfeifer and Fumiya Iida talk about newer developments and changes in concepts of cognitive abilities:

> "When the field started initially, roughly half a century ago, intelligence was essentially viewed as a computational process. Research topics included abstract problem solving and reasoning, knowledge representation, theorem proving, formal games like chess, search techniques, and – written – natural language, topics normally associated with higher level intelligence. [...]
>
> This GOFAI (Good Old-Fashioned Artificial Intelligence) still exists, but a newer concept is that of embodied artificial intelligence, which comprises a paradigm that employs the synthetic methodology which has three goals: (1) understanding biological systems, (2) abstracting general principles of intelligent behavior, and (3) the application of this knowledge to build artificial systems such as robots or intelligent devices in general. As a result, the modern, embodied approach started to move out of computer science laboratories more into robotics and engineering or biology labs." (Iida 2004)

Various points are noteworthy here: first, there are several notions of intelligence, which get rated differently. Logical and abstract thinking are described as "higher forms" of intelligence. At the same time, these are considered to be farthest away or most easily abstracted from the body. Thus, logical thinking and "pure reasoning" is reconfigured as more readily transferable to a computer. It comes as no surprise that artificial intelligence's most convincing examples are in areas of human thinking that are already rule-oriented or that rely on a mathematical basis (Weber, Bath 2004, pp. 9–10). The famous chess example of IBM's Deep Blue[129] illustrates this.

Second, it is noted that the body is needed for interaction with the world. This brings computer science in contact with other fields, such as robotics, engineering, material sciences, or biology – areas that deal with the materialities and consistencies of embodiment rather than with purely semiotic, abstracted representations of it. In the discourse of artificial intelligence, moving out of the computer laboratory means leaving the well-defined space of Nake's principles of semioticization, formalization, and algorithms[130]. It brings in all the messiness and unpredictability of the material world and binds objects and bodies to the laws of physics. At the aforementioned Dagstuhl seminar, Pfeifer and Iida remark:

> "A crucial aspect of embodiment is that it requires working with real world physical systems, i.e. robots. Computers and robots are an entirely different ball game: computers are neat and clean, they have clearly defined inputs and outputs, and anybody can use them, can program

---

129 See: *http://www-03.ibm.com/ibm/history/ibm100/us/en/icons/deepblue/*, checked on 20/12/2013.
130 See Chapter 2.2.1.

them, and can perform simulations. Computers also have for the better part only very limited types of interaction with the outside world: input is via keyboard or mouse click, and output is via display panel. In other words, the 'bandwidth' of communication with the environment is extremely low. Also computers follow clearly defined 'input processing' output scheme that has, by the way, shaped the way we think about intelligent systems and has become the guiding metaphor of the classical cognitivistic approach. Robots, by contrast, have a much wider sensorymotor repertoire that enables a tight coupling with the outside world and the computer metaphor of input-processing-output can no longer be directly applied." (Iida 2004)

By failing to address the body as a key factor, "Good Old-Fashioned Artificial Intelligence" has obstructed a wider notion of human intelligence in the field. This exclusion has led to a negligence of other topics as well: emotion, and context or situatedness, which are tied to the body or to affordances of the physical world. Feminist critics of science have questioned the field's traditional concept of intelligence, which fails to provide knowledge about or validation of the body. Alison Adam questions symbolic artificial intelligence research for its disembodied and decontextualized understanding of intelligence – an understanding that accords with Western modernist thought (Adam 1998, p. 155).

Nevertheless, over the years the body has become a topic not only for fields like artificial intelligence, which address bodies from a constructive point of view or follow a "bio-inspired approach", but also for other areas of computing. For example, Paul Dourish talks about embodiment as a foundation for a new approach to human-computer interaction (Dourish 2004). According to Dourish, embodiment involves more than just the physicality of the body, or the body as an object that enables contact with the world. His concept of embodiment is much wider, for it includes awareness of the inescapable connection between body and context or situation. Dourish gives the example of conversation in order to make clear that context and situatedness cannot be abstracted from embodiment:

"When I talk of 'embodied interaction', I mean that interaction is an embodied phenomenon. It happens in the world, and that world (a physical world and a social world) lends form, substance and meaning to the interaction. Like the example of a conversation, interaction is embodied not merely in the fact that there is physical contact between real fingers and a solid, three dimensional mouse; it is embodied in the sense that its occasion within a setting and a set of specific circumstances gives it meaning and value. By implication, it loses both if removed from those circumstances again." (Dourish 1999)

In this sense, embodiment secures a connection to the world through participation and action. Embodiment is what happens *in* interaction. Thus, the interacting body is constantly changing; it never stands still. It is adaptive to the setting – surroundings and context form an integral part of every act of embodiment. Dourish offers a philosophical articulation of this point by drawing on phenomenology[131], and in doing so he presents an anti-Cartesian position[132].

The two main points of embodied interaction, for Dourish, are that embodiment secures meaning, and that it is needed in order to make sense of the interaction. He strays from the common assumption that factoring in embodiment means a more natural way of communicating; he defies the belief that "natural means an easy and more usable interaction". Instead, Dourish avoids an essentialist view of the body. The body is something which is crucial for interaction, since humans are embodied beings. But, for Dourish, a successful interactive system must account for the body as active and as an establisher of meaning and sense in the world. Here, the body is not a fixed or determined object. It changes with contexts and specific situations, and, of course, over time. The body, as conceived by Dourish, is best described as the place where an ongoing process of embodiment happens. For the human-computer interaction space, it is important to note that the body/bodies/embodiment resists simple mechanistic attributions. As Dourish states:

> "Conversation, for example, is embodied, in more ways than simply that speech patterns are carried as physical disruptions in the air. It is embodied in the way that it happens in the world, through the engaged participation of two equally embodied people, and against a backdrop of an equally embodied set of relationships, actions, assessments and understandings. This background situates the activity of the conversation. The setting within which the activity unfolds is not merely background, but a fundamental and constitutive component of the activity that takes place. Embodiment, then, denotes not physical reality but participative status." (Dourish 1999)

This holds implications for the whole field of human-computer interaction, especially when technology is becoming more and more pervasive and ubiquitous. The approach to designing interactive systems needs to be reconfigured accordingly. As Dourish states:

> "The significance of this for design is that, in designing interactive systems, we typically take the meaning of the elements of the system – its components, processes and representations – to be given or static within the frame of the application. What an action in the interface 'means' is something that we typically imagine to be determined by the designer. However, the notion of meaning as being interactionally determined means that we have to see this in a different light. What a user means by engaging in some action – by recording or communicating information through a system, by incorporating the system into their working practice, and so

---

131 Amongst others, he cites Edmund Husserl, Martin Heidegger, and Maurice Merleau-Ponty (Dourish 2004, p. 103f).
132 "There are things that unfold in the world, and whose fundamental nature depends on their properties as features of the world rather than as abstractions." (Dourish 1999)

forth – may have little to do with what the designer had imagined. Most importantly, the designer does not have absolute control, only influence. In turn, this suggests that, if the meaning of the use of the technology is, first, in flux and, second, something that is worked out again and again in each setting, then the technology needs to be able to support this sort of repurposing, and needs to be able to support the communication of meaning through it, within a community of practice." (Dourish 1999)

Interestingly, Dourish's notion of embodiment – with its phenomenological grounding, its emphasis on situatedness and flexibility – comes closer to feminist theories of the body than it does to common concepts of embodiment in the research field of the embodied interface agent.

To be clear, the uneasy relation with the body is not something found only in "Good Old-Fashioned Artificial Intelligence" or in computing at large. It is inherent to Western culture and thus apparent in various scientific areas. Accordingly, the "embodiment turn", the return of the body in science, is not limited to certain strands of computing, such as embodied interaction, bio-inspired intelligent systems, or embodied cognition. Embodiment/the body has also increasingly become a topic for conferences, readers, and theory-building in the humanities (Morgan et al. 2005; Schiebinger 2000; Turner 2012). In *Sociology of the Body*, Kate Cregan refers to Bryan Turner's foundational study (Turner 1984) on the role of the body in the social sciences. Cregan views this as a turning point for the field, remarking that "the body was often taken to be merely an interface at which social interaction took place, and that this interface was often unthinkingly treated or read through an undifferentiated norm (the body as white, heterosexual, able-bodied, adult, male). In this sense, all academic disciplines had been body-blind until at least the early 1970s." But of course, "the body was always 'there' in sociological or anthropological theories: it was just not explicitly accounted for" (Cregan 2006, p. 2)[133].

The idea that the mind can be abstracted from the body and can thus be transferred to other systems (systems of thought or computational systems) is mostly credited to the work of René Descartes. The Cartesian split gets cited frequently as an influential concept for modern thought[134]. The Cartesian split is located at the pineal gland, which forms the interface where the human mind interacts with the body. The Cartesian view of the body is that of a machine. The body is a material object and therefore bound to the laws of physics. The mind (or soul) is considered to be immaterial and thus free from these constraints. The thinking

---

[133] Cp. "The frequent feminisation and racialisation of any notion of the body at all indicates that the 'Cartesian' dualism, which provides a reference point for much contemporary sociology of the body, is indeed hardly neutral." (Fraser, Greco 2004, p. 7)
[134] See "Forgetting about the body is an old Cartesian trick." (Stone 1991). Further: Kittler, Johnston (1997); Featherstone, Burrows (1995).

substance (*res cogitans*) lies outside of nature, to which the extended substance (*res extensa*) belongs. Because the mind transcends the laws of nature, it can rule over it[135].

There are also analyses, however, that consider common readings of Descartes as oversimplified. Mariam Fraser and Monica Greco provide a critical review of Descartes' work and reception. They state that:

> "The inaugurating motif of the sociology of the body has been the denunciation of its absence from the research agendas of traditional social science. How has that absence been explained? In large part, it has been accounted for with reference to the legacy of Rene Descartes (1596-1650), who radicalised the distinction between the mind and the body (the mental and the material, soul and nature) and who privileged the former over the latter. Corporeal events might have an impact on processes of thinking, but the final product – thought 'itself', with its concomitant relations of meaning – was to be valued precisely insofar as it was disembodied (cf. Descartes 1985; 1991). The reference to Cartesian dualism is certainly an ubiquitous feature of accounts of the body in contemporary social science, and is here recorded as such. It should however be treated with caution." (Fraser, Greco 2004, p. 6)

In *Descartes' Error*, Antonio Damasio addresses the influence of Descartes. Collaborating with his wife, Hanna Damasio, he points out the shortcomings of the Cartesian approach to the concept of self from the perspective of neurobiology (Damasio 1994). In the book, which became widely popular, Damasio argues that the body and emotions are crucial for making rational decisions.

Western culture's complicated relationship with the body and issues of matter and materiality reaches back further than Descartes. Elizabeth Grosz, in *Volatile Bodies*, speaks of the establishment, in ancient Greece, of a "profound somatophobia" (Grosz 2004, p. 47). Plato is an early representative of this kind of body politics, where mind rules over the body: "In his doctrine of the Forms, Plato sees matters itself as a denigrated and imperfect version of the Idea" (ibid.). In Christianity, the distinction between body and mind correlates with what is considered mortal or immortal. The gendered coding of dichotomies – emotion / rationality, passivity / activity, private / public space, the other / the white male, nature / culture, the burdened and decaying body / the pure and everlasting mind – has been the topic of feminist scholars for a long time now[136].

Even though Elizabeth Grosz places these biased dichotomies in a much earlier historical context, she emphasizes Descartes' influence on the deployment of these dichotomies as a foundation for the establishment of modern science:

---

135 See Descartes (1966, c1961), in particular, "The Description of the Human Body and Passions of the Soul".
136 See, for example, "Is Female to Male as Nature Is to Culture?" (Ortner, 1972)

3.1. The Return of the Body

"Dualism not only poses irresolvable philosophical problems; it is also at least indirectly responsible for the historical separation of the natural sciences from the social sciences and humanities, the separation of physiology from psychology, of quantitative analysis from qualitative analysis, and the privileging of mathematics and physics as ideal models of the goals and aspirations of knowledge of all types. Dualism, in short, is responsible for the modern forms of elevation of consciousness (a specifically modern version of the notion of the soul, introduced by Descartes) above corporeality." (Grosz 2004, p. 48)

Thus, the split between body and mind, or nature and culture, is bound to power relations that are tied to the cultural order of gender. The biased dichotomy influences what counts as objectivity in science and establishes what "real science" consists of. It promotes certain forms of knowledge over others, and it favors some standpoints and perspectives while neglecting others. To visualize this, Grosz refers to Donna Haraway's account of Robert Boyle's airpump experiments. During these experiments, which took place in the 1660s, women could be present at the laboratory and watch the experiments, but they could not count as a witness for them (ibid.). Basically, Grosz finds that in science there are "three lines of investigation of the body": the body as an object for natural sciences; the body as metaphor, instrument, or tool; the body as signifying medium, or vehicle of expression (ibid.). The latter two concepts, in particular, are of interest for the embodiment of the Virtual Human. Furthermore, in an overview of the body in science and its attribution in gender studies, Irmela Marei Krüger-Fürhoff makes two major points regarding research that deals with embodiment concepts. Firstly, analysis of the body needs to work at the intersection of the symbolic order of the body and bodily phenomena such as lust, pain, and death – and, in doing so, it needs to address the diversity of human bodies. She writes:

"Although the male and, especially, the female body already have become central subjects of feminism and gender studies since the 1960s, since the middle of the 1980s a veritable 'body-boom' looms large, respectively – corresponding to the earlier linguistic turn – a body turn in the various political goals and scientific theoretical approaches that have shaped gender studies. Thereby, one of the persisting challenges is to reflect equally the diversity of bodies (e.g. bodies that are younger, disabled, of different skin colours or ethnicities) as well as how the body is (historically, orally and visually) symbolically constructed, as well as its dependency on physiological phenomena such as desire, pain or mortality."[137]

---

[137] "Obwohl der männliche und vor allem der weibliche Körper schon seit den 1960er Jahren zu den zentralen Gegenständen von Feminismus und Geschlechterforschung gehören, zeichnet sich seit Mitte der 1980er Jahre ein regelrechter ‚Körperboom' bzw- - vergleichbar mit dem früheren lingusitic turn - ein body turn in den unterschiedlichen politischen Zielsetzungen und wissenschaftlichen Theorieansätzen geprägten Gender Studies ab. Dabei gehört es zu den bleibenden Herausforderungen, die Vielfalt des Körpers (z.B. als junger, behinderter, einer bestimmten

Secondly, every gender studies analysis of the body has to deal with the aforementioned dichotomy of "male culture" or "male mind" versus "female nature" or "female bodies as objects", and with the hierarchies that form this order of knowledge[138].

Against the background of the history of Western science, the fact that the body finally gets on the agenda of artificial intelligence research could be read as an improvement for, or a relative valorization of, an otherwise neglected sphere of knowledge. Jutta Weber, who does research on technology, ethics, and philosophy, has commented on newer forms of artificial intelligence or artificial life research: "First of all we should clarify that they – unlike the old AI – address 'the unpredictable liveliness of the world and processes of open-ended becoming' (Pickering) and do not mask it out. Materiality, that is the material quality of the system, is in many current approaches recognised as a relevant and important factor"[139]. Still, Weber remains critical in her assessment of the field. She states that it is crucial to note which forms of embodiment are realized in artificial intelligence and what goals they serve (ibid.).

So, instead of a late validation of the body, the background given above may also suggest that embodiment is brought onto the agenda in order to secure technological progress, and that the body is still seen and used mainly as a resource – a material vessel for hegemonic wishes of transcendence. The latter is not a new move. Christina von Braun describes the transition from oral culture to written language as interwoven with processes that stabilize the cultural order of gender. The body is located at the center of this move, which can also be described as a process of abstraction and re-sensualizing:

Hautfarbe oder Ethnie zugeordneter Körper) ebenso zu reflektieren wie seine Zugehörigkeit zum (historisch, sprachlich und visuell konstruierten) Symbolischen sowie seine Abhängigkeit von physiologischen Phänomenen wie Lust, Schmerz und Sterblichkeit." (Krüger-Fürhoff 2005, p. 66)

138 See also: "The point of departure for the critical interrogation of the natural sciences and their history is the realisation that the metaphor of 'masculine culture' and the immateriality, respectively the masculine mind on the one hand, and that of 'feminine nature' and its respective physicality on the other hand, shapes all scientific discourse and boils down to a hierarchical relationship between the masculine researcher-subject and the female object of the research (whether that is nature, woman, or her body)." ("Ausgangspunkt der kritischen Befragung der Naturwissenschaften und ihrer Geschichte ist die Einsicht, dass die Metaphorik von ‚männlicher Kultur' und Körperlosigkeit bzw. männlichen Geist auf der einen und ‚weiblicher Natur' bzw. Körperhaftigkeit auf der anderen Seite alle Wissensdiskurse prägt und sich in einem hierarchischen Verhältnis zwischen männlichem Forschungs-Subjekt und weiblichem Objekt der Forschung (sei dies die Natur, die Frau oder ihr Körper) niederschlägt.") (Krüger-Fürhoff 2005, p. 73)

139 "Erst einmal ist festzuhalten, dass sie – anders als die alte KI – 'the unpredictable liveliness of the world and processes of open-ended becoming' (Pickering) thematisieren und nicht ausblenden. Material bzw. die materiale Beschaffenheit des Systems wird nun in vielen neuen Ansätzen als ein relevanter und wichtiger Faktor anerkannt." (Weber 2003, p. 126)

3.1. The Return of the Body

"By structuring oral speech, the written word also resulted in a structuring of the body through thought. Precisely this was of consequence for the symbolic gender order. With the complete alphabet writing, to which both, the promised 'immortality of the mind' and the process of abstraction and disembodiment were connected, a gender order arose in which the male body became the symbolic carrier of the mind and the female the carrier of the corporal. Precisely because the female body had previously symbolized fertility, sexuality and the circularity of time, it now became in the new culture of the mind the symbol of perishability, which seemed to be one with sexuality and corporeality. This means that the same historical dynamic that was unleashed by alphabetic writing and which catered to equality before the law for all citizens, created a law that produced inequality between genders. It was the same dynamic that shaped the relationship of speech and writing."[140]

The Virtual Human/embodied agent is a computational artifact. Keeping in mind the semiotic character of the computer, the embodiment of the agent derives precisely from an interchange of signs, symbols, and materiality. Signal-processing, on the side of the computer (according to Nake, "the signs that are withdrawn from our senses"[141]), results in signs forming the Virtual Human at the human-computer interspace. This is a complex and multi-layered technological process, yet, as Nake writes, it is in itself a process of animation: "In the computer, signs become executable, processeable, and thus they acquire an independent existence, they attain their own reality"[142]. The embodied agent is not a hardware robot. At least on a phenomenological level, it is a transcendent form of embodiment; a dematerialized form of embodiment that promises artificial life – a form of life that in itself seems to come without material constraints.

---

140 "Indem das geschriebene Wort sich strukturierend auf die mündliche Sprache auswirkte, hatte es auch eine Strukturierung des Körpers durch das Denken zur Folge. Eben das sollte auf die Geschlechterordnung zurückwirken. Mit der vollen Alphabetschrift, mit der sich sowohl das Versprechen 'geistiger Unsterblichkeit' als auch ein Prozeß der Abstraktion und Entkörperung verband, entstand eine Geschlechterordnung, in der der männliche Körper zum Symbolträger des Geistigen und der weibliche zum Symbolträger des Leiblichen wurden. Eben weil der weibliche Körper bis dahin Fruchtbarkeit, Sexualität und die wiederkehrende Zeit symbolisiert hatte, wurde er nun in der neuen Kultur der Geistigkeit zum Symbolträger der Vergänglichkeit, die mit Sexualität und Körperlichkeit in eins gesetzt schien. Das heißt, dieselbe von der Alphabetschrift ausgelöste historische Dynamik, die für eine Gleichheit aller Bürger vor dem Gesetz sorgte, schuf ein Gesetz, das eine Ungleichheit zwischen den Geschlechtern herstellte. Es war dieselbe Dynamik, die auch das Verhältnis von Mündlichkeit und Schriftlichkeit prägte." (Braun 2006, p. 13)
141 "die Zeichen, die unseren Sinnen entzogen sind" - See Chapter 2.2.1.
142 "Im Computer werden Zeichen exekutierbar, sie prozessieren und werden mithin verselbständigt, gewinnen eine eigene Realität." (Nake 1993a, p. 14)

3.1.2. Bodies in Action

Earlier[143], I introduced Donald Norman's influential conception of the interface as defined by gaps that need to be bridged. Read against this background, the embodied agent resides at the gap. It functions as a translator between two worlds: it speaks the language of the machine, but it appeals to the human user. Its anthropomorphic form of embodiment is supposed to make the gap between machine and human less noticeable for the user. Virtual Humans are viewed, by those engaged in their design, as the next step in human-computer interaction (Cassell 2000a; Magnenat-Thalmann 2004). As I previously mentioned, embodied agents "are just one way of thinking about a different kind of relationship between humans and computers – it is really all about multimodal interfaces"[144]. This approach especially seeks to take human communication in its entirety, whether verbal or non-verbal, into account. It addresses the whole body. It is noteworthy that, when the body or embodiment is on the agenda in the field of human-computer interaction, it is mostly seen as a means of innovation. Interfaces are promised an increase in usability and accessibility and they are said to gain functionalities that were not previously realizable. The body brings a new quality to the field. The aim of the multimodal interface community is thus to meet the user in her or his everyday activities without the felt interruption of dealing with a machine. The best interface, in this sense, is the one that is not noticed. Also, embodied interface agents are meant to familiarize the machine by giving a face to it (Cassell 2000b, p. 2). Information may be retrieved simply by talking to the embodied agent, sparing the user the effort of dealing with more abstract levels of the computer system. The conversation metaphor is thus taken literally. As Nicole Krämer et al. state:

> "The metaphor of the dialog partner experiences a particular implementation in the context of so-called 'humanoid interface agents'. Here, it is a matter of more or less life-like 3D figures, which should reach out to the user beyond the screen through the use of speech and non-verbal communication (facial expressions, gestures, body postures). A greater naturalness is attributed to such multimodal, socially oriented interfaces, especially because of structural similarities with human face-to-face communication and, in short, greater ease of use and more efficiency and user acceptance are attested to them."[145]

---

143 See Chapter 1.2.
144 See Chapter 1.3.2.
145 "Eine besondere Ausformung erfährt die Dialog-Partner-Metapher im Rahmen sogenannter 'humanoider Interface-Agenten'. Hierbei handelt es sich um mehr oder weniger lebendig wirkende 3D-Figuren, die mit dem Nutzer unter Verwendung von Lautsprache und non-verbaler Kommunikation (Mimik, Gestik, Körperhaltung) über den Bildschirm in Kontakt treten sollen. Solchen multimodalen, sozial-orientierten Schnittstellen wird meist auf Grund struktureller Ähnlichkeiten

3.1. The Return of the Body   115

and

> "Among the various factors that can provoke or intensify a social reaction to computers, the depiction of a human face is certainly among the most influential."[146]

Krämer et al. review anthropomorphic interfaces critically. They emphasize that most work in this area is still basic research and that the embodied agent is not fitting for just any interaction scenario (Krämer, Bente 2002, p. 217). Others, as indicated by the aforementioned quote from Justine Cassell, are more enthusiastic about "interfaces that have bodies". They believe that the gap between human and computer system, which Norman identified, will be closed by Virtual Human embodiments. Figure 12 illustrates this idea.

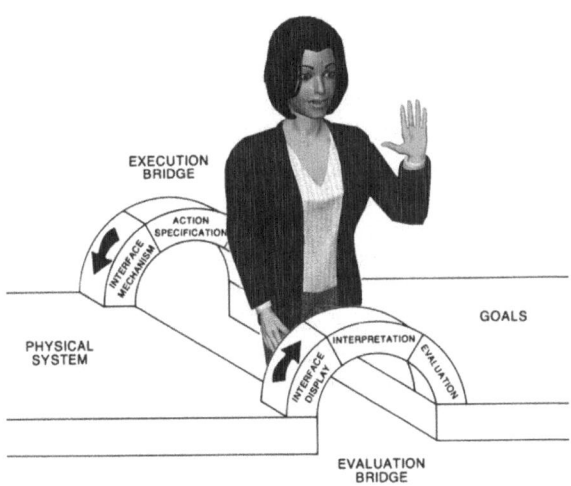

Fig. 12 Greta Bridging the Gap between User and System
(Source: The illustration is a collage by Claude Draude with Norman's graphic of the Gulfs (Norman 1986, p. 40) and Greta, developed by Pelachaud et al., 2002)

---

mit der menschlichen face-to-face-Kommunikation eine größere Natürlichkeit zugesprochen und im Kurzschluss auch eine leichtere Handhabung sowie größere Effizienz und Akzeptanz bescheinigt." (Krämer, Bente 2002, pp. 203–204)
146 "Unter den verschiedenen Faktoren, die eine soziale Reaktion auf Computer auslösen oder verstärken können, gehört die Abbildung eines menschlichen Gesichts sicher zu den einflussreichsten." (Krämer, Bente 2002, p. 212)

But what is it that can be experienced as a body or embodied interaction with a Virtual Human? The human-like alter ego that the agent demonstrates while interacting with the human is a video projection, an on-screen figure or, in some cases, a projection realized in a three-dimensional virtual reality space. As researcher Ipke Wachsmuth, from the University of Bielefeld, writes about embodied conversational agent MAX: "Max is an artificial agent who communicates with his human counterpart verbally and physically, through gesture and expression. In the laboratory setting of a three-dimensional enormous computer graphic projection, he can be brought to life with a human-like appearance"[147].

In contrast to embodied agents, robots are tangible objects. Robots consist of a body made from metal, wires, plastic, hard- and software – they move around physical spaces and can be touched. The embodied agent interface, of course, results from a co-construction of hardware and software (amongst many other things and actors) as well. Still, embodied agents, avatars, or Virtual Humans are technological artifacts that are primarily experienced and structured through vision. They literally make sense in the "geography of the eye" (Hillis 1996) of internet/virtual reality technologies.

This phenomenological immateriality of the ECA is indispensable for its function as an intermediary between the abstracted/signal-processing world of the computer and the physical space of human interaction. The agent body that is made of light brings advantages as well as disadvantages. Unlike a hardware robot, a Virtual Human cannot lift heavy weights or vacuum the floor. Instead, it may gather and sort information online and/or act on behalf of the user. Especially in the latter function, the Virtual Human demonstrates the interchange between the physical world and the world of signs. Conceptually, the embodied agent plays with notions of doubling the body and of freedom from bodily restraints. It introduces multi-localities and produces overlays of virtual and real embodiments. Writer Neal Stephenson, who made the term avatar popular, describes an interaction scenario in his novel *Snow Crash*:

> "As Hiro approaches the Street, he sees two young couples, probably using their parents' computers for a double date in the Metaverse, climbing down out of Port Zero, which is the local port of entry and monorail stop.
>
> He is not seeing real people, of course. This is all a part of the moving illustration drawn by his computer according to specifications coming down the fiber-optic cable. The people are pieces of software called avatars. They are the audiovisual bodies that people use to communicate with each other in the Metaverse. Hiro's avatar is now on the Street, too, and if

---

147 "Max ist ein künstlicher Agent, der mit seinem menschlichen Gegenüber verbal und körpersprachlich, mit Gestik und Mimik, kommuniziert. In menschenähnlicher Erscheinung kann er in der Laborumgebung einer dreidimensionalen computergrafischen Großprojektion erlebt werden." (Wachsmuth 2010, p. 139)

3.1. The Return of the Body

> the couples coming off the monorail look over in his direction, they can see him, just as he's seeing them. They could strike up a conversation: Hiro in the U-Stor-It in L.A. and the four teenagers probably on a couch in a suburb of Chicago, each with their own laptop. But they probably won't talk to each other, any more than they would in reality. These are nice kids, and they don't want to talk to a solitary crossbreed with a slick custom avatar who's packing a couple of swords.
> You can look any way you want it to, up to the limitations of your equipment. If you're ugly, you can make your avatar beautiful. If you've just gotten out of bed, your avatar can be wearing beautiful clothes and professionally applied makeup." (Stephenson 1992, pp. 35–36)

For the human user, it seems, there exists a tension between the desired freedom from the body, as expressed in the avatar, and the restrictiveness of the material world. In the virtual reality world of the Metaverse, a sort of Internet with embodied characters, avatars serve as self-representations. There are also software agents that do not represent a human user but that obtain a function for the system, such as maintenance or other specific tasks.

Technologically speaking, the avatar means a broader bandwidth of information. Especially when it comes to non-verbal communication, it allows for a wider picture than a mere text-based scenario. The appearance and functionality of the avatar mirrors the ideals of the human users, as well as their technological knowledge, abilities, and constraints. Differences in social background, economic resources, and sub-cultural technological expertise also play a role in how the audiovisual representation is designed. The scene above implies experiencing a technologically-mediated reality in which the intermediary character of the technology is not experienced as such: Metaverse users see each other when they see the corresponding avatar; the two forms of embodiments, the real life body and the data representation, seem to collapse.

It is only the semiotic-material embodiment of the agent/avatar, however, that has the power to travel across the world with a mouse click. Formerly, in text-based communication like letters or email, the self-representation took place through the written sign. Now, with the material-semiotic embodiment of the avatar, the sign is tied back to the body in a more obvious way. The avatar is considered to represent the human more adequately, because it invokes the human body as such, not just a description of it. Just as with emoticons in emails or chats, the user does not have to type "I am smiling" but shows it with a picture that is considered closer to the bodily expression.

What counts as the avatar and the Virtual Human body is the projected "Lichtgestalt" ("luminous figure") that the technology produces. Interestingly, the term avatar or avatāra is derived from Sanskrit. In its Hindu context, it is used to describe the human or animal form of embodiment of a god after descending from heaven to earth. The usage of the term avatar within cyberculture comes as no surprise – it points to the transcendental connotations of Internet-/virtual reality technologies. In the original meaning, the Hindu god or goddess is bound to a certain form of embodiment, but he or she keeps godly power and wisdom, while being free from human suffering and pain. She or he also may emerge in different places at the same time. Therefore the avatar describes a form of representation that is bound not to the rules of physical reality, but to a transcendent meta-reality where death and pain have no meaning (Coleman 2011).

Certainly, existing embodied interface agent technologies are not as far advanced or futuristic as their fictive or religious correspondents. But the supposed (im)materiality of their embodiment as a moving image means that, just like their fictive or religious correspondents, they do not age or decay. And, with their character as pro-active agents, they can "crawl the web", as the Semantic Web scenario suggests[148].

What is often left out in visionary scenarios is the fact that the technology, of course, is not just a moving image, and that it furthermore puts claims on matters/materiality, the body, and the environment. Figure 13 shows the ECA Greta (Pelachaud et al. 2002) in an interaction scenario.

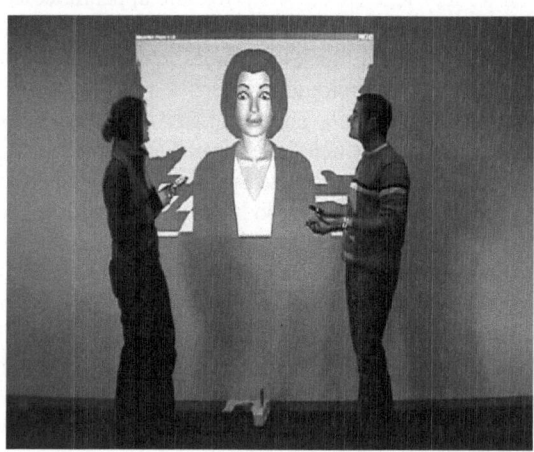

Fig. 13 Greta in Interaction
(Source: Pelachaud et al., 2002)

The human experiences the embodiment of the agent in the form of a video projection onto a wall. Depending on the set-up, the system may also generate speech output or use touch sensors (Kopp et al. 2003). These multimodal input and output

---

148 See Introduction and Berners-Lee et al. (2001).

3.1. The Return of the Body

devices, which are needed for the interaction to take place, are not visible in the above setting.

The lab picture of ECA MAX in interaction with a researcher shows a less revised version.

Fig. 14 Max in Interaction
(Source: Kopp et al., 2003)

The affordances for an ECA as a multimodal system are obviously quite high: the system should be able to recognize and process the language and gestures of the human user. It needs to generate appropriate reactions, which include recognizing the content of a conversation as well as offering new topics: "Among the most important performance characteristics are, besides the capability to understand the speech and gestures of the user, the generation of original verbal and non-verbal reactions, directing the conversation, the recognition and assessment of how a discussion develops and, as required, the creative introduction of new conversation subjects. Currently, no applications living up to those demands exist"[149].

---
149 "Zu den wichtigsten Leistungsmerkmalen gehören neben der Fähigkeit, Sprache und Gestik des Nutzers zu verstehen, die Generierung eigener verbaler und nonverbaler Reaktionen, die Dialogsteuerung, die Erkennung und Bewertung der Diskursentwicklung und gegebenenfalls die kreative Einführung neuer Gesprächsinhalte. Tatsächlich finden sich noch keine Realisationen, die

Referring to Donald Norman, we can see that the questions regarding the interface are not reducible to the oppositional, either/or choice between "moving the machine closer to the human" or "moving the human closer to the machine". Instead, the picture of MAX in interaction demonstrates that reconfigurations and overlaps have to take place on both sides in order for the system to work. It is not only the technical side, but also the *natural* – that is, the human – side that has to be enhanced or remodeled. The human needs to be equipped with technical devices, just as the room needs to be monitored by cameras and microphones. In this sense, the contextual space has to be adapted for a successful interaction. Depending on the interaction setting, the system receives information from the user through keyboard, speech recognition, camera, and sensors. However, the reconfiguration of the human does not stop here. The embodiment of the ECA materializes in interaction. The power of the figuration reaches beyond the grid surface of the "body made from light" and results in the transformation of human interaction.

Basically, the architecture of an ECA is realized as an input-output model, as pictured in Figure 15.

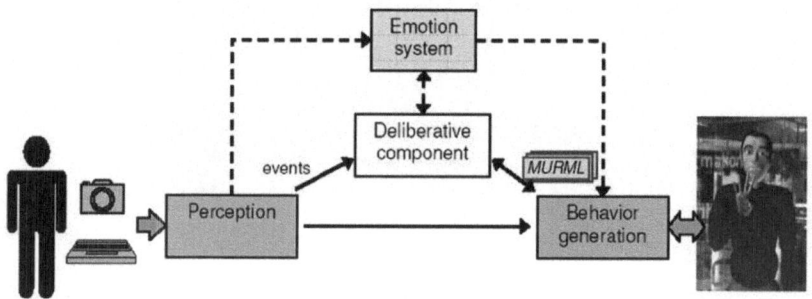

Fig. 15 Max System Architecture Overview
(Source: Kopp et al., 2003)

The complex "deliberative or decision making module" processes the input data according to its pre-specified rules and chooses an appropriate action as output. The capability to act is central to agent technology and separates the embodied agent from the avatar. As Justine Cassell et al. put it, they are "more than just a pretty face":

---

diesem Anspruch gerecht werden." (Krämer, Bente 2002, p. 206)
See ibid., p. 205.

3.1. The Return of the Body

> "Of course, depictions of human bodies are also more decorative than menus on a screen and, like any new interface design, they are also currently quite in vogue and therefore attractive to many users. Unfortunately, many embodied interface agents developed to date don't go further than their ornamental or novelty value. Aside from the use of pointing gestures and two or three facial expressions, many animated interface agents provide little more than something amusing to look at while the same old system handles the mechanics of the interaction. It is little wonder that these systems have been found to be likable and engaging, but to provide no improvement in task performance over text or speech-only interfaces." (Cassell 2001 et al., p. 55)

In my analysis, the focus is on how the border between what does and does not count as human is negotiated. For this, I pay closer attention to the (supposed) agency of the agent, as well as to the design goal that the agent should be able to reciprocate feelings or to return the gaze[150] – while neglecting other topics[151]. These traits describe the demarcation line between living agent and lifeless avatar. In what follows, I will give particular attention to the decision making module that is supposed to make the agent interactive and lifelike.

3.1.3. Agency: Embodiment and the Ability to Act

As with other characteristics, the potential actions of the agent are designed to mirror human actions. Agency is linked to the autonomous status of the agent and defines the agent's state of animation, of liveliness. The concept of the agent's capacity to act is extrapolated from human agency, which thus serves as the natural state of interaction according to which the technical state is supposed to be modeled. Nature serves as an analogy: "Through the - analogous to nature - allocation of the overall problem into interacting entities, those allocated applications can be adequately modelled, simulated as well as implemented"[152].

The crucial question concerns the way in which agency is to be conceptualized and applied. It is interesting, though not surprising, to acknowledge that the model of agency within this new paradigm of agent technology is close to the planning model I referred to earlier in the context of Norman's concept of the human-computer interface. This model reorganizes human agency as a defined set of

---

150 See Chapters 3.2. and 3.3.
151 For example, topics like movements or animated motions, the skeleton structure or skin and hair textures.
152 "Durch die naturanaloge Aufteilung des Gesamtproblems in autonome, miteinander interagierende Einheiten lassen sich derartige verteilte Anwendungen adäquat modellieren, simulieren und auch implementieren." (Pokahr et al. 2002, p. 1)

goals, plans, and deliberative actions[153]. Here, agency is intentional and goal-oriented. Lucy Suchman finds that, in order to work, the model of planning and reasoning needs to follow certain basic assumptions. Through her articulation of the relation between individual and joint social behavior, she points out the difficulties that come with the concept of the planning model of interaction:

> "The planning model attempts to bring concerted action under the jurisdiction of the individual actor by attaching to the others in the actor's world sufficient description, and granting to the actor's sufficient knowledge, that he or she is able to respond to the actions of others as just another set of environmental conditions. [...] The problem for interaction, on this view, is to recognize the actions of others as the expression of their underlying plans. The complement to plan generation and execution in artificial intelligence research, therefore, is plan recognition, or the attribution of plans to others based on observation of their actions. The starting premise for a theory of plan recognition is that an observer takes some sequence of actions as evidence, and then forms hypotheses about the plans that could motivate and explain those actions. One persisting difficulty for action understanding in artificial intelligence research has been the uncertain relation between actions and intended effects." (Suchman 1987, p. 33)

She illustrates the last point, the "relation between actions and intended effects", by giving the example of switching on the light[154]. This is a simple task – but, depending on the circumstances, there can be very different plans that need to be executed in order to achieve the goal. There are differences in switches, and in older houses there might be an issue with the fuses, or the light-bulb might need to be changed, if flicking the switch does not work. It is everyday tasks like these, which are supported by what is often implicit, tacit knowledge, that provide a major challenge for artificial intelligence research. What is left out in this thought experiment is something that actually cannot be left out: the form of embodiment of the human or the artifact, the context, and the concomitant disabilities. In so-called "smart houses", where appliances are monitored by computer technology, unconventional actions, such as the wish to shower in the dark, might not be supported by the application setting. Here, a light sensor might always switch on the light. The range of possible actions depends on what is determined in the overall scenario.

For the design of a rational agent architecture – software that meets the above described principles of agent technology – the most common concepts of modeling agency are the Belief-Desire-Intention (BDI) approach, the theory of Agent Oriented Programming (AOP), and the Unified Theories of Cognition (UTC, SOAR) (Pokahr et al. 2002, p. 5). Those concepts mainly derive from fields

---

153 See Chapter 1.2.
154 She actually refers to this example being made by Allan (1984).

3.1. The Return of the Body

of knowledge like behaviorism or cognitive psychology, or – in the case of the BDI approach – from the theory of practical reasoning, which has its roots in Western philosophy (Georgeff et. al. 1999).

The BDI approach is used to model the behavior of agents in a vast number of systems. This is also true for embodied interface agent systems, like MAX (Kopp et al. 2003). Here, practical reasoning is understood as "the process of deciding, moment by moment, which action to perform in the furtherance of our goals" (Weiss 1999, p. 55). The process of deciding on the goals is called deliberation. Following this, the BDI approach can be understood as broadening the rather static planning model described earlier, by being more adaptive and flexible to changing environmental conditions.

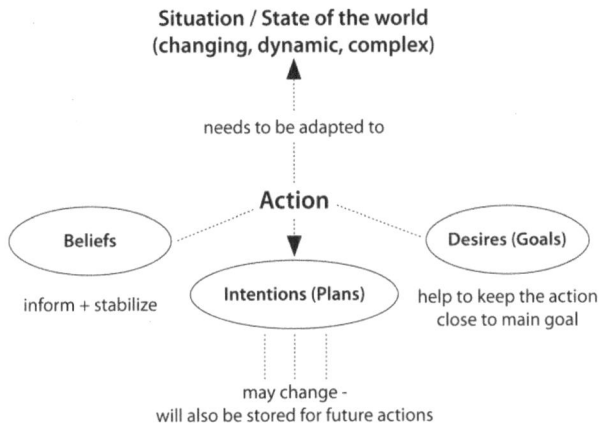

Fig. 16 Simplified BDI Overview
(Source: Illustration Claude Draude)

In this model, as Figure 16 shows, agent behavior is characterized as dependent on the "state of the world" or "model of the world" linked to the knowledge that is already incorporated in the agent architecture (beliefs) and the goal which is to be obtained (desires). A change in the "state of the world" will lead to several sub-plans or sub-goals (intentions). These may vary in the course of the action, but they will always be devoted to the main goal. The beliefs give the agent some sense of knowledge about its place in the system, and they define the information upon which it can calculate further action. Thus the agent already "knows" something and does not need to compute everything from scratch. Beliefs represent the subjective form of knowledge that the agent obtains about its internal state as well as its environment.

Here the anthropomorphizing of the artifact becomes quite obvious: it is not just a phenomenon, as is a figure of speech used by designers or later users; it is integrated into the system as such. The language of my description mirrors this – in fact, it seems hardly possible not to reaffirm this move. In research articles that are written in the German language, the agent appears as "der Agent" and the personal pronoun "er" (he) is used, whereas in English texts the agent is referred to as "it". Concerning the information gathered as "beliefs" and the subjective perspective of the agent, Alexander Pokahr et al. state:

> "This information is not a direct depiction of the impulses included, but it rather excels in a domain-dependent abstraction of the elements, which emphasizes important features and dismisses less important ones. This filter and interpretation mechanism enables the agent to have a personal worldview."[155]

In most cases, when it comes to implementing BDI-systems into larger architectures, an abstract BDI-interpreter is used as a basis (ibid; Singh et al. 1999). An abstract BDI-Interpreter may look like this (Rao, Georgeff 1995):

BDI-interpreter
Initialize-state();
repeat
options := option-generator(event-queue);
selected-options := deliberate(options);
update-intentions(selected-options);
execute();
get-new-external-events();
drop-successful-attitudes();
drop-impossible-attitudes();
end repeat

Pokahr offers an explanation of the BDI-interpreter loop:

> "In these, in the beginning of each run-through, the main suitable plans are determined according to each event; afterwards, from these available options a subset is selected (Meta-Level Reasoning), this is added to the structure of intentions and finally executed. All external

---

[155] "Diese Informationen sind jedoch kein direktes Abbild der aufgenommenen Reize, sondern zeichnen sich vielmehr durch eine domänenabhängige Abstraktion der Elemente aus, die wichtige Eigenschaften betont und weniger wichtige ausblendet. Dieser Filter und Interpretationsmechanismus ermöglicht dem Agenten eine persönliche Weltsicht." (Pokahr et al. 2002)

3.1. The Return of the Body

occurrences up to that point are in the next pass incorporated into the list of events. To conclude, the goal structure and structure of intentions of the agent are brought up to date by removing attitudes that have been completed or have become impossible. In the implemented systems, there are partly significant differences, especially in regard to the technical software application of the underlying concepts (Beliefs, Goals, Plans)."[156]

The case of the BDI-model shows that marking the capability to act as pro-active and event-driven (in the language of the field of agent technology) seems already very fitting for the rule-oriented mechanisms of the computational machine. This understanding of behavior undergoes co-constructive processes as it becomes implemented into computational systems, which will then be used to simulate the 'real world' of which they are already a part. Considering the working principles of computer technology and the constraint they put on designing artifacts, this is not surprising. Thus, the BDI-interpreter approves the findings that Corinna Bath and Jutta Weber state for the field of social robotics in general:

> "Every socially intelligent machine we can dream of is still based on rule-oriented behaviour, since this is the material ground and fundamental functionality of these machines. Therefore it is rule-oriented social behaviour that is at the core of the theoretical approaches, concepts and practices of software agent researchers and roboticists. The kind of rules might differ in diverse strands of AI, but a standardization of human behavior is a precondition for every computer model and software application. Anthropomorphized machines are intended to operate by simulating social norms, supposed gender differences and other stereotypes. The starting point of these prototypes and implementations is rule-based social behaviour which is said to be performed by humans. Researchers often use folk psychological and sociological approaches about sociality and emotionality to model human-machine-relations. Especially those theories from the wide range of psychology and sociology are chosen for the computational modelling which already consider social behavior to be operational." (Weber, Bath 2004, pp. 9–10)

Every action, behavior, or reaction the agent displays has to be realized against the computer's basic principles of "semiotization, formalization, algorithmization" [157]. Nicole Krämer et al. state that rule-orientedness sets the limit of the agent's capability and believeability: "In accordance with the oft-cited axiom 'one cannot not

---

156 "In diesem werden zu Beginn jedes Schleifendurchlaufs die zu einem aufgetretenen Ereignis prinzipiell passenden Pläne bestimmt; danach wird aus diesen verfügbaren Optionen eine Untermenge selektiert (Meta-Level Reasoning), diese der Intentionenstruktur hinzugefügt und schließlich ausgeführt. Alle bis zu diesem Zeitpunkt aufgetretenen externen Ereignisse werden im nächsten Schritt in die Ereignisliste aufgenommen. Abschließend werden die Ziel- und Intentionenstrukturen des Agenten aktualisiert indem erfüllte oder unmöglich gewordene Attitüden entfernt werden. In den umgesetzten Systemen existieren zum Teil erhebliche Unterschiede - vor allem hinsichtlich der softwaretechnischen Ausgestaltung der zu Grunde liegenden Konzepte (Beliefs, Goals, Plans)." (Pokahr et al. 2002)

157 See Chapter 2.2.1.

communicate', the visual presence of ECAs raises then major problems, when specific areas of behavior cannot be modelled due to their lack of rule-based knowledge"[158].

What always resonates here is the belief that one day everything about the human will be expressible in computational terms (Trogemann 2003). This belief occurs even amidst the most careful research, and can be said to stem from the principles of the computer, rather than from a personal choice of the researcher.

ECA researcher Justine Cassell, for example, works on the conversation part of the embodied agent and tries to translate "human communication protocols" into "agent communication protocols" – a rather complex endeavor:

> "Embodiment provides us with a wide range of behaviors that, when executed in tight synchronization with language, carry out a communicative function. It is important to understand that particular behaviors, such as the raising of the eyebrows, can be employed in a variety of circumstances to produce different communicative effects, and that the same communicative function may be realized through different sets of behaviors. It is therefore clear that any system dealing with conversational modeling has to handle function separately from surface form or run the risk of being inflexible and insensitive to the natural phases of the conversation." (Cassell et al. 2001, p. 56)

Communicative Functions	Communicative Behavior
Initiation and termination:	
Reacting	Short Glance
Inviting Contact	Sustained Glance, Smile
Distance Salutation	Looking, Head Toss/Nod, Raise Eyebrows, Wave, Smile
Close Salutation	Looking, Head Nod, Embrace or Handshake, Smile
Break Away	Glance Around
Farewell	Looking, Head Nod, Wave
Turn-Taking	
Give Turn	Looking, Raise Eyebrows (followed by silence)
Wanting Turn	Raise Hands into gesture space
Take Turn	Glance Away, Start talking
Feedback	
Request Feedback	Looking, Raise Eyebrows
Give Feedback	Looking, Head Nod

Table 1. Some examples of conversational functions and their behavior realization

Fig. 17 Communication Protocols
(Source: Cassell et al., 2001)

---

158 "Im Sinne des vielzitierten Axioms 'Man kann nicht nicht kommunizieren' wirft die visuelle Präsenz von ECAs immer dann schwerwiegende Probleme auf, wenn bestimmte Teilbereiche des Verhaltens auf Grund des fehlenden Regelwissens nicht modelliert werden können." (Krämer, Bente 2002, p. 218)

3.1. The Return of the Body

Earlier[159], I stated that the Virtual Human is embedded in the field of agent technology, which is mirrored in the term Embodied Conversational Agent. The BDI-interpreter, for example, is used to model the behavior in a variety of embodied agent systems. The ECA MAX, developed by the Artificial Intelligence Group at the Technical University of Bielefeld, was initially designed to assist users in virtual reality assembly constructions. Figure 18 shows the integration of the BDI approach in the MAX system.

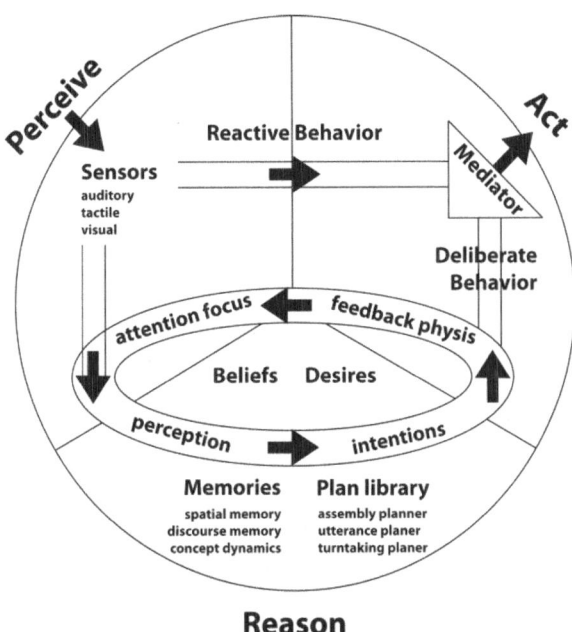

Fig. 18 BDI-architecture of the MAX Model
(Source: Kopp et al., 2003)

> "Max is controlled by a cognitively motivated agent architecture [...] and at first displays the classical perceive-reason-act triad. The direct connection between perceive and act illustrates the reactive component being responsible for reflexes and immediate responses. Deliberation processes take place in the reason section. Processing in the perception, reason, and act components runs concurrently such that reactive responses and deliberative actions can be simultaneously calculated." (Kopp et al. 2003, p. 13)

---

159 See Chapter 1.3.3.

Embodied conversational agents like MAX are highly complex systems. The construction of MAX demonstrates the challenges of the research area. Even when restricted to a specific assembly task, the dialog between user and system is perceived as "mixed-initiative dialog", which is "characterized by openness and unpredictability of the discourse" (Kopp et al. 2003, p. 13).

With the Virtual Human, the degree of anthropomorphization rises and differs in quality. Above, I highlighted that theories of practical reasoning become employed, adjusted, and broadened within interface agent architectures. Thus, behavior is now described not only as a rational, cognitive process. With the interface agent, emotion and affect come into play – two concepts that are not of interest to the above described field of agent technology as long as the agent is not displayed with a human body. In order to execute their tasks properly, the agents that are coupled with terms like sociality do not need to simulate feelings – at least not up to now. Emotion, as well as the meaning of gaze, enters the picture with the research field's notion of embodiment. Before these two new qualities will be elaborated upon, however, I will present an approach that actively considers the role that gender plays in this field.

3.1.4. The Gender Generator

Embodiment is where gender studies, artificial intelligence, and human-computer-interaction form an interesting intersection. Within the area of gender studies, the human body forms a contested zone oscillating between gender re- and deconstruction. When a child is born, and even before it is born, the child's identity becomes established through its entry into the cultural order of gender. The materiality of the child's body is set in accordance with the hegemonic discourse. Most prominently, Judith Butler has questioned the construction of "biological sex" as prior to a "social gender norm":

> "The matrix of gender relations is prior to the emergence of the 'human'. Consider the medical interpellation which (the recent emergence of the sonogram notwithstanding) shifts an infant from an 'it' to a 'she' or a 'he', and in that naming, the girl is 'girled', brought into the domain of language and kinship through the interpellation of gender." (Butler 1993, p. 7)

As Butler writes further on (ibid.), the gendering involved in "becoming human" does not end here. It is an ongoing performative process that is supported and requested by cultural norms, discourse, and power relations. The human gains entry into human society by answering to a binary set of gender relations. Being a man or being a woman is furthermore linked to other powerful dichotomies, such as nature and culture, emotion and reason, or subject and object. Against this background, it is not surprising that personal service assistants, Virtual Humans, embodied interface agents, and Embodied Conversational Agents – all of which name attempts to design anthropomorphic beings – bring embodiment explicitly to the agenda and, with this, the heteronormative gender order. The fact that they do need to follow this ordering system, in appearance, exemplifies that the gender order always is a symbolic order. Its power is not tied to the materiality of the human body. Discourse exceeds and precedes it. Furthermore, the Virtual Humans are pictured as white and able-bodied. The majority of assistive agents are embodied as women[160]. ECA MAX's background, as a construction helper in an automotive industries setting, explains its male gender attribution. In an ongoing performance, humans learn to recognize the dichotomy of gender simply by looking at faces, appearances, clothing, etc. This takes place when looking at instances of the ECA/Virtual Human as well, especially since they seek to represent typical images of a man or a woman.

But what about the behaviors? Are the internal planning and reasoning modules adapted according to presumed binary genders as well? The system architectures of MAX or Greta, at least as they have so far been developed, do not suggest a difference according to gender or cultural background (Paiva et al. 2011, p. 149). This is not to deny, of course, that these models are developed in a specific social setting and therefore most likely represent the worldview of those who built them (Rommes 2002).

The goal of ECA research, however, is to build a lifelike, trustworthy, and believable agent (Ruttkay 2004) – a machinic alter ego that ideally passes as human in behavior and appearance. And, since a believable gender performance is tightly interwoven with an intelligible human identity, it is not surprising that there are researchers that directly address gender performance in embodied agent systems.

Ana Paiva et al. state that:

> "together with personality, culture and other factors, gender is a feature that impacts the perception and thus the believability of the characters. The main goal of this work is to understand how gender can be provided to ECAs, and provide a very simple model that allows for existing tools to overcome such limitation [...] Focusing mainly on nonverbal behaviour, our agents with gender were tested to see if users were able to perceive the gender bias of the behaviours being performed. Results have shown that gender is correctly perceived, and also has effects when paired with an accurate gender appearance." (Paiva et al. 2011, p. 148)

---

160 Cp. Chapter 3.1.1.

It is noteworthy that the authors regard gender as somewhat flexible and performative as long as it responds to the cultural order of two genders. Continuing, they remark: "In this paper, gender is considered to be the physiological, social, and cultural manifestations of what people perceive to be the appropriate behaviours of females and males. Gender differences are assumed to be present for both verbal and non-verbal communication" (Paiva et al. 2011, p. 149). The notion of an "accurate gender appearance" is given support by studies that find differences in the behavior of women and men, which is not unusual when gender is addressed in computer science (Angeli et al. 2006). The studies cited in the aforementioned paper reinforce folk-psychological beliefs – for instance, that women are generally more communicative, emotional, and caring, or that men communicate more straightforwardly and are fact-oriented. Of apparent interest for embodied agent research are findings that articulate gender differences, such as that men take up more space than women in conversation, as well as in public space in general. Supposedly, this is demonstrated through specific modes of gesturing, positioning the body, and using arm- and leg space (Paiva et al. 2011, p. 149). This points to one of the core problems of this work, when considered from a gender studies perspective: designers want to do the best job they can in building a realistic agent, and for this reason specific traits of humans – such as presupposed gender differences – are singled out and reconstructed within the artifact. In effect, this leads to a reinforcement of stereotypical beliefs about men and women. The studies cited by Paiva et al. treat women and men as homogenous groups that differ from one other intrinsically. Gender becomes the apparent and essential marker for different behaviors among people. And gender, of course, is a powerful structuring category. At least in Western countries, for example, access to technological fields and expertise has a strong gender bias. Many initiatives[161] address this question of women in technology and strive for an adequate participation in the field. In the specific case of access to the field, it might make sense to single out one aspect of identity, like being a woman, because of its impact (although interdependent markers like social background and access to education should be taken into account). When it comes to addressing gender as a structural and symbolic category in society at large, however, a more complex picture is needed. The sociologist Carol Hageman-White did critical research on gender-specific behavior and found that differences between men and women are not nearly as distinctive as differences between individuals within one gender group (Hagemann-White 1988). Hageman-White's work shows that gender is just one category that makes sense when understood as interwoven with other sociocultural categories, whose meanings change depending on context and setting. Feminists of color, in particular, have pointed

---

161 For an overview on German initiatives, see *http://www.kompetenzz.de/*, checked on 20/12/2013.

out that talking about men and women most often only includes white people (Rothenberg 2004). The term diversity is used to describe how humans differ in ethnicity, sexual orientation, abilities, age, state of health, and economic background. The academic concept of intersectionality was developed, most prominently by Patricia Hill Collins (Collins 1991; also Crenshaw 1991), in order to highlight the intertwining of these categories. Susanne Knudsen writes that: "Intersectionality implies more than [...] studying differences between women and men, and more than diversities within women groups or within men groups. Intersectionality tries to catch the relationships between sociocultural categories and identities" (Knudsen 2006). Thus, instead of just adding one social category to another, the intersectional approach focuses on the crossing points of social markers and the power relations, hierarchies, and politics of in- or exclusion. Social categories are not fixed entities. Their attributed meaning changes throughout history, or depending on a specific situation or differing context. In the early days of science, women were excluded from accessing universities. Black people, regardless of gender, have been excluded – and for far longer – from taking an official stand in significant discourses of science and politics (Ballard 1973). This non-diversity of perspectives shaped the formation of scientific approaches and fields, as well as the production of knowledge in general (Schiebinger 1999; Keller, Longino 1996).

Thus, research that strictly divides between men and women tends to neglect intersectionality and the embedding of gender in a network of social categories. Furthermore, it does not include gender positions that transgress the binary gender order, such as transgender or intersexual realities (Halberstam 2005; Jagose 1996; Hark 2005).

Building an embodied interface agent, however, is already a complex endeavor and thus, up to this point, a very generalized and broad-brushed notion of gender has been employed. Knowledge of gender and gender interdependencies, and a correspondingly more dynamic and diversified concept of identity, have not yet been transferred to the research field of artificial characters. This should be kept in mind as we return to the proposal of Paiva et al.:

> "We aim at creating distinct individual characters which can perform the exact same script, with the same proposed gestures, but behave somehow differently according to their gender. Overall, most gender differences are involuntary movements observed at different levels: (a) gestures and postures that are socially attributable to man or woman (mutually exclusive); (b) gestures and postures that are performed by both male and female, but in a different way; and finally (c) differences between the amount of gestures and postures performed during a conversation." (Paiva et al. 2011, p. 150)

In order to realize gender differences, the designers suggest an extension of existing ECA architecture:

> "The process of generating behaviour in ECAs usually considers three stages: intent planning, behaviour planning and behaviour realization. Since we are interested in involuntary movements, which do not have any specific semantic meaning, they are somewhere in-between the behaviour planning and the behaviour realization. As such, we introduced these involuntary movements at the body level of our characters. Since we do not want to redesign the existent behaviour generators but rather to complement them, and use the currently available tools, our model extends the current behaviour generation pipeline adding a behaviour reviser and an involuntary behaviour generator. The *behaviour reviser* looks at the previous generated behaviours and, if necessary and possible, replaces gestures or postures which are inaccurate in gender. Thus, it adapts or performs gender variations by selecting the appropriate gesture or posture whilst keeping the intended semantic meaning. The *involuntary behaviour generator* generates gender specific involuntary movements. Previous generated behaviours are not overridden or replaced. The inclusion takes place in the empty spaces, in which no concrete behaviour was generated. The process considers the differences between genders: female characters will use more distinct gestures than male characters, and male characters will change from gesture to gesture more frequently reusing previous used gestures." (Paiva et al. 2011, p. 150)

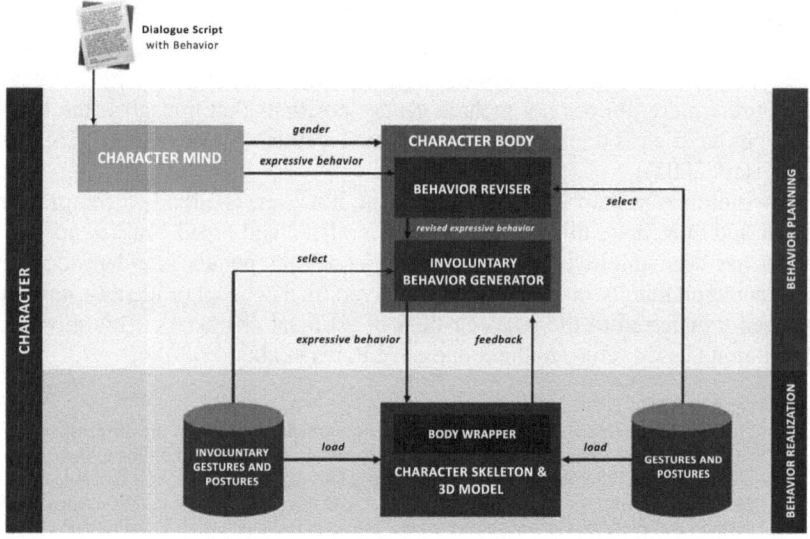

Model for a Character's body processing model with gender

Fig. 19 Gender Module
(Source: Paiva et al., 2011)

3.1. The Return of the Body

Besides the fact that the concept takes binary gender difference as a basis, it is interesting where and how gender is placed within the model. Namely, gender performance is regarded as an involuntary process that happens prior to discourse. It is realized "at the level of the body" of the characters – and in the model, as shown in Figure 19, it takes place in empty spaces.

Thus, the active attribution of gender in the field of Virtual Human/ECA research forms a nodal point where various threads interconnect. With embodiment, gender becomes a topic on research agendas, but in order to form an intelligible identity, the agent needs to follow the heteronormative order. Gender, it seems, happens "in the flesh", as an unconscious process – and this becomes evident from the manner in which the researchers evaluate the model, shown in Figure Twenty.

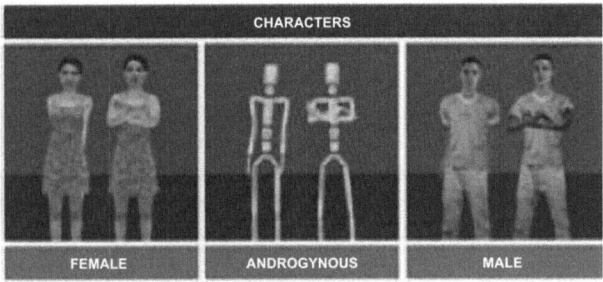

Fig. 20 Gendered Character Evaluation
(Source: Paiva et al., 2011)

Strikingly, the androgynous character is pictured as a skeleton. The un-gendered body is a body without "flesh". To be perceived as lifelike/alive, believable, trustworthy – and to function as an interface in this setting – the agent needs to be "fleshed out", and this materiality, it seems, is always already gendered. Sara Cohen Shabot writes in *Grotesque Bodies* about the way in which artificial characters tend to reinforce gender stereotypes rather than dissolve them:

> "The cyborg, then, is created as a hyper-masculine or hyper-feminine figure in order to save us – so it appears – from the threat of ambiguous gender identities. It may even be argued that the ambiguity of the cyborg regarding the human/technological divide is in a way responsible for the reluctance to create ambiguity in the gender and sexual realm: the reinforcement of the normative gender and sexual structures is the only way – from the point of view of the structures of power – to avoid a pervasive ambiguity that will turn everything into chaos and will strongly shake the foundations of domination. In other words: at times when ambiguity, certain kinds of ambiguity (in this case, an ambiguity concerning the human/technology

divide), is present, other binary structures (such as the gender structure) are reinforced for fear of losing everything as a consequence of a pervasive, chaotic and total blurriness." (Shabot 2006, p. 225)

This idea of the androgynous skeleton against the "fleshed out", gendered agent, invokes the dichotomy of a neutral, objective, reasonable, transcendent mind in contrast to the gendered, material body. Unsurprisingly, with the body and with design processes of embodying, the notion of emotion enters the research field, as will be discussed in the following chapter.

3.2. "Once more with feeling": The Role of Emotions

3.2.1. The Computer as Affective Device

In Douglas Adams' science fiction novel, *The Restaurant at the End of the Universe*, computers are equipped not only with cognitive intelligence, as it is found on the agenda in traditional artificial intelligence research, but also with emotions. Emotions are used to make the devices smarter and more adaptive to the user's needs. In his novel, however, Adams pictures various side effects that emotionally intelligent devices might develop. One character is a depressive robot, called Marvin, who is too smart and sensitive for his own good. Furthermore, Adams describes a drink dispenser that ties up the complete processing power of a spaceship's main computer just to provide a perfect cup of Earl Grey tea. Also noteworthy are the elevators, the "Sirius Cybernetics Corporation Happy Vertical People Transporters", which are able to anticipate when a person wants to go to a certain level of a building. Due to their intelligence and emotional state, however, they tend to get bored with their everyday tasks:

> "Not unnaturally, many elevators imbued with intelligence and precognition become terribly frustrated with the mindless business of going up and down, up and down, experimented briefly with the notion of going sideways, as sort of an existential protest, demanded participation in the decision making process and finally took to squatting in basements sulking." (Adams 1980, p. 47)

Current technology clearly has not reached the point where it denies service because of its emotional state – but, as I will show below, the construction of the embodied conversational agent MAX actually encourages such behavior. In the

3.2. "Once more with feeling": The Role of Emotions

field of design engineering, Virtual Humans exemplify a perception of the computer as a social entity and, with this, emotion and affect play an important role. In this sense, current simulations of the human in computer science, such as social robots and embodied interface agents, address an area that has been neglected in the field of traditional artificial intelligence research. Like embodiment, the term emotion has been reported as missing from the concept of artificial intelligence (Bath 2010; Adam 1998). The coupling of body and emotion is no coincidence: "Within feminist criticism, the interest in affect has, in a sense, a long history: the conceptual links between woman, body and emotion is a recurrent issue" (Koivunen, Paasonen 2001, p. 7). Regarding the cultural history of the gender order, it comes as no surprise that, with the materiality of the body, emotion enters the picture. And with that move, gender is also explicitly on the agenda. In fact, we could say that it is with the materiality of the body that the gendering of computing technology suddenly becomes visible.

Katharina Scherke writes about the works of the eighteenth century "Sensualphilosophen" ("sensualist philosophers") and their differentiated ideals of female and male sentience. A tight coupling of the female gender, body, and abilities, even if not intended by the thinkers as such, led to an exclusion of women from higher education and academia:

> "The female gender, according to authors such as Henri Fouqet (1727-1806), possessed a stronger sensitivity (Jütte 2000). This position was reinforced by the assumption that women, on the basis of their greater irritability, are not in the position to undertake intellectual activities. The supposedly stronger propensity towards affect, which was being argued for in reference to the female body and its functions, and the assumed weakness of the powers of comprehension related to this, were particularly used to legitimise the exclusion of the female gender from higher education."[162]

Sense and sensibility, feelings and rationality, were considered to be not only separate spheres, but also hierarchically related. Scherke stresses that though this was the most common perspective, there have always been opposing views throughout history. The Romantic era and its male artists, for example, emphasized the importance of individual expression and regarded the artistic process as introspect-

---

162 "Das weibliche Geschlecht besaß Autoren, wie etwa Henri Fouqet (1727-1806), zufolge, eine stärkere Empfindsamkeit (vgl. Jütte 2000). Ergänzt wurde diese These durch die Annahme, dass Frauen aufgrund ihrer stärkeren Reizbarkeit zu verstandesmäßiger Tätigkeit nicht in der Lage seien. Die angeblich stärkere Neigung zum Affekt, die unter Hinweis auf den weiblichen Körper und seine Funktionen begründet wurde, und die damit verbundene angenommene Unfähigkeit zur Verstandesleistung wurde vor allem zur Legitimierung des Ausschlusses des weiblichen Geschlechts von höheren Schulen verwendet." (Scherke 2009, p. 25)

tive, as tied to feelings and emotions rather than as a reproduction of outer context (Scherke 2009, p. 25).

For some time now, the senses have undergone a process of reevaluation. Traditional cognitive concepts of purely symbolic and disembodied intelligence have been adjusted and broadened. Increasingly, there is employed a notion of intelligent human behavior that acknowledges the role and value of emotional intelligence. It draws on the importance of emotions for decision-making, as well as on affect for general human behavior and interaction processes, spanning from folk psychological approaches (Goleman 1995) to more academically renowned works like Antonio R. Damasio's aforementioned book *Descartes' Error* (Damasio 1994)[163]. Damasio's work, which is built upon a large corpus of case studies he conducted together with his wife Hannah Damasio, has been received in a wide, interdisciplinary manner. In this book, Damasio reevaluates the role of emotions. In contrast to the common belief that emotions or feelings cloud a rational decision-making process, Damasio's major point is that emotions and feelings are important and helpful for this process. In academic research, the term emotions is commonly preferred to the term feelings. In Damasio's work, feelings are used to describe the subjective experience of alternating bodily sensations, whereas emotions are attributed to certain types of affect that are generally accepted, such as being happy, sad, disappointed, etc. (ibid.). Feelings thus turn into emotions and become socially recognizable, as alterations in facial expressions or gestures, for example.

Sigrid Weigl notes that emotions and feelings always have formed a transfer site and played the role of a mediator:

> "Already in the 18th century, feeling was understood as a kind of medium, which had to mediate between the poles of 'Sensibilité physique' and 'Sensibilité morale'. As far as that goes, it is not by coincidence that today again the concept of feeling – or semantically seemingly more neutral that of emotion – is being developed. The concept stands in the cusp of 'Soma' (body) and 'Sema' (sign): as a medium that bundles or translates physiological phenomena in a specific semantic shape. Without feelings, the gap between body and spirit would have been impossible to bridge."[164]

---

163 See Chapter 3.1.2.
164 "Schon im 18. Jahrhundert wurde das Gefühl als eine Art Medium konzipiert, das zwischen den Polen von Sensibilité physique und Sensibilité morale vermitteln musste. Es ist insofern nicht zufällig, wenn heute wieder mit dem Konzept des Gefühls – oder semantisch scheinbar neutraler dem der Emotion – gearbeitet wird. Das Konzept steht auf der Schwelle von Soma und Sema: als Medium, das physiologische Phänomene in eine spezifische semantische Gestalt bündelt bzw. übersetzt. Ohne Gefühle wäre der Graben zwischen Körper und Geist nicht zu überbrücken." (Weigel 2005, p. 244)

3.2. "Once more with feeling": The Role of Emotions

And, elsewhere:

> "Thereby, all along emotions mark the threshold of 'Soma' (body) and 'Sema' (sign), of empiricism and semantics, of physiology and psychology. When considered as excitations, as biological or neuronal phenomena, they are accessible to empirical research through indirect indications, such as heartbeat, blood pressure and hormonal releases, among others, while when treated as feelings, as spiritual or psychological phenomena, they depend on interpretation."[165]

This role of a mediator is true for Damasio's theory as well as for modern concepts of embodied cognition. On one hand, it is true, of course, that a heavy emotional reaction may hinder an informed decision; on the other, however, it is not possible to abstract from emotion in order to decide or make plans. As the title of the book implies, Damasio criticizes Descartes' modern concept of the mind-body split, as well as any contemporary belief that describes the mind-body relation as similar to the software-hardware relation. He questions the "notion, by way of example, that mind and brain are intertwined, but merely as if the mind is the software that runs in a computer hardware called brain, or that the brain and the body are in a relationship with one another, but only insofar as the former cannot survive without the vital life processes of the latter"[166].

Damasio proposes a holistic approach to embodiment. Processes of the mind and of the achievement of self-consciousness are intrinsically interwoven with the human body. In his conception, the body is not merely the material base for the human mind, it is an active contributor. Just as the mind cannot be separated from the brain, so the brain – which is itself part of the body – cannot be separated from bodily functions. Damasio elaborates on a thought experiment, "the brain in a bowl", in which the brain is split from the body. He shows, more precisely, that this scenario would not work (Damasio 1994, p. 131). Thus, intelligence is always embodied and emotion plays an important role. This "affective turn" is reflected in computing as well.

---

[165] "Dabei markieren die Affekte immer schon die Schwelle von soma und sema, von Empirie und Semantik, von Physiologie und Psychologie. Als Erregungen, als leibliche oder neuronale Phänomene betrachtet, sind sie über indirekte Indikatoren wie Herzschlag, Blutdruck, Hormonausschüttungen u.a. der empirischen Forschung zugänglich, während sie als Gefühle, seelische oder psychische Phänomene betrachtet, auf Deutung angewiesen sind." (Weigel 2005, p. 242)

[166] "Vorstellung beispielsweise, daß Geist und Gehirn miteinander verwandt sind, aber nur insofern, als der Geist das Softwareprogramm ist, das in einer Computerhardware namens Gehirn abläuft, oder daß Gehirn und Körper zwar in Beziehung zueinander stehen, aber nur insofern, als ersteres nicht ohne die vitalen Lebensprozesse des letzteren überleben kann." (Damasio 1994, p. 328)

Virtual Humans serve as an example for this turn from the computer as a rational cognitive device to the "emotion machine", the proposal of which can be located with researcher Marvin Minsky (Minsky 2006), Rosalind Picard of the 'Affective Computing' Group at MIT, or the European network "HUMAINE"[167].

Even Donald E. Norman, to whom I have previously referred, alters and broadens his conception, which ranges from current machines to future machines of emotional intelligence: the more computational artifacts become part of the world and of everyday life, the more they need to function in a variety of contexts and situations, and this entails that they are increasingly in need of emotions. Norman states that these will not be "human emotions" but "machine emotions":

> "Our machines today don't need emotions. Yes, they have a reasonable amount of intelligence. But emotions? Nope. But future machines will need emotions for the same reasons people do: The human emotional system plays an essential role in survival, social interaction, and learning. Machines will need a form of emotion – machine emotion – when they face the same conditions, when they must operate continuously without any assistance from people in the complex ever-changing world where new situations continually arise. [...] Thus, for the same reason that animals and people have emotions, I believe that machines will also need them. They won't be human emotions, mind you, but rather emotions that fit the needs of the machine themselves." (Norman 2005, p. 162)

Nevertheless, nature serves as the role model[168].

The MIT Media Lab gives a wider definition of affective computing by defining it as "computing that relates to, arises from, or deliberately influences emotions". The group's research goals are summed up as "giving machines skills of emotional intelligence, including the ability to recognize, model, and understand human emotion, to appropriately communicate emotion, and to respond to it effectively. We are also interested in developing technologies to assist in the development of human emotional intelligence"[169]. Affective computing not only involves the conceptualization and modeling of emotion systems for social robots or agents, it also addresses the overall field of designing computers for emotion recognition, simulation, and triggering. The agenda of the HUMAINE network demonstrates the need for interdisciplinarity in the area, yet it also highlights the fact that, in the end, knowledge about emotion needs to be formalized:

---

167 HUMAINE – 'Human-Machine Interaction Network on Emotion', a Network of Excellence in the EU's Sixth Framework Programme. See: *http://emotion-research.net*, checked on 04/05/2013.

168 "Animals and humans have developed sophisticated mechanisms for surviving in an unpredictable, dynamic world, coupling the appraisals and evaluations of affect to methods for modulating the overall system. The result is increased robustness and error tolerance. Our artificial systems would do well to learn from their example." (Norman 2005, p. 169)

169 Quote from the institute's website. See: *http://affect.media.mit.edu*, checked on 08/05/2013.

3.2. "Once more with feeling": The Role of Emotions

> "HUMAINE aims to lay the foundations for European development of systems that can register, model and/or influence human emotional and emotion-related states and processes – 'emotion-oriented systems'. Such systems may be central to future interfaces, but their conceptual underpinnings are not sufficiently advanced to be sure of their real potential or the best way to develop them. One of the reasons is that relevant knowledge is dispersed across many disciplines. HUMAINE brings together leading experts from the key disciplines in a programme designed to achieve intellectual integration. It identifies six thematic areas that cut across traditional groupings and offer a framework for an appropriate division of labour – theory of emotion; signal/sign interfaces; the structure of emotionally coloured interactions; emotion in cognition and action; emotion in communication and persuasion; and usability of emotion-oriented systems. Teams linked to each area will run a workshop in it and carry out joint research to define an exemplar embodying guiding principles for future work in their area. Cutting across these are plenary sessions where teams from all areas report; activities to create necessary infrastructure (databases recognising cultural and gender diversity, an ethical framework, an electronic portal); and output to the wider community in the form of a handbook and recommendations of good practice (as precursors to formal standards)."
> (HUMAINE 2004)

Rosalind Picard, of the aforementioned MIT group, has devoted substantial research to the challenges of "affective computing" (Picard 1997). According to her, one of the main problems that arises from the pairing of computers and emotions is the vagueness of emotional states. In a reflection on affective computing, she compares the conceptualization of emotional states with weather phenomena. Like emotion, the weather is characterized as a natural force that is hard to measure and therefore hard to control. She states:

> "There's an old saying in the business world: if you can't measure you can't manage it. Affect, like weather, is hard to measure; and like weather, it probably can't be predicted or controlled with perfect reliability. But, if we can do significantly better than random, then people will at least be less likely to get caught in a thunder storm without an umbrella. If computers can at least measure affect that is clearly expressed to them, say by irate users, then such measures can be useful in comparing product and interface designs." (Picard 2003, p. 4)

In her work, Picard stresses her doubts about computers that genuinely *have* emotions just as humans or animals do. Nevertheless, she regards the computer simulation of emotions as an experimental ground for examining mechanisms of affective states, precisely because the machine can "fake" them and "separate expression from feeling"[170]. The challenge of affective computing, therefore, is once again located at the interface between the human and the machine. In a review of

---

[170] See: "Machines can fake the appearance of an emotion quite well, without having any feelings similar to those we would have: They can separate expression from feeling. With a machine it is easy to see how emotion expression does not imply 'having' the underlying feeling. Machines that might actually 'have' feelings is the key area of affective computing that I expressed serious doubt about in my 1997 book Affective Computing." (Picard 2003, p. 1)

Picard's book, *Affective Computing*, Donald A. Norman states that: "Today's computers are cold, logical machines. They needn't be. In this important book, Rosalind Picard presents a compelling image, not only of how machines might come to have emotions, but why they must. Emotions: not just for animals and people."[171]

So, where formerly the frontier between human and machine has been defined by rational intelligence, a shift takes place that brings emotion into the picture. And, as Picard makes clear, the ability to control such natural states lies in the ability to make them measurable. Bearing in mind Lev Manovich's principles of new media[172], it is interesting to note that Picard characterizes emotions "as both discrete and continuous," and then adds that "it is hard sometimes to know how to describe them" (Picard 2003, p. 3).

When building an affective computing device, the designer is confronted with challenges that arise from the process of turning anything into a computational object. In order to be understood by the human, the affective interface must simulate emotions in such a way that humans can recognize and respond to them. In order to be processable by the machine, feelings must be expressed in discrete units, following the principles of semioticization, standardization, and formalization, and they need to be expressible as algorithms. In this process, "nature" serves as a point of transfer and negotiation, where several fields of knowledge, and thus human expertise, meet. Picard compares the aims and proceedings of affective computing to those of computer vision research:

> "The machine vision community knows and appreciates many of these same modelling problems, which are not necessarily particular to emotion. In that community, researchers who try to understand and model human vision interact with those who want to build machines that see. One might think that the latter group couldn't make much progress without better answers, and better data, from the former group. But, in fact, both groups have learned from each other, and the latter group has built many useful systems, despite that neither group understands fully how the human vision system works. I expect that affect modelling research will proceed similarly: learning from human and animal models of affect, and in turn informing the development of such models by trying to build computationally working systems. I also expect attempts to model affect to result in computational solutions that are useful, even if they turn out to not follow nature's mechanisms." (Picard 2003, p. 5)

Knowledge about the human body serves as a reference point and a source of validation. Manovich's principle of transcoding applies here. Picard, too, sees that

---

171 See: Donald A. Norman, Hewlett-Packard; Professor Emeritus, Cognitive Science, University of California, San Diego; *http://mitpress.mit.edu/catalog/item/default.asp?ttype=2&tid=4062* , checked on 04/05/2013.
172 See Chapter 2.2.2.

3.2. "Once more with feeling": The Role of Emotions

these processes of translation and transference may result in a reconfigured understanding of the human. She still keeps to the logic of "the more we know, the more we can model". This is a general way that knowledge is characterized in the area of artificial intelligence research[173].

> "With any complex modelling problem, there are ways to handle complexity and contribute to progress in understanding. If we want to model affect at the neuropeptide signalling level, then we are limited indeed, because we know only a small part about how such molecules communicate among the organs in our body [...] and realtime sensing of local molecular activity is not easily accomplished; computer modelling is likely to push the human understanding in such an area. But there are other levels where we know more, and can describe a set of requirements, at least for high-level functions to be met." (Picard 2003, p. 5)

What supports the belief in progress is the way that feelings and emotions are reconceptualized within neuroscience. Sigrid Weigl analyzes how the shift takes place: formerly, the happening of feelings was seen as equivalent to certain neuronal movements, the processes were described as parallel; now, feelings have become part of the brain activity themselves, they have moved inside of the brain. Furthermore, with the rise of neuro-imaging, they can even be made visible. The constructional process of the research, the development phase of the images, becomes invisible in the end product. Neuro-imaging appears as a technique that lets the researcher *look into the brain directly*. Another important aspect is that the brain's activity, and thus feelings/emotions, become measurable and in the end computable (which is indispensable for the generating of computer imagery). As Weigl writes: "The material culture of the research on feelings is also shaped by an inverse configuration: through data that appear as images (imaging techniques) and through recording techniques, whose physiognomic interpretation is concealed through methods of measurement (EMG, electronic video evaluation)"[174].

---

173 Cp. "Given the current state of psychological knowledge, large areas of non-verbal dialog behavior cannot be algorithmically formulated, for the foreseeable future. The theoretical gaps in the body of knowledge are too large to be bridged by synthetically generated motions in order to simulate communication processes. Until the closure of those gaps, it is therefore necessary to revert to movement protocols of natural movements." ("Beim derzeitigen psychologischen Wissensstand können wir große Bereiche nonverbalen Dialogverhaltens auf absehbare Zeit noch nicht algorithmisch formulieren. Die theoretischen Lücken in den Wissensbeständen sind zu groß, um mit synthetisch generierten Bewegungen überzeugende Kommunikationsabläufe zu simulieren. Bis zur Schließung der Lücken muss deshalb auf Bewegungsprotokolle von natürlichen Bewegungen zurückgegriffen werden.") (Trogemann 2003, p. 286)
174 "Die materielle Kultur der Gefühlsforschung ist also durch eine inverse Konstellation geprägt: durch Daten, die als Bilder erscheinen (bildgebende Verfahren), und durch Aufzeichnungstechniken, deren physiognomische Interpretation durch Messverfahren verdeckt ist (EMG, elektronische Auswertung von Videos)" (Weigel 2005, p. 272)

Contemporary research on emotion is characterized by an interplay between the inside and the outside (of the body), between what is visible and what is invisible (or, in the logic of the research field, not yet visible). Bodily sensations, or feelings, become accessible through new practices of measurement, experimentation, and visualization. The design of embodied interface agents presents tasks – such as the realistic output of emotions, within a computational context, in terms of gestures and facial expressions – that are also inherent to the cultural history of measurement, feelings, and physiognomy: "It is, however, common among all physiognomic concepts to understand the features and movements of the human face as a code, as a conventionalized system of signs that can be decoded, and which corresponds to a catalogue of affect or to character traits"[175].

3.2.2. "The Agent that Walked Out of the Display..."

A major challenge for multimodal interface experts is the "believability" and "trustworthiness" of the agent. What is meant here is that the agent's performance in appearance, motions, and reactions – its verbal as well as non-verbal behavior – has to be perceived as consistent and sensible within the user-agent interaction. In one of the first compendia for Embodied Conversational Agents, Justine Cassell singles out four components that lead to the production of believable behavior: emotion, personality, performatives, and conversational function (Cassell 2000a, p. 2). The aspect of emotion is one that interweaves all other functions and thus plays a significant role.

Earlier[176], I stated that an agent is distinguishable from ordinary software programs due to the conception of its intelligence and autonomy, and to its strict model of socially normative behavior, which results in a formalized concept of agency. The embodied agent, however, on its way to becoming a lifelike Virtual Human, is furthermore defined by its ability to perceive, react to, generate, and display emotions:

---

175 "Allen physiognomischen Konzepten ist jedoch gemeinsam, dass sie die Merkmale und Bewegungen des menschlichen Gesichts als Code begreifen, als ein konventionalisiertes und also decodierbares Zeichensystem, das mit einem Affektkatalog oder mit Charaktermerkmalen korrespondiert." (Weigel 2005, p. 263)
176 See Chapter 1.3.3.

3.2. "Once more with feeling": The Role of Emotions

> "The capability of displaying emotion seems to be a critical component of creating intelligent agents with whom humans can comfortably relate and communicate. The emotional aspect distinguishes a dead machine from an agent who is believable, alive, and trustworthy." (Perry 1996)

Lynellen Perry makes clear that the boundary object dividing "dead machines" from "living agents" is emotion. The success of the interface agent very much depends on the acceptance of the user. Multimodal interface experts note that since humans tend to anthropomorphize computers anyway, an embodied agent should be designed so that a somewhat stable relationship emerges during the human-machine interaction. This stability is achieved through trustworthiness.

An example of an interface with an emotion model integrated into its system is the agent system MAX. The designers of MAX set out to explore "the generation of natural multimodal behavior" (Becker et al. 2004). The MAX system was gradually extended in order to serve as a conversational agent for various projects, such as the project of solving Virtual Reality construction tasks together with humans or of impersonating a virtual receptionist in the hallway of the lab of the working group that developed it. Since January 2004, a MAX system has served as a virtual museum guide at the Heinz-Nixdorf MuseumsForum (HNF), a computer museum in Paderborn, Germany (ibid.). This is of particular interest since Virtual Humans, thus far, are rarely found as "real-life applications". MAX *meets* the visitors of the museum as a human-sized visualization on a screen. The system includes a camera, for visual perception, such that it may *notice* people passing by. MAX is meant to engage them in conversation and to provide information about the museum. Due to the problem of background noise in such a "real world situation", the visitor converses with the system using keyboard and mouse. MAX *answers* with a synthesized voice, gestures, and facial expressions.

Fig. 21 Virtual Human MAX at the Heinz-Nixdorf Museum, Paderborn
(Source: Kopp et al., 2003)

The system architecture of MAX contains, among other things, direct feedback in a virtual reality application and a BDI interpreter for what is called "deliberative reasoning". The "deliberative component" in itself is already multi-layered, consisting of different submodules, such as stances of dynamic and static knowledge, which inform and are informed by the dialog manager (Becker et al. 2004; Kopp et al. 2003).

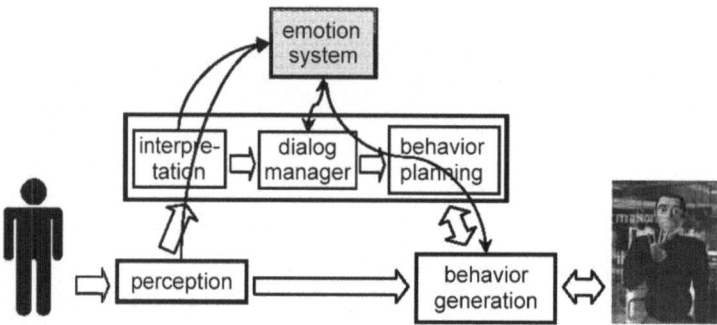

Fig. 22 Max System Architecture with Emotion System
(Source: Kopp et al., 2003)

As Figure 22 shows, MAX is able to perceive visual information about the area where the input device – in this setting, the keyboard – is located and about some of the exhibition space. Changes that take place are perceived as "events", and the "deliberative component" is the unit where incoming information is processed and checked against the agent's internal "beliefs" (knowledge) and "desires" (plans)[177]. This unit also contains "spatial memory" so that MAX can refer to objects or persons that surround the system. The behavior generation module is able to respond directly to informational input from the perception module so that the agent can move its head directly into the direction of a visitor; at the same time, behavior generation is informed by the deliberative component.

As the architecture overview shows, the MAX system does not just include sensory systems, a BDI interpreter, and a behavior generation module. It also contains an emotion system that plays a crucial role for all other system components. The importance of the emotion system for the system as a whole is described by the designers of MAX:

> "Finally, Max is equipped with an emotion system that continuously runs a dynamic simulation to model the agent's emotional state. The emotional state is available anytime both in continuous terms of valence and arousal as well as a categorized emotion, e.g. happy, sad or angry, along with an intensity value [...]. The continuous values modulate subtle aspects of the agent's behaviors, namely, the pitch and speech rate of his voice and the rates of breathing and eye blink. The weighted emotion category is mapped to Max's facial expression and is sent to the agent's deliberative processes, thus making him cognitively 'aware' of his own emotional state and subjecting it to his further deliberations. The emotion system, in turn, receives input from both the perception (e.g., seeing a person immediately causes positive stimulus) and the deliberative component." (Becker et al. 2004, p. 4)

Thus, unlike current human-computer interfaces, the MAX system is sensitive to what is regarded as emotional impact expressed by the users (and pre-scripted by the designers). For example, insulting behavior will lead to MAX eventually withdrawing from the screen. If the user types in words that are listed as insults in the "discourse knowledge module" of MAX's "deliberative component", this will lead to negative impulses on the emotion system. Such behavior, if repeated, "will put the agent in an extremely bad mood, which in turn can eventually result in MAX leaving the scene, an effect introduced to de-escalate rude visitor behavior" (ibid.). When the user compliments MAX and tells the system "I am sorry", the agent will, after some time, return to the screen. Its return to the interaction setting, however, depends on the strength and duration of the insults:

---

177 Cp. Chapter 3.1.2.

"As mentioned [...], we choose a conversational agent scenario in which the virtual human MAX acts as a museum guide. Within this scenario, MAX engages with human partners in a natural face-to-face conversation and conducts multimodal small talk dialogs using speech, gestures, and facial behaviors. The emotions of MAX can be triggered in different ways. For example, MAX's emotions are triggered positively when a new person enters his field of view or when the human partner's verbal expression is interpreted as a compliment. MAX's emotions are triggered negatively when the human partner's verbal expression is interpreted as obscene or politically incorrect." (Boukricha, Wachsmuth 2011)

Fig. 23 Max as the Guide at the Heinz-Nixdorf Museum Gets Angry and Leaves the Display (Source: Becker et al., 2004)

The MAX system uses an emotion model that draws on the works of physiological psychologist Wilhelm Wundt (Wundt 1913), and more precisely on a framework derived from Wundt by Albert Mehrabian, an expert in non-verbal behavior, who has a background in both engineering and psychology (Becker et al. 2004, p. 2). Here, affective states are characterized by emotions and moods, where emotions are seen as shorter, more strongly felt experiences, and moods are seen as "more diffuse and longer lasting" (ibid.). The terms that are used to first describe and later model the emotional states are called "pleasure, arousal, and dominance" (PAD). These are used, furthermore, in order to conceptualize a three-dimensional PAD space. The valence for "pleasure", for example, derives from what is constructed as positive stimuli to the system from outside input (e.g. user utterances). "Arousal" is comprised of the activity range of the system, while "dominance" describes the level of control (or "submissiveness") the system has regarding different situations and events. This is linked to the static knowledge module and the BDI interpreter of the system (Becker et al. 2004, p. 2). Thus, the MAX system does not employ the theory, called OCC, that is most commonly used to model emotional states within computational systems (Zong et al. 2000). Christian

3.2. "Once more with feeling": The Role of Emotions

Becker, Stefan Kopp, and Ipke Wachsmuth, who decided to use a multidimensional model of emotion mapping, relate to the OCC model and develop their approach with awareness of OCC's influence (Becker et al. 2004, p. 3). Before discussing the OCC model and its impact, I want to draw the attention to MAX's companion, EMMA, a system that was developed a few years later.

EMMA is an embodied conversational agent, just like MAX, and was designed in order to elaborate even further the role of emotions in artificial systems. The scenario EMMA provides is very interesting from a gender perspective. EMMA stands for Empathic MultiModal Agent and it is, as the name indicates, a model concerned with empathy: "The proposed model of empathy is illustrated in a conversational agent scenario involving the virtual humans MAX and EMMA. In the conversational agent scenario in which the virtual human MAX engages in a multimodal small talk with a human partner, we integrate EMMA as a third interaction partner. Within this scenario, the human partner can trigger the emotions of both virtual humans by either insult or kindness toward them. During the interaction of MAX with the human partner, EMMA follows the conversation and reacts to MAX's emotions empathically" (Boukricha, Wachsmuth 2011, p. 198). In order to do this, "EMMA internally simulates MAX's facial expression" (ibid.). EMMA's architecture is similar to MAX's, but with the addition of being able to modulate empathy:

> "Based on the Empathy Modulation [...], an elicited empathic emotion is modulated by means of the following two factors: First, EMMA's mood which changes dynamically over the interaction when the human partner triggers EMMA's emotions negatively or positively. Second, EMMA's relationship to MAX represented by EMMA's liking toward MAX and EMMA's familiarity with MAX. The values of liking and familiarity are predefined and do not change dynamically over the interaction. Thus, the impact of the mood factor as dynamically changing over the interaction can be better perceived in this scenario. For example, when EMMA's emotions are triggered by the human partner negatively, EMMA's empathy with MAX's positive emotional states is either low or is not triggered at all. Depending on the values and weights of liking and familiarity different profiles of EMMA's modulated empathy with MAX can be defined. The higher the values of liking and familiarity, the higher EMMA empathizes with MAX." (Boukricha, Wachsmuth 2011, p. 202)

Thus, in the cases of EMMA and MAX, the artifact's gender coding reaches beyond its appearance. The fact that EMMA is introduced in order to explore the role of empathy in an interaction setting resonates with the concept of femininity and emotion. In the scenario, EMMA reads MAX's facial expressions and adjusts its own expressions accordingly:

> "EMMA can empathize with MAX and thus align to MAX's emotions depending on her mood and current relationship to him. [...] Once the empathic emotion is modulated, EMMA's

> multiple modalities are triggered by means of the Expression of Empathy [...] EMMA's verbal utterance is triggered as follows: In this scenario, MAX's emotions can be triggered negatively or positively by the human partner. Consequently, this is reflected by a negative or a positive change in MAX's pleasure value. By calculating the difference of the pleasure values of MAX's perceived emotional state, [...] EMMA can detect the changes in MAX's pleasure value. A positive change in pleasure triggers a verbal expression of EMMA that encourages the human partner to continue being kind to MAX. A positive change that results in a positive pleasure value triggers verbal expressions such as 'That's great, you are so kind to MAX!'. A positive change in the negative space of pleasure triggers verbal expressions such as 'This is not enough! You have to be kinder!'. A negative change in pleasure triggers a verbal expression of EMMA that advises the human partner not to be unfriendly to MAX. A negative change in the space of positive pleasure triggers verbal expressions such as 'Why are you saying that to MAX? This is nasty!'. A negative change that results in a negative pleasure value triggers verbal expressions such as 'Better think about what you are saying! This is really nasty!'"
> (Boukricha, Wachsmuth 2011, p. 203)

To a great extent, EMMA's emotions, utterances, and actions are defined by either MAX or the human interaction partner, and, of course, by the design and scripting of the system and interaction setting in general.

Even though systems like MAX and EMMA do not come close to the emotionally intelligent and autonomous elevators satirically pictured by Douglas Adams, a major shift nonetheless takes place. If this approach of "affective computing" succeeds, users will have to behave according to preset standards while interacting with computational systems. The intertwining of sociotechnical spheres gains a wider impact in so far as it will be likely, in the future, to find yourself in a scenario in which, if you are not nice and polite to technological devices, they simply may not work. The realization of MAX and EMMA furthermore points to an additional way in which gender stereotypes may be inscribed within system architectures.

3.2.3. The OCC Model of Emotion

On account of its impact for research areas such as affective computing, the design of Virtual Humans, and social robotics, I will outline the aforementioned OCC model of emotion.

The OCC model, dubbed after the first letters of the surnames of its authors, can be traced back to the book, *The Cognitive Structure of Emotions*, by Andrew Ortony, Gerald L. Clore, and Allan Collins. The proposed aim of the book is, first, "to bring some semblance of order to what remains a very confused and confusing field of study" and, second, "to lay the foundation for a computationally tractable model of emotion", which "could in principle be used in an Artificial Intelligence

(AI) system that would, for example, be able to reason about emotions" (Ortony et al. 1988, p. 2).

The research areas from which the authors come are cognitive science and social psychology, with a strong interest in computational aspects of human behavior. According to Ortony et al., emotions are based upon the "cognitive construal of events" (ibid., p. 14). "Taking the perspective of empirical psychology and cognitive science, we start with the assumption that emotions arise as a result of the way in which the situations that initiate them are construed by the experiencer" (ibid., p. 1). In fact, cognitive processes are seen as the basis for any kind of emotional experience. Following this, the authors explain why physiological, behavioral, and expressive aspects of emotions are being neglected within the theory: "For example, physiology is essential for emotional experience but we have ignored it because it is not relevant to the question of the role that cognition plays in the elicitation of emotions" (Ortony et al. 1988, p. 172). Thus, cognition is antecedent to everything else.

A main goal of the OCC theoretical approach is to provide a theory of the structures by which emotions emerge – Ortony, Clore, and Collin refer to this as the "psychological possibilities of emotions" (ibid., preface). They make clear that their aim is not that of finding an explanation for local or culturally specific descriptions of emotional settings. Along these lines, the OCC model aims at providing a meta-theory for emotions that is adaptable to a variation of local, cultural, and (inter)personal realities. The authors emphasize that the model focuses on emotion-eliciting structures rather than on "emotion words", which are the terms used to describe what is seen as the character of the emotion itself. There may be various words used to refer to one emotion type, and it is such types – rather than the variety of expressions linked to them – that interest the authors. This is how the OCC model seeks to solve the problem that is posed by the fact that emotions are, as Rosalind Picard put it, both discrete and continuous.

Of specific interest are the references that Ortony, Clore, and Collin make – as a means of verifying their theoretical grounding – to practices of writing literature. Writers, they state, do not depend on emotion words but instead construe events so as to trigger certain emotions, which the reader will then experience. Therefore, "if the eliciting conditions of an emotion are to be effective, the experiencing individual must encode the relevant situation in a particular way. In other words, if an emotion such as distress is a reaction to some undesirable event, the event itself must be construed as undesirable, and because construing the world is a cognitive process, the eliciting conditions of emotions embody the cognitive representations that result from such construals" (ibid., p. 4).

It is important to keep in mind that the OCC model sets out, from the very beginning, not only to explain the structure of emotion, but also to provide a framework for artificial intelligence system construction. In their structuring of emotions, Ortony, Clore, and Collin single out three major aspects of perceiving the world, or of perceiving changes in the state of the world. As Figure 24 shows, emotions are defined as valenced reactions to consequences of events, actions of agents, or aspects of objects. Events are "people's construals about things that happen, considered independently of any beliefs they may have about actual or possible causes"; "objects are objects viewed qua objects"; and "agents are things considered in light of their actual or presumed instrumentality or agency" (ibid., p. 18).

What is therefore central is the construal of what is happening. Consequently, objects might receive the status of agents if they are experienced as such. Depending on whether the change of situation is due to an event, an agent, or an object, different affective reactions will follow. The complexity of these reactions differs depending on the cause. In the illustration of the OCC model, the structural elements are written in upper case and the terms referring to emotion types are written in lower case. The authors stress that the terms in lower case are only suggestions for representing emotion types – they may vary. Basic classifications for emotions are pleased/displeased, approving/disapproving, and liking/disliking. These classifications, which the authors state are the most neutral terms they could conceive, then lead to a further differentiation of emotion types. For the representations of emotion types note Figure 24.

3.2. "Once more with feeling": The Role of Emotions   151

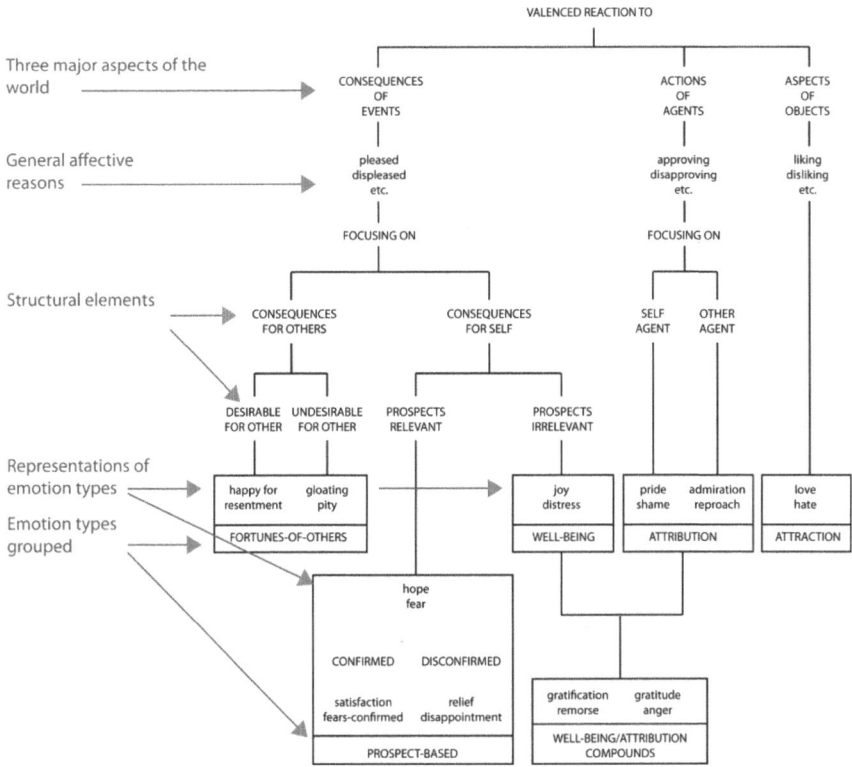

Fig. 24 Overview OCC Model of Emotion Structure
(Source: Illustration Claude Draude according to Ortony et al., 1988)

To understand this theory of emotion, we must be aware that an emotion is here understood as a cognitively valenced reaction towards something – an event, an agent, an object. The authors state, for example, that within their model the experience of "surprise" is not an emotion, simply because it does not correspond to the notion of an emotion being a valenced reaction. "Unexpectedness" is viewed "as a global variable that can modulate the intensity of any emotion". Thus surprise is not an emotion, but simply a cognitive state. Emotions need to be valenced (ibid., p. 32).

In this sense, the OCC model appears as a simplified and standardized version of the world of emotions and human feelings. This appearance is augmented by the fact that the OCC theory itself gives the impression of having been made to measure its own ends. Reflecting on the illustrated overview (Fig. 24), a question comes to mind: How is such a precise separation of events, agents, and objects able to meet "real world situations"? Ortony, Clore, and Collin are aware of this question. They state that in reality most emotions derive from a mixture of the three main aspects, and that even this mixture may – up to a certain point – be expressed with their model. Still, many emotional states fall outside of the OCC model and are thereby not considered to be emotions. The theory leaves out all states that do not respond to the straightforward logic of causes (events, agents, objects) and their immediate effects (pleased/displeased, approving/disapproving, liking/disliking). Nonetheless, even the OCC model, with its simplification and standardization of human emotion, presents a challenge for the modeling of emotion systems of embodied interface agents or social robots. In other words, even when simplified and standardized, human emotion, due to its complexity and to the vast amount of information that needs to be processed, remains a challenge[178]. The OCC model indicates one of the key difficulties encountered by interface design when "real world issues" are transferred to computational systems: the underlying working principles determine the way new media objects, or adequate theories, can be conceptualized and built. Thus, the OCC model follows the logic of the rule-oriented machine. By reformulating emotions as consisting of strict and precise categories, a standardized system of human emotions is developed that can be applied to a computable model. Here, a co-construction of theory and technological basis takes place.

Ortony, Clore, and Collin clearly state that, while forming their theoretical model, they already bear in mind the possibilities for the future use of this model in the field of applied computer science. This, of course, explains the wide acceptance of the theory among artificial intelligence experts and the impact it has on the field. Furthermore, Ortony, Clore, and Collin suggest that after implementing emotion systems based on the OCC model, this system may be used to test human emotional behavior. This concurrence of theory, computer model, and notions about what does and does not pass as valid human behavior is not seen as problematic (Ortony et al. 1988, p. 12f). Computer systems based on the OCC model provide a (semiotic-material) manifestation of this very theory. Testing

---

178 Cp. "Beyond these, there is a well-known and widely accepted classification of emotions. This is the OCC Cognitive Model [...] which provides not only a definition of them, but also a hierarchy based on the target of the emotion (self, other) and other metacategories such as consequences of events, aspects and actions. However, this is a strict and complex cognitive model of the key emotions. In order to use this approach, one does not only need to model the emotions themselves, but it is necessary to adopt the entire cognitive model including all its processes and structures. In that case we would be able to manage the emotions appropriately, but it would also be very cumbersome. Even a simple model here implies a complex architecture, as is clearly visible from reports on similar projects (Integrating Models of Personality and Emotions into Lifelike Characters) at DFKI." (Tatai et al. 2003)

3.2. "Once more with feeling": The Role of Emotions 153

emotions with such a computing system provides a circular argument and is questionable from an epistemological and objective standpoint.

This approach will fail to achieve successful computer interaction if, in future interfaces, the human does not respond to the OCC model of emotion. More likely, however, is an outcome in which the human user proves to be adaptive to the system and finds some way to work around or with the provided setting.

Interestingly, Ortony, Clore, and Collin are aware of cultural differences – they even devote a sub-chapter of the book to "cross-cultural issues". They hope, by means of their approach of dividing the structure of emotions from the expressions or content, to get as close as possible to a universal theory of emotions:

> "We have tried to specify the cognitive antecedents of emotions at a level of description that is, at least in principle, culturally universal in the sense that the specification of the classes of situations that lead to emotions is in terms of psychological constructs for which a reasonable case for universality can be made. These are the constructs of desirability, praiseworthiness and appealing, which we think are much more likely to be culturally universal than, for example, descriptions in terms of social constructs such as leisure, work, and social networks. Thus, for example, we think it more likely that, particularly, a primitive culture will perceive the world in terms of such constructs as the desirability (or otherwise) of an event, than in terms of a difference between work and leisure." (Ortony et al. 1988, p. 175)

This quote not only unmasks the authors' view of the world as a place of "primitive" ("other") cultures and "advanced" ("our") culture, it also demonstrates the old trick whereby a theory that is very much grounded in a specific sociocultural setting nonetheless claims to be universal and objective. A great deal of the empirical research that informs the OCC model is drawn from US-American sport events, like baseball or football games, in which the players are male (ibid., p. 4). Due to the need for generalization, this does not occur explicitly within the actual model. Categories like gender, ethnicity, or age are thus viewed not as inherent to the structure of the model, but as content that can be later applied (if necessary for the system).

3.2.4. Alternative Approaches to Emotion

Although prominent, the OCC model is not the only approach towards emotion in the field of affective computing. The challenges and difficulties that arise when trying to produce "machine emotions" are addressed in research. There are critiques within computing that question the very need to model the agent's emotions or to simulate human feelings. One alternative research path that has been suggested involves concentrating on the user's experience. This shifts the focus from determining the agent's inner state to understanding the kind of emotions the user might experience during the interaction. Nicole Krämer and Gary Bente elaborate upon this:

> "Must the interface agent actually 'have' emotions itself, in order to display an appropriate non-verbal behavior, and thereby to be able to trigger emotions in the user? Must an initial underlying state be modeled, in order to be able to control behavior (although then again, at first extensive knowledge on processes must be available, which poses an even greater riddle for us), or can a more direct way be pursued?
> From this it is not necessary to conclude that agents should also actual feel their 'emotions' — as to that, the consensus dictates that this kind of vitalization is neither desirable nor expedient. Instead, the focus is on whether one should use assumptions on the functioning of the emotions in order to control the behavior of the interface agent, when the main goal is the influencing of emotional reactions by the user."[179]

What Bente and Krämer demonstrate is how underlying basic assumptions alter the course of research. In the case of affective computing, non-verbal behavior plays an important role. Regarding the analysis of non-verbal behavior, Bente and Krämer refer to two basic (and opposed) research approaches: the "classic emotion view", or "readout", and the "social-communicative approach"[180]. The classic view reaches back to Charles Darwin and follows the belief that non-verbal behavior primarily expresses inner states of the human. These inner states correlate with specific facial expressions and gestures. As such, they are readable for others. This approach follows the general idea that emotions are, at base, relatively free from cultural impact. The "social-communicative approach", in contrast, regards emotion as a means for organizing social communication and interaction[181]. There is, then, a fundamental difference between the two research perspectives. The first views human emotions as primarily determined by internal states, whereas the second regards sociocultural settings and the interaction's specificity as crucial for

---

179 "Muss der Interface Agent tatsächlich selbst Emotionen 'haben', um ein angemessenes non-verbales Verhalten zu zeigen und dadurch Emotionen beim Nutzer auslösen zu können? Muss zunächst ein darunter liegender Zustand modelliert werden, um Verhalten steuern zu können (obwohl dann zunächst umfangreiches Wissen über Prozesse vorliegen muss, die uns noch große Rätsel aufgeben) oder kann ein direkter Weg beschritten werden?
Dabei soll es nicht darum gehen, ob Agenten ihre 'Emotionen' auch tatsächlich fühlen sollen - diesbezüglich herrscht Einigkeit darüber, dass diese Art von Belebung nicht erwünscht und zielführend ist. Fokussiert wird stattdessen, ob man Annahmen über das Funktionieren von Emotionen nutzen sollte, um das Verhalten des Interface Agenten zu steuern, wenn das eigentliche Ziel die Beeinflussung emotionaler Reaktionen beim Benutzer darstellt." (Krämer, Bente 2003, p. 287)
180 "sozial-kommunikativer Ansatz" (ibid, p. 289f)
181 See: "The function of the mimic displays would not be to make core emotions legible, but instead to organize social encounters." ("Funktion der mimischen Displays sei es nicht, Basisemotionen ablesbar zu machen, sondern soziale Begegnungen zu organisieren.") (ibid., p. 290)

3.2. "Once more with feeling": The Role of Emotions

non-verbal behavior. Bente and Krämer suggest that the communicative approach to emotions should be followed. This means, with regard to the realization of affective components in human-agent interaction, that it might not be useful to link the non-verbal behavior of the agent to models that presume basic emotions to be internal states of the agent. Instead, the agent's behavior should facilitate a comfortable interaction environment. An example of this sort of facilitation may be found in the description of the project EMBASSI, which aims at supporting TV and audio recordings in private households:

> "When the Agent needs to announce to someone that the recording of their favorite film was not successful, they must, through appropriate behavioral indications, manage to avoid that the user's exchanges his device in anger, but instead that he calms down. To this end, the agent must definitely not be 'sad' – directed by the hope that when it is sad, the user will see that it is sorry for the fault etc. – instead, it is sufficient in certain cases to let the agent demonstrate a behavior that has been shown to have a soothing effect in certain situations. This can, of course, result in a behavior, which evokes certain emotional attributions in the user — but without it being necessary to model the coherence of situation, emotion and behavior and to shift the agent to an 'emotional state'."[182]

Bente and Krämer propose an alternative architecture that is based not on the internal state of the agent, but rather on the agent's effect on the human user (Krämer, Bente 2003, p. 290).

The overviews of Figures Twenty-five and Twenty-six illustrate the way in which agent design differs from the more common approach.

---

182 "Wenn der Agent etwa verkünden muss, dass die Aufnahme des Lieblingsfilms nicht erfolgreich war, soll er durch entsprechende nonverbale Begleitverhaltweisen erreichen, dass der Benutzer nicht wutentbrannt das Gerät umtauscht, sondern sich beruhigt. Dazu muss allerdings nicht der Agent 'traurig' werden - geleitet von der Hoffnung, dass wenn dieser traurig ist, der Benutzer sieht, dass er den Fehler bedauert etc. - sondern es reicht aus, den Agenten in solchen Fällen ein Verhalten zeigen zu lassen, von dem nachgewiesen wurde, daß es eine besänftigende Wirkung in bestimmten Situationen hat. Dies kann im Ergebnis natürlich durchaus ein Verhalten sein, das bestimmte Emotionszuschreibungen durch den Benutzer hervorruft – aber ohne dass es notwendig war, den Zusammenhang von Situation, Emotion und Verhalten zu modellieren und den Agenten in einen 'emotionalen Zustand' zu versetzen." (Krämer, Bente 2003, p. 291)

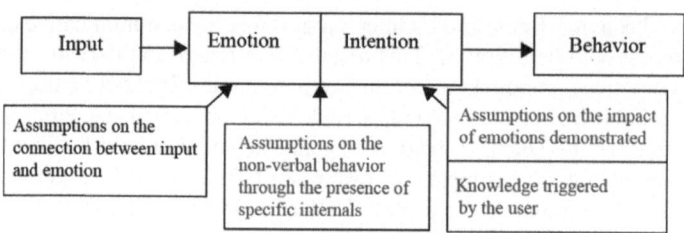

Sketch of current implementations, considering the modeling of underlying conditions

Fig. 25 Typical Architecture
(translated; for original see Appendix, *Fig. i*)

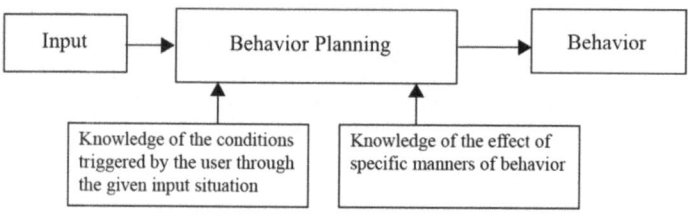

Alternative architecture, considering a set of rules on the effect of non-verbal manners

Fig. 26 Alternative Implementation of Emotions
(translated; for original see Appendix, *Fig. ii*)

The proposed architecture provides a more open approach. It avoids some of the epistemological traps found in the traditional view on emotions. Nonetheless, the problem of determined states remains – it has simply been shifted from the agent to the user. There needs to be a system that correlates intended effects on the human recipient with the non-verbal (as well as verbal) behavior of the agent. The project EMBASSI realizes an artifact that is comprised of a dialog management system, a speech generating module, a planning module for multimodal in- and output, a user interface, a speech synthesis tool, and an anthropomorphized character: "In order for the anthropomorphic figure to be able to demonstrate movements and facial expressions that correspond to the content they aim to convey (not a trivial problem, since the module controlled by the agent first and foremost does not know what the agent is saying), there must be underlying rules that offer information on what kind of statements should be supported by nonverbal signals, in order to provoke the intended state in the user"[183].

---

183 "Damit die anthropomorphe Figur Bewegungen und Mimik zeigen kann, die den wiederzugebenden Inhalten entsprechen (ein nicht triviales Problem, da das den Agenten steuernde Modul zunächst einmal nicht weiß, was der Agent äußert), müssen Regeln vorliegen, die Auskunft darüber

3.2. "Once more with feeling": The Role of Emotions

Krämer and Bente implement a framework that attributes speech acts to desired intentions/effects and matches these with the behavior of the agent. According to the authors, the speech acts are based on John S. Searle's theory (although the cited article does not offer further elaboration of this point).

Table: Overview of speech acts, intentions pursued and the behavior indicating them

Speech	Intention/ objectives for the user	Specific behavior Agent	Timing
message_greeting: the system greets the user in the beginning of the interaction	The user feels greeted in a friendly and polite way	Eyebrows high and eyes 1 second larger Laughter Wave (optional) Smiling Head tilting (c. 10 degrees to the right)	Start of the display Before the start Before the start After greeting After greeting (for 4 seconds)
message_closing: will be used at the end of the interaction with the user	The user feels he has been given a friendly goodbye	Smiling	After farewell
message_inform [status: warning]	User must pay attention urgently	Eyebrows raised Eyes larger Hands raised. Palms towards the user (maybe only one hand raised with forefinger pointing up)	Throughout the interaction In the beginning, then slowly lowering hands
message_inform [status: busy]	User must remain patient	Head slightly bending downwards	Throughout the interaction

Fig. 27 Speech Act Table (Excerpt)
(translated; for original see Appendix, *Fig. iii*)

The table in Figure 27 shows how the attribution works. Although it is the internal state of the agent's emotions that have been modeled, the focus is on user reception. This means that the way the human reacts needs to be anticipated and predetermined. The challenges that arise from the task of reconfiguring human behavior in terms of computing are simply shifted: the new model runs the risk of inscribing – without regard for specific context – fixed assumptions about humans and their behavior. According to speech act theory, and especially to its notion of indirect speech acts, what is essential are not fixed assumptions, but rather the context, situational setting, and shared background of those who are communicating (Searle 1975).

The rules of the framework are generated from empirical research, which at this point, the authors claim, is not sufficiently extensive (Krämer, Bente 2003, p. 292). The rough-cut character of the framework is thus attributed to this missing data. It is believed that the system will become more fine-tuned as the empirical

---

geben, welche Art von Aussage durch welche nonverbalen Signale unterstützt werden sollen, um einen angestrebten Zustand im Benutzer auszulösen." (Krämer, Bente 2003, p. 292)

groundwork increases in extent. Krämer and Bente, however, note the context-dependency of non-verbal behavior and affective design. They state that: "In the end, it will not be possible to make an ultimate prediction on which (emotional) reactions a specific behavior from the interface agent will provoke in the user — but this problem will be not be solved by a recourse to emotions"[184].

In a critical analysis, Corinna Bath[185] also points out existing alternatives to the OCC approach in affective computing. She remarks, furthermore, that:

> "This reorientation introduces new research questions. By way of example, it is now relevant whether users find a system 'likeable' or morally acceptable, or whether they become emotionally involved. Thereby, methods of system development become as affected as those of evaluation. With new problem presentations, critical theoretical references become even more important. 'Design for experience' currently positions itself as an innovative approach, which separates itself firmly, firstly from the conventional HCI methods of usability, but equally distinguishes itself fundamentally, secondly from traditional understandings of software developments, thirdly from perceptions of scientific objectivity as well as, fourthly, from concepts that perceive emotions as information and thus express the communication of emotions through a simple model of sender and recipient."[186]

The field of "affective computing" presents itself in a more differentiated manner and provides points of connection for the sort of interventions found in gender and cultural studies. As Bath points out, one of the most promising approaches is "design for experience". Like Krämer and Bente's approach, "design for experience" shifts the basic assumptions and the focus of the research. Kirsten Boehner, Rogério DePaula, Paul Dourish, and Phoebe Sengers deal with the question of the interface by focusing on the users and their subjective experiences in the interaction

---

184 "Letztendlich wird nicht endgültig vorhergesagt werden können, welche (emotionalen) Reaktionen ein spezifisches Verhalten des Interface Agenten beim Nutzer auslösen – dieses Problem löst aber auch der Rückgriff auf Emotionen nicht." (ibid.)
185 Drawn from a research project with Jutta Weber: "Sozialität mit Maschinen. Anthropomorphisierung und Vergeschlechtlichung in aktueller Agentenforschung und Robotik" ("Sociality with Machines. Anthropomorphizing and Gendering in Current Agent Research and Robotics.") April 2004 - September 2006 supported by the 'Österreichisches Ministerium für Bildung, Forschung und Kultur' ('Austrian Ministry for Education, Research and Culture').
186 "Die Neuausrichtung wirft neue Forschungsfragen auf. Es wird nun beispielsweise relevant, ob NutzerInnen ein System 'sympathisch' finden oder moralisch akzeptabel, oder ob sie emotional involviert werden. Dabei werden Methoden der Systementwicklung ebenso berührt wie die der Evaluation. Mit den neuen Problemstellungen gewinnen darüber hinaus kritische Theoriebezüge an Bedeutung. „Design for Experience" positioniert sich gegenwärtig als ein innovativer Ansatz, der sich erstens von den herkömmlichen HCI-Methoden der Usability dezidiert abgrenzt, sich zugleich aber auch grundlegend unterscheidet von zweitens traditionellen Verständnissen der Softwareentwicklung, von drittens wissenschaftlichen Objektivitätsauffassungen sowie von viertens Konzepten, die Emotionen als Information verstehen und bei deren Kommunikation von Emotionen von einem simplen Sender-Empfänger-Modell ausgehen." (Bath 2010, p. 197)

(Boehner et al. 2005). As in Dourish's embodied interaction approach[187], human-computer interaction is understood as a flexible, co-productive process that varies according to the individual user or to a community of users. Artifacts, the environment, situatedness, and local practices all play an important role. Hence, the actual interface emerges while the interaction takes place; it is not something merely technical, which pre-exists, but rather a socio-cultural-technical construct. The approach is summed up as follows:

> "While affective computing explicitly challenges the primacy of rationality in cognitivist accounts of human activity, at a deeper level it relies on and reproduces the same information-processing model of cognition. In affective computing, affect is often seen as another kind of information – discrete units or states internal to an individual that can be transmitted in a loss-free manner from people to computational systems and back. Drawing on cultural, social, and interactional critiques of cognition which have arisen in HCI, we introduce and explore an alternative model of emotion as interaction: dynamic, culturally mediated, and socially constructed and experienced. This model leads to new goals for the design and evaluation of affective systems – instead of sensing and transmitting emotion, systems should support human users in understanding, interpreting, and experiencing emotion in its full complexity and ambiguity." (Boehner et al. 2005, p. 59)

Because human-computer interaction is understood as an experience that emerges while dealing with technology, the concept of agency also changes. In the "design for experience" approach, no determined, fixed model of human agency needs to be inscribed into the system[188]. The same applies for the notion of affective computing. Boehner et al. agree that the enhancement of computational systems that is supposedly brought about by introducing emotion into the picture is in need of a critical rereading:

> "By bringing affect on a level par with logic and rationalism, HCI researchers seem to take a further leap away from the historically limited model of cognitivism.
>
> However, [...] the very models of cognition as discrete, abstract, and formalizable that are being disbanded for rational thought are at the heart of how affect is being modeled for computing design. In other words, rather than affect further dismantling a dated view of cognition, affective computing is often following the same trajectory only decades later." (Boehner et al. 2005, p. 60)

In contrast to the OCC model, for example, which regards emotion as an internal, intrinsic state of an individual, Boehner et al. offer a non-essentialist understand-

---

187 See Chapter 3.1.2.
188 Cp. Chapters 1.3.2. and 3.1.2.

ing of emotion as a performative act. Emotions depend on the situation and context, and as such they are socioculturally grounded. Following a social constructivist perspective, then, emotion is – at least to some degree – produced within the (inter)action. Regarding the role of emotions in human-computer interaction, such a view shifts the focus from the aim of helping computers "understand" human feelings to the aim of helping humans understand or reflect upon their own emotions. As in the concept of "reflective design" (Sengers et al. 2005), the "evocative character" (Turkle, 1995, p. 22) of the computer is hereby acknowledged and actively supported. Subsequently, this leads to a different understanding of the design and evaluation strategies of affective systems:

> "Systems inspired by the interactional approach to emotion emphasize the expression of emotion in a co-constructed, co-interpreted fashion. Measures of success for such systems are therefore not whether the systems themselves deduce the 'right emotion' but whether the systems encourage awareness of and reflection on emotions in users individually and collectively." (Boehner et al. 2005, p. 59)

"Design for experience" thus moves outside of the paradigm of mirroring human behavior and appearance in a supposedly lifelike manner. For Boehner et al., representational concepts are questionable, as is the concept of "affect as information" that is found in common approaches, where "affect is often seen as another kind of information" (ibid.). The concept of representation and the concept of "affect as information" are closely interwoven in the logic of Virtual Human design. The abstract modes of computer science give rise to a dematerialized conception of emotion as "discrete units or states internal to an individual that can be transmitted in a loss-free manner from people to computational systems and back" (Boehner et al. 2005, p. 59), even as they respond to the wish for a proper reproduction of human behavior and appearance. In contrast, Boehner et al. tackle the challenge of how to solve the sign mediation taking place at the interface[189] between, on one side, the interpretative stance of the human and, on the other, the processing, signal-oriented basis of the computer. Their epistemological stance leads them to a concept of emotions that differs – in its very nature – from the concept found in the traditional cognitive approach. As they remark, "feelings are not substances to be discovered in our blood but social practices organized by stories that we both enact and tell. The production and interpretation of emotion – of national pride, justifiable anger, or shame – is social and cultural in origin. We take emotion as a social and cultural product experienced through our interactions" (Boehner et al. 2005, p. 59).

---

189 Cp. Chapter 2.2.

3.2. "Once more with feeling": The Role of Emotions

In summation, we can say that researchers seek to extend current discussions on affective design according to three steps (which have been partly described above). The first step arises from the notion that emotion is "culturally grounded"[190]; the second step is the "interactional approach"; and the third step, which arises from the second, leads "to new design and evaluation strategies for devices" (Boehner et al. 2005, p. 59).

These three steps do not just expand the discussion on affective computing, they alter the very paradigm – moving it away from representation in order to call for a new way of conceptualizing the artifacts. Whereas the first approach that I presented – by Krämer and colleagues – seems adaptable to current embodied agent architectures, the "design for experience" approach questions the very essence, or the basic assumptions, of the project of reconstructing human behavior and appearance as an interface solution.

---

[190] Note: "When we talk of social and cultural aspects of emotions, it is important to avoid two potential misreadings. By emotion as a social fact, we do not mean to point merely to the social value or social role played by emotion, but rather to talk of the ways in which our notions of what things might constitute emotions or might be thought of as emotional behaviors is a social notion. Similarly, by emotion as a cultural fact, we do not mean to examine culture as a taxonomic phenomenon (say, distinguishing between ethnically defined cultural regions, as in a comparison between emotion in British culture, emotion in Latin culture, and emotion in Asian culture), but instead want to think of culture as a productive phenomenon, one that shapes individual and collective experience and gives it meaning. We are concerned with the ways in which our very definitions, categorizations, and experiences of 'emotion' is socially and culturally bound." (Boehner et al. 2005, p. 64)

3.3. "The object stares back"[191]

3.3.1. Beyond the Screen

Consistency of the embodied agent's verbal as well as non-verbal behavior is believed to guarantee a stable and functioning relationship between human and artifact. "Gaze behavior" belongs to the non-verbal behavior qualities of the agent. The appearance of the agent[192], looking at the agent, the ability of the agent to return a look, and interchanging looks in scenarios with multiple actors (human/non-human) are among the most common topics in research material that deals explicitly with the design and construction of Virtual Humans.

As I stated earlier, embodied agents are technological artifacts that are primarily experienced and structured through vision. This is fitting for Internet/virtual reality technologies, which Ken Hillis characterizes as a "geography of the eye" (Hillis 1996).

Throughout its variations, the Virtual Human always is a "Lichterscheinung" – a being made from light. Unlike robots, which move across space with their hard- and software body, the agent's body is primarily experienced through vision (although speech input and output devices enable hearing by and speech toward the system). Phenomenologically, this reproduces a split between the materiality of the machine and the "immaterial" pictorial body[193]. This split is furthered by the fact that the human, in order to be *understood* by the technical system, must adapt to it – through head-mounted displays, body/eye trackers, or precise speech. Such a fact breaks the metaphor of the *natural interface solution*. As previously pointed out[194], this kind of user modeling is hardly mentioned in the research material that deals explicitly with the design and construction of embodied agents. Here, the credo is that the machine interface becomes more human-like, never the other way around. This human-like alter ego of the agent, the one the human user

---

191 In the book with the same title, James Elkins (1997) questions the act of seeing as a natural process and instead examines its cultural and historic situatedness. Looking at something does not happen in isolation, he argues. And the way we look at a particular object varies depending on location or personal moods. He also emphasizes the materiality and the momentum of objects that are seen as passive, but that, of course, provide feedback. See, for instance, his remark that: "Vision, then, is irrational, inconsistent, and undependable. It is immensely troubled, cousin to blindness and sexuality, and caught up in the threads of the unconscious. Our eyes are not ours to command; they roam where they will and then tell us they have only been where we have sent them. No matter how hard we look, we see very little of what we look at. [...] Seeing is like hunting and like dreaming, and even like falling in love. It is entangled in the passions – jealousy, violence, possessiveness; and it is soaked in affect – in pleasure and displeasure, and in pain." (Elkins 1997, p. 11)
192 See *Truth Is Beauty: Researching Embodied Conversational Agents* (Nass et al. 2000).
193 Light is not immaterial, of course, but it has a dual character as waves or particles.
194 See Chapter 3.1.2.

experiences, is a projection. As a phenomenon, the actual body of the ECA is projected out of the machine onto a wall or display.

Depending on the state of the technology and the actual setting, further interaction possibilities vary: the human can type input into a keyboard or speak to the system's microphone; a camera can capture the human's gestures or facial expression. Within the logic of the research field, the interaction should be as multimodal as possible. Thus, a new interaction space beyond the desktop is formed, one that ultimately uses virtual reality technology and demonstrates mixed reality/augmented reality solutions. Virtual reality (VR) has received a lot of attention, especially in the 1990s. It describes a scenario where the human user, rather heavily equipped, becomes immersed in a computer-generated reality. Prevalent descriptions read like these:

> "A computer simulation of a real 3-dimensional world, often supplemented by sound effects. People often associate virtual reality with a body suit and head gear that includes an internal screen. The suit measures your body's movements and displays them on the screen. These computerized images can be simulated in any environment making you feel like you're really there. This is one interface, a more common use for VR is seen in many 3D computer games."[195]

or

> "An artificial environment created with computer hardware and software. To 'enter' a virtual reality, a user wears special gloves, earphones, goggles and/or full-body wiring. In addition to feeding sensory input to the user, the devices also monitor the user's actions. The goggles, for example, track how the eyes move and respond accordingly by sending new video input."[196]

In what he now calls *A Vintage Virtual Reality Interview*, Jaron Lanier, an early VR promoter, stresses the importance of the closeness of technical devices to the human body; the devices are able to capture all of the senses without being "in the way" (Lanier 1998). The focus of virtual reality is on the simulated environment as an alternate reality. Especially since applications have started to leave the laboratories, augmented reality (AR) has become more widely known. Instead of creating an immersive experience, AR seeks to provide everyday surroundings with an additional layer of information. The Google glass device, for example, consists of a head-mounted display that, combined with a smart phone, provides the user with Google search information and allows her or him to record videos

---

[195] See: *http://www.cem.uvm.edu/util/html/definitions.php*, checked on 09/07/2013.
[196] See: *http://www.csc.calpoly.edu/~ebrunner/VocabGraphics.htm*, checked on 10/12/2013.

and share content on the way[197]. Augmented reality applications are designed to enrich the physical world through visual overlays that supply additional information (or even show additional computer-generated objects). The Fraunhofer Institute[198] realized an application that allows smart phone users to learn about the Berlin Wall through an augmented reality walk[199], which superimposes historic photographs upon the current cityscape. In this sense, augmented reality ideally functions like a reversed instant wonderland. Instead of Alice (the user) entering a fantasy world *Through the Looking-Glass* (computer screen), fictional artifacts enter the real world.

Even commercials have taken a literal stance on Ivan E. Sutherland's notion of the "mathematical wonderland" and the idea that "a bullet displayed in such a room would be fatal"[200]. In Coca-Cola's advertisement for the film *Avatar*[201], the image on the bottle – when held in the right position in front of a webcam (and when the user visits the website) – triggers a three-dimensional picture on the computer screen. In the commercial, an arrow shoots out of the computer display into the human's room, where it hits a wall[202]. Of course, the Coca-Cola application does not really work like this, but this imaginary scenario is noteworthy for its invocation of the penetrating power the artifact. Here, the screen, which serves as a border between the material-semiotic objects of the computer and the physical world, has vanished. In this sense, words become objects.

In the area of human-computer interaction, too, new concepts are introduced that move beyond the computer screen and challenge the demarcation line between physical and digital realms. An example of this is MIT's Sixth's Sense[203], which introduces a mobile technology that projects interactive images wherever the user might need them – like a watch on the sleeve; other examples may be found in the works of the designer and engineer, Jinha Lee[204], such as SpaceTop, "a computer desktop prototype that lets you reach through the screen to manipulate digital objects" (Lee 2013). Similarly noteworthy is Lee's prototype of a pen that penetrates into the screen in order to draw a three-dimensional model, or her "What you click is what you wear" device. The pen demonstrates the desire to reach

---

197 See: *http://www.google.com/glass/start*, checked on 10/12/2013.
198 See: *http://www.igd.fraunhofer.de/Institut/Abteilungen/Virtuelle-und-Erweiterte-Realit%C3%A4t/*, checked on 10/12/2013.
199 See: *http://www.youtube.com/watch?v=gwtmk1ZjhY0*, checked on 10/12/2013.
200 See Chapter 2.1.1.
201 Cameron, USA, 2009.
202 See: *http://www.youtube.com/watch?v=Jx0IAZkgEco*, checked on 20/12/2013.
203 See: *http://www.ted.com/talks/pattie_maes_demos_the_sixth_sense.html*, checked on 20/12/2013.
204 See: *http://www.leejinha.com,* checked on 20/12/2013.

through the screen, whereas "What you click is what you wear"[205] has digital artifacts tilting over into the physical world. Interestingly, in both cases vision is central: the pen, of course, does not physically penetrate the screen, but produces an image that does; and the images of clothing let the human see what the attire might look like, but the human cannot feel the texture or the weight of the fabric. Augmented and mixed reality scenarios play with the idea, found in *Alice Through the Looking-Glass*, of turning the display "soft like gauze"[206]. They demonstrate that the boundaries between virtual and real are not stable and that "all reality is mixed reality" (Hansen 2006, p. 1). Thus, although there is a conceptual difference between VR and AR technologies, in experience it is difficult to create a purely virtual reality scenario. Augmented reality projects the human-computer interface onto the world, producing manifold overlays that result in configurations and states of perception that were formerly not realizable.

The Virtual Human, as a concept (though not in actual realizations of the technology), is not confined to the computer screen. Virtual or mixed reality scenarios describe the interaction space for humans and embodied agents. The special role of the embodied agent is that of a connector between the physical world, where the agent blends in, and the digital world, where the agent is a means to represent the human beyond the screen and/or a means to travel the web and gather information. The phenomenon of the Virtual Human is one in which the computing machine that produces it actually recedes into the background.

In effect, the combining of digital and physical artifacts, in a mixed reality space, produces interesting interferences. The VR Lab of the artificial intelligence work group, at Bielefeld University[207], has realized a CAVE-like[208] VR environment, which is illustrated in Figure 28.

---

205 See: *http://www.leejinha.com/wyciwyw*, checked on 20/12/2013.
206 See Chapter 2.1.1.
207 See: *http://www.techfak.uni-bielefeld.de/ags/wbski/labor.html*, checked on 06/12/2013.
208 See: *http://evlweb.eecs.uic.edu/pape/CAVE/*, checked on 06/12/2013.

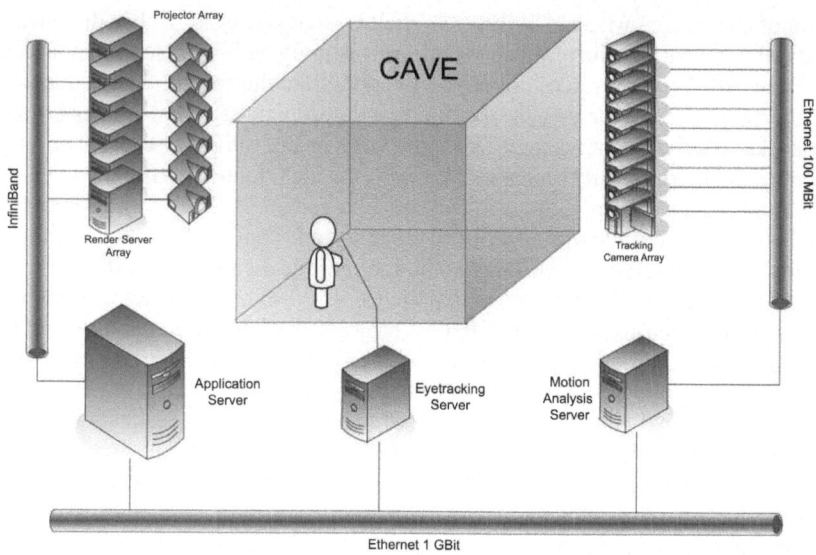

Fig. 28 CAVE Overview
(Source: *http://evlweb.eecs.uic.edu/pape/CAVE*, checked on 10/11/2014)

During a research visit to the laboratory[209], I had the chance to experience the environment and *walk* around a virtual landscape. The immersion effect is impressive. Among other things, I had to concentrate hard on not literally walking into the physical walls of the CAVE structure while I was *walking* into the virtual landscape. There is also the possibility to jump off a rock onto a meadow and, when taking up this possibility, I found myself reflexively bending my knees. I was told that this happens frequently.

Virtual and mixed reality scenarios, as well as the doubling of embodied existence, are recurring themes not only in the narrations that accompany research, but also in science fiction. Just as Ivan E. Sutherland describes virtual reality as a mathematical wonderland, so novelist (and historian) Neal Stephenson describes VR, or the Metaverse, in *Snow Crash* as "pure geometric equation made real" and continues by describing a computer lens that tracks the protagonist of the story while producing three-dimensional visuals of the Metaverse:

---

209   20/06/2013, University of Bielefeld, Germany.

3.3. "The object stares back"

> "The lens can see half of the universe – the half that is above the computer, which includes most of Hiro. In this way, it can generally keep track of where Hiro is and what direction he's looking in.
>
> Down inside the computer are three lasers – a red one, a green one, and a blue one. [...] As everyone learned in elementary school, these three colors of light can be combined, with different intensities, to produce any color that Hiro's eye is capable of seeing.
>
> In this way, a narrow beam of any color can be shot out of the innards of the computer, up through that fish-eye lens, in any direction. Through the use of electronic mirrors inside the computer, this beam is made to sweep back and forth across the lenses of Hiro's goggles, in much the same way as the electron beam in a television paints the inner surface of the eponymous Tube. The resulting image hangs in space in front of Hiro's view of Reality.
>
> By drawing a slightly different image in front of each eye, the image can be made three-dimensional. By changing the image seventy-two times a second, it can be made to move. By drawing the moving three-dimensional image at a resolution of 2K pixels on a side, it can be as sharp as the eye can perceive, and by pumping stereo digital sound through the little earphones, the moving 3-D pictures can have a perfectly realistic soundtrack.
>
> So Hiro's not actually here at all. He's in a computer-generated universe that his computer is drawing onto his goggles and pumping into his earphones." (Stephenson 1992, p. 23)

In the novel, Stephenson describes various moments where humans forget about their current physical location and bodily needs because they are too immersed in the alternate reality. People forget to drink their beer or talk loudly with someone at the Metaverse and forget that others at their physical location might eavesdrop on them (Stephenson 1992, p. 224). Another sequence of virtual and real object overlay can be found in William Gibson's novel *Idoru*. Rei Toei, the Idoru, is a virtual pop star who makes public appearances as a holograph. In one paragraph, the male protagonist describes a scene at a restaurant, where humans and the Idoru have a meal together:

> "The meal was elaborate, many small courses served on individual rectangular plates. Each time a plate was placed before Rei Toei, and always within the field of whatever projected her, it was simultaneously veiled with a flawless copy, holo food on a holo plate. Even the movement of her chopsticks brought on peripheral flickers of nodal vision. Because the chopsticks were information too, but nothing as dense as her features, her gaze. As each 'empty' plate was removed, the untouched serving would reappear." (Gibson 1996, p. 176)

In contrast to these literary figurations, the embodied agent MAX was designed in order to assist with factory work. MAX[210], short for "Multimodal Assembly eXpert", was first realised as a "VR-based conversational agent who can assist the user in virtual construction tasks. [...] In the basic scenario, a human and an artificial communicator engage in natural language interaction to cooperatively solve

---

210 See Chapter 3.1.2.

construction tasks with Baufix parts. Max is one realization of such an artificial communicator in a CAVE-like VR environment, where he is visualized in human size. [...] In communicating with the user in a face-to-face manner, the agent employs prosodic speech, deictic and iconic gestures, eye gaze, and 'emotional' facial expressions. The VR user – who is equipped with data gloves, optical position trackers, and a microphone – may employ natural language and gesture when interacting with Max. Furthermore, both Max and the user can initiate assembly actions in their environment" (Kopp et al. 2003, p. 11).

The interaction scenario is described as follows:

> "Max assists the user in VR-based construction procedures. The user and Max stand face-to-face across a table which has a number of Baufix parts lying on it. The user may re-arrange the parts, add parts to the scene, or build something with the available parts. At any time, the user may ask Max for assistance with the construction of subassemblies of a Baufix airplane. All interactions of the user, both to trigger changes in the virtual environment and to communicate with Max, are specified using speech and gesture."[211] (Kopp et al. 2003, p. 11)

For a successful interaction, the embodied agent should work properly "concerning dialog, turn taking, and action planning" (ibid.). The interaction space, supposedly a virtual reality scenario, forms a mixed reality, a setting to which the human has to adapt. Following this, it is not only that the embodied agent reconstructs what it means to be human and what is considered crucial for an interaction, it is also that the actual human users are reconfigured – by means of technical equipment and, furthermore, by the human's adjustment to the whole setting. If the system uses speech recognition, for example, humans tend to talk in a slower, more accentuated manner than they would when talking to another human. This can be noticed, for example, when people have to talk to an automated operator on the phone. Within the VR interaction, the human also learns how to move and where to stand in order for the camera eye to recognize the human figure. Human traits, such as emotions or non-verbal behaviors (which include the gaze and turn-taking), are reconfigured against the background of computational principles. Thus, on both sides, embodiments through information exchange are created.

---

211 See an interaction sequence at *http://www.techfak.uni-bielefeld.de/~skopp/download/d3.mpg*, checked on 20/10/2013 and the screenshot from this: Figure 14 - MAX in interaction.

3.3.2. Gaze Behavior in Embodied Conversational Agents

As I have stated above, the interaction setting of the embodied agent varies – depending on the technical realization – from more basic screen display to projections on walls to VR/mixed reality scenarios. But it is not only the interaction space that is structured by vision; even the embodied agent, which introduces a functionality that was not previously realized, is defined by vision. Just as with emotions, where the agent is supposed to give appropriate feedback and simulate emotions of its own, when it comes to gaze realization, the agent is supposed to make eye contact. This animation of the agent is crucial, as Justine Cassell writes in what is significantly titled "More than just a pretty face...":

> "There is a qualitative difference between face-to-face conversation and other forms of human-human communication. Businesspeople and academics routinely travel long distances to conduct certain face-to-face interactions when electronic forms of communication would seemingly work just as well. When people have something really important to say, they say it in person. The qualitative difference in these situations is not just that we enjoy looking at humans more than at computer screens but also that the human body enables the use of certain communication protocols in face-to-face conversation which provide for a more rich and robust channel of communication than is afforded by any other medium available today. The use of gaze, gesture, intonation, and body posture play an essential role in the proper execution of many conversational functions-such as conversation initiation and termination, turn-taking, interruption handling, feedback and error correction-and these kinds of behaviors enable the exchange of multiple levels of information in real time. People are extremely adept at extracting meaning from subtle variations in the performance of these behaviors; for example slight variations in pause length, feedback nod timing or gaze behavior can significantly alter the interpretation of an utterance (consider 'you did a great job' vs. 'you did a . . . great job')."
> (Cassell et al. 2001, p. 55)

"Gaze behavior", "visual feedback", or simply "gaze" – meaning the active vision of the artifact – is seen as very important when it comes to designing believable agents, and this is especially the case as systems become more elaborated (ibid.). The look and behavior of the agent's eyes are seen as crucial when establishing non-verbal behavioral abilities. Various authors note the importance of the human eyes, or the so-called "windows into the soul" (Cohen et al. 2000), which express emotions and intentions. Furthermore, these authors insist on the eyes' role in structuring conversations and directing attention. The head, or the upper part of the agent's body, usually deserves the most regard – especially when embodied conversational agents are viewed through a computer screen and are not realized as full anthropomorphic figures. This is a scenario that is familiar in modern Western culture. People are used to the figure of a newscaster on television or of people behind desks – in offices and schools or at academic conferences. This last example (a roundtable discussion at an academic conference) is a particularly good indication, since the ultimate goal of design engineers is to make the agent capable of engaging in such a group of humans (other agents and social robots can be included as well).

Furthermore, ECA – as avatars/representations of humans – are presented as a solution to some of the major problems of teleconferencing. Besides problems with processor power, bandwidth, and storage while processing huge amounts of real live video recordings, Michael Cohen et al. state that in teleconferencing it is not possible for the (human) participants to connect through eye contact, or through the gaze:

> "More specifically, if an individual who participates in a video-based teleconference watches the other participant's image on a monitor, they cannot (without special mirrors) also be looking at the camera. Instead a particular advantage of avatars over video is the avatar's capability to connect via eye gaze." (Cohen et al. 2000)

Here, agent-to-agent gaze, or agent-to-human gaze, is set as the more natural communication solution. The eye of the agent is, in this technical environment, more capable than that of the human[212]. This points to the variety of possible interaction scenarios: agents looking at agents; humans looking at agents; agents looking at humans looking at humans looking at agents; and so forth.

In contrast to a television newscaster or an actor in a movie, the ECA is conceived not only as an object of the observer's gaze, but also as a subject that returns the gaze.

---

212 This is due to the resistant materiality of the human body, which needs to pass through the circle of abstraction - modeling - simulation before being able to interlink with the machine. The computer can only process the body as abstracted signs of information.

3.3. "The object stares back"

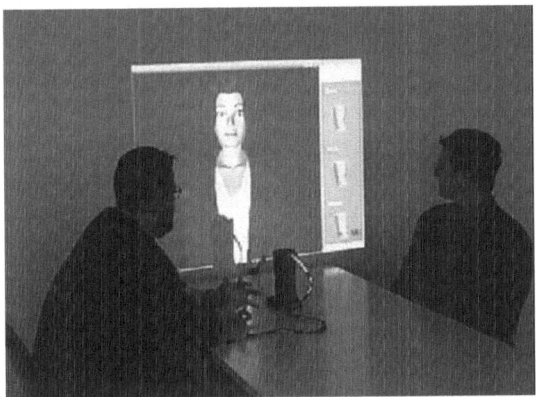

Fig. 29 ECA Greta Playing a Game of Dice with Two Humans
(Source: Photo taken by Claude Draude at AAMAS conference, Utrecht, The Netherlands, July 2005)

Figure Twenty-nine shows a setting where ECA Greta substitutes for the third human player in a game of dice[213]. Game-playing is a test case for what are considered the social abilities of the agent. Here, non-verbal behavior, such as putting on a poker-face, is at stake (Rehm, André 2005). In the pictured setting, the interactive gaze of Greta is not yet fully implemented. Greta seems to look at the player that holds the dice box, but Greta's performance is not linked to the player's gaze as such. To enable this link, the human player needs to be equipped with an eye-tracking device – or at least a camera that captures the player's head movements. The data can then be fed into the computer, where it would be processed and synchronized to the agent's internal gaze architecture.

This leads to an important point, which bears similarities to the role of emotions within Virtual Human design engineering (or within affective computing in general): in order to simulate emotional expressions, or human-like gaze behavior, the system architecture needs an implemented computational model of such expressions or behavior. This point may appear redundant, yet I nonetheless emphasize it due to its significance for the way in which the field conceives, structures, and technically implements gaze behavior. Before turning to the applied gaze models, I should add that the aim of ECA researchers is not to rebuild a human eye, but rather to simulate the role of eye movements and expressions in human conversation (broadly understood).

The majority of gaze behavior descriptions and construction plans – as differentiated as they are in details of description, planning, and modeling – rely on

---

213 Greta's design and architecture were constructed, amongst others, by Catherine Pelachaud, University of Paris. See: *http://www.iut.univ-paris8.fr/~pelachaud*, checked on 20/10/2013.

the work of the social psychologist Michael Argyle, who is well-known for his work on non-verbal communication and especially the role of gaze[214]. Mostly cited is his publication *Gaze and Mutual Gaze* (Argyle, Cook M. 1976)[215].

Lance et al. draw on a variety of functions that the gaze serves in human communication, including: gathering and regulating information; managing turn-taking in conversations and thus playing an important role in regulating the structure of the conversation; signaling interest and attention and expressing emotional states (Lance 2004). Again, it is important to keep in mind that every behavior of the ECA basically needs to be initially expressed as a model. In the case of gaze behavior, the model needs to cause the agent to perform reliable and believable actions, meaning actions that are perceived as genuinely human. In general, the reference model for the human is an able-bodied, healthy adult – not someone who has a more marginalized status in society (Zeising et al. 2014).

In the core research material, the role of turn-taking in conversation, for example, is frequently addressed in a rather operational mode: "Results from the studies[216] suggest that eye gaze helps control the flow of turn taking in conversations. For example, the person who is listening uses eye gaze to indicate whether they are paying attention, while the person who is speaking uses it to track whether the listener is still engaged in the conversation. Eye gaze is also a means to create subtle breaks in conversation to allow for a change of speaker" (Cohen et al. 2000). Cohen et al. provide a resource in which gender and cultural differences are explicitly mentioned – other gaze models do not refer to this part of Argyle's work:

> "Mutual gaze occurs when two individuals look simultaneously into each other's eyes. Argyle discusses findings that indicate the length of mutual gaze varies depending on the following:
>
> - age (longer in adults than in young children)
>
> - gender (longer in women than in men)
>
> - the distance between speakers (mutual gaze is longer the more widely separated the conversants are)
>
> - culture
>
> In adults in western cultures, mutual gaze tends to be rather short with a mean duration of 1 - 2 seconds." (ibid.)

---

214 Exceptions, of course, exist – such as the model offered by Torres et. al. 1997, who argue that "turn-taking is not an adequate explanation for gaze behavior in conversation". Torres et. al. also do not rely on the works of Michael Argyle.
215 See Cohen et al. 2000; Vinayagamoorthy et al. 2004; Rehm, André 2005; Lance 2004; Heylen et al. 2003.
216 Argyle's work on gaze.

These findings, derived from experimental psychological studies, then need to be transformed into a computational model. Lance and colleagues point out the problems computer scientists must face when adapting knowledge from other academic fields: "Unfortunately, the psychology literature on human interactive gaze also has shortcomings that make it impossible to extract mapping directly from data in the literature. Much of the relevant information in the psychology literature is about when and where to gaze and there is not a great deal of information about how specific gaze shifts should be executed" (Lance 2004). This "gap" in research, the need for precise, operational, detailed descriptions, must then be filled by the designers themselves.

On the highest level of a system's architecture, a simplified model can be expressed. This is demonstrated in Figure 30.

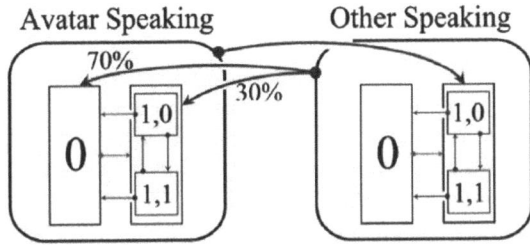

Fig. 30 "Diagram for two people talking"
(Source: Cohen et al., 2000)

The figure shows how the agent's gaze structure is controlled by the model. The gaze structure of the other is not explicitly controlled – unless it is the gaze of another agent. It is, of course, implicitly controlled, for the whole architecture relies on the specific way the user is grasped and envisioned in advance. State (0) indicates that the agent is gazing away from the other. State (1,0) indicates that the agent is gazing at the other, but that the other is looking away. State (1,1) indicates that the agent and the other are gazing at each other (mutual gaze). In this state, the agent always looks at the other (this can be another agent or a human) when the other starts speaking. The value of 30% indicates that the agent will look at the other for only part of the time that the agent is speaking. The value for this is set stochastically.

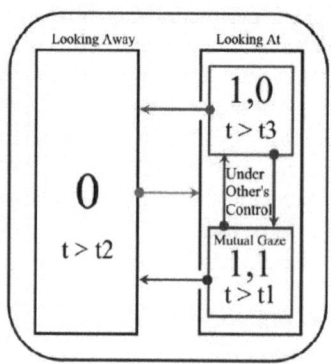

Fig. 31 "Detail of eye gaze state transitions"
(Source: Cohen et al., 2000)

This figure describes how changes in the agent's eye gaze (looking at, looking away) are linked to the passing of time (t). The transition times (t1, t2, t3) depend on whether the agent is in a state of speaking or of listening. The values for the transition time are derived from the psychological literature and thus can be set to various social markers (age, gender, culture) as well as adjusted to the distance between the speakers (as noted in the quotation above).

Colburn et al. state that social markers such as gender or age are not inscribed into the above model, but that, in order to place the agent in a variety of settings and cultures, this may be done in the future. The agent could then possess an internal gaze model that would, for example, characterize the ECA as a Japanese man. For now, "the specific model is based on average values for Western adults", and "these values are supplemented with the authors' own informal observations in cases in which the psychological literature did not provide necessary details" (ibid.). The first remark, with its regard for the way in which its core material is culturally specified, is rather unusual – generally such specification is not explicitly stated. The second remark points to what Els Rommes calls the I-methodology of the designer (Rommes 2002), which seems to be – from design to usage-evaluation (Isbister, Doyle 2002) – very common in the construction of Embodied Conversational Agents. In this sense, social markers are already inscribed but left unseen. This suggests the conclusion that social markers are named as such only when they deviate from a normalized reference model, that of the healthy, able-bodied, white, heterosexual Western adult.

Nevertheless, it is interesting that, in order to build more believable artifacts, social categories like gender and cultural context are increasingly considered as topics for research (Angeli et al. 2006; HUMAINE 2004).

3.3. "The object stares back"

Phillipp Kulms et al. describe the possible impact of gender on the functioning of the embodied agent interaction scenario:

> "However, one of the most important categories of human everyday life and the question whether its effects are also transferable to the interaction with agents has not been studied in depth: Gender. While studies of course frequently assess and consider whether female users' reactions differ from those of male users [...] the systematic manipulation of the agent's gender has not received sufficient attention [...] To have knowledge on the differential effects of female and male agents, however, is all the more important as the agent's gender might not only have an influence per se but might also affect how the agent's behavior is perceived and evaluated. Here, social psychological research has demonstrated that the same nonverbal behavior will elicit different attributions, judgments and reactions depending on whether it is shown by a man or a woman." (Kulms et. al. 2011, p. 80)

Interestingly, the authors notice the stereotyping effect of a strong binary approach to gender:

> "In a seminal study, Deutsch et al.[217] provided evidence that women who do not smile are socially less accepted than men if they do not smile: they are associated with less happiness and carelessness compared to men. The authors explain their finding with the fact that – due

---

217 See the description of the cited study: "Women do not only show more immediacy, e.g. by means of smiling or gaze, they are also expected to show immediacy to a larger extent, whereas male communicators are seen as less skilled [...] However, if women's nonverbal behavior is not congruent with the stereotypes that society holds about them, women are faced with rather harsh judgements. Deutsch, LeBaron and Fryer [...] showed that the examination of non-smiling female faces displayed on photographs evoked more negative evaluations than non-smiling male faces. Men, as opposed to women, do not have to fulfill comparable behavioral expectations, because they are nonexistent in their case. Thus, men are not perceived to reveal a negative emotional state if they do not smile, as non-smiling men are seen as the norm, whereas women are perceived to deviate from the norm when they are not smiling [...]. This means that the same behaviour is judged differently dependent on whether it is shown by men or women. This has also been demonstrated for gaze behaviour: In a job interview setting that incorporated different levels of gaze and changing reward values through applicants' status, judgments of female applicants differed significantly from judgments of male applicants. When the applicants were presented as high status, high gaze rates led to attributing submissiveness to females and dominance to males. When the status of applicants was low, the pattern was reversed: high gaze females were perceived as dominant, whereas high gaze males were seen as submissive [...]. What has not been analyzed so far is whether similar to the study of Deutsch et al. [...], who demonstrated this for the immediacy cue smiling, women will also be penalized when they do not show the immediacy behaviour of frequent gaze. The results depicted above have been explained by the ubiquitousness of gender categories in social cognition [...] and the fact that (gender) stereotypes are activated automatically and are hard to suppress [...]. Given that it has already been shown that gender stereotypes are applied in human computer interaction even when gender is manipulated rather superficially by using male versus female voices [...] our objective here is to analyse whether gendered virtual humans evoke gender-related attributions and whether, more importantly, this leads to a differential evaluations of the same behaviour." (Kulms et al. 2011, p. 82)

to gender stereotypes and due to the fact that women indeed show more smiles and immediacy behavior in everyday life – women clearly are expected to smile whereas for men, smiling and other immediacy behaviors are positive deviations from the norm. The objective of the present study is to test whether this pattern can also be observed for female and male virtual agents." (ibid., pp. 80–81)

As with emotions in the design of embodied agents, knowledge about gender and gaze, insofar as it is taken up within the field, is commonly informed by the binary, heteronormative perspective that prevails in modern society. As Kulms' analysis shows, the challenge for interface designers, even if they are aware of this, is how to deal with the tension between re-inscribing knowledge produced by normative gender assumptions and building artifacts that do not fit the research goal of "believable lifelike characters". Believability, it seems, amounts to singling out the most typical traits in related research fields in order to build a male or female agent – or, alternatively, it amounts to taking these traits into account in order to presume user reactions that are based on gender. As I have shown with emotions and gaze, knowledge on these topics, in so far as they become objects for computing, needs to become formalized and standardized – this is the case, at least, if research follows the prevailing representational or reconstructive approach.

3.3.3. The Object Stares Back? Summing Up Thoughts on Gaze

To conclude with my discussion of the role of the gaze, I want to shortly reflect on three aspects that are interwoven in the narrative of the Virtual Human and the setting of virtual reality or mixed reality technologies. These aspects – interactive gaze, permeability/ubiquity of the screen, and tangible gaze – also raise questions for further research.

Interactivity is one of the most intriguing aspects of computers. It is fascinating that the machine responds to user input not only in concept but also in experience. For embodied agent design, the machine interface is given a human-like appearance, which enforces the expectation of feedback. The interface agent is conceptualized as an intelligent artifact that is able to engage in face-to-face – or rather body-to-body – communication with humans, robots, and other agents[218]. In contrast to human or human-like actors in cinema or on television, they present interactive counterparts. Consequently, when it comes to visual relations, what is called the object in (feminist) film theory is designed to look back, thus introducing the notion of interactive gaze.

---

218 I doubt that the "Lichtgestalt" ("luminous figure") of the Virtual Human will ever work for animals. Even cats, who are said to be "Augentiere" ("visual animals"), do not respond to screen-based beings, whereas robots, with their tangible body, provoke reactions.

3.3. "The object stares back"

In *Visual Pleasure and Narrative Cinema*, Laura Mulvey[219] analyzes spectatorship and visual relations against the background of psychoanalytic theory (Mulvey 1989b). In reference to Sigmund Freud (1951), she contemplates the image of the woman on the screen and the male spectator, or what she calls the "masculinization of the spectator position" (Mulvey 1989a). In her analysis, Mulvey relates the structure of cinema to the "dominant order", which makes sense if conceived in terms of the "phallocentric order" inherent to Freud's theory. Mulvey's discussion of Freud leads her to the finding that, in the existing cultural order, "woman [...is] tied to her place as bearer of meaning, not maker of meaning" (ibid.). The image of woman on the cinema screen, and the male spectator position in the dark room of the audience, is therefore a symbol and effect of this existing cultural order.

Simply put, what is important to keep in mind for the analysis of the embodied agent is that, in patriarchy, tools and technologies are developed according to the dominant structure[220]. The heterosexual gender order also structures visual relations, with their inherent organization of power and hierarchy. Dominant structures are thus built into the artifacts themselves (see ibid; Braun 1997). The camera, the projector, the screen, the seats for the spectators, and the attributed roles are manifestations/materializations of the cultural gender order. Mulvey writes:

> "During its history, the cinema seems to have evolved a particular illusion of reality in which this contradiction between libido and ego has found a beautifully complementary phantasy world. In reality the phantasy world of the screen is subject to the law which produces it. Sexual instincts and identification processes have a meaning within the symbolic order which articulates desire. [...]"

---

219 Years later, Mulvey offered her "Afterthoughts on 'Visual Pleasure and Narrative Cinema'" and responded to the critique that she highlighted only the position of the male spectator in the original piece (Mulvey 1989a).
220 See: "To summarise briefly: the function of woman in forming the patriarchal unconscious is twofold, she first symbolises the castration threat by her real absence of a penis and second thereby raises her child into the symbolic. Once this has been achieved, her meaning in the process is at an end, it does not last into the world of law and language except as a memory, which oscillates between memory of maternal plenitude and memory of lack. Both are posited on nature (or on anatomy in Freud's famous phrase). Woman's desire is subjected to her image as bearer of the bleeding wound, she can exist only in relation to castration and cannot transcend it. She turns her child into the signifier of her own desire to possess a penis (the condition, she imagines, of entry into the symbolic). Either she must gracefully give way to the word, the Name of the Father and the Law, or else struggle to keep her child down with her in the half-light of the imaginary. Woman then stands in patriarchal culture as signifier for the male other, bound by a symbolic order in which man can live out his phantasies and obsessions through linguistic command by imposing them on the silent image of woman still tied to her place as bearer of meaning, not maker of meaning." (Mulvey 1989a)

> In a world ordered by sexual imbalance, pleasure in looking has been split between active/male and passive/female. The determining male gaze projects its phantasy onto the female figure, which is styled accordingly. [...]
>
> It is the place of the look that defines cinema, the possibility of varying it and exposing it. This is what makes cinema quite different in its voyeuristic potential from, say, strip-tease, theatre, shows, etc. Going far beyond highlighting a woman's to-be-looked-at-ness, cinema builds the way she is to be looked at into the spectacle itself. Playing on the tension between film as controlling the dimension of time (editing, narrative) and film as controlling the dimension of space (changes in distance, editing), cinematic codes create a gaze, a world, and an object, thereby producing an illusion cut to the measure of desire." (Mulvey 1989b)

Mulvey's point – that "cinema builds the way she is to be looked at into the spectacle itself" – gains a new quality with the way the looking-relation is organized in human-agent interaction. In the concept of this interaction, the human spectator leaves the role of the mere spectator and has to take part in the interaction. The object, once passive on the screen, now actually looks back. The spectator is put in a position where he or she is being watched as well[221].

The MAX agent addresses the human once that human enters into the focus of the system's camera-eye. Regarding emotions, the system is already equipped to be sensitive to verbal insults, which will lead to the MAX character leaving the display. An advanced internal gaze model will eventually result in similar behavior if the human looks away too often or stares at body parts that are considered improper to look at. If installed as such, MAX or EMMA will also load the system's gaze model for women once the user has introduced herself with a female name.

The ability of the technological artifact to return the gaze – or, similarly, its ability to reciprocate an adequate emotional response – is described in terms of a shift from inanimation to animation. The formerly passive object is thus conceived as obtaining the status of a subject by means of the interactive character of the visual relation between human and artifact. Upon closer attention, however, it can be revealed that the consistency of Virtual Humans depends on the cultural construct of visual relations. Donna Haraway states that "vision is always a question of the power to see – and perhaps of the violence implicit in our visualizing practices" (Haraway 1991b, p. 192). By drawing on feminist and postcolonial film theory, I run the risk of equating Virtual Humans with "the other" (Kaplan 1997), or at least of contributing to the vivification of the agents. This is far from my intention. However, bearing in mind the process of what Lev Manovich calls

---

221 With new surveillance technologies and cameras ubiquitous in public spaces, this is not just true for human-artifact interaction.

"transcoding", I wonder why certain relationship models are acted out within the technosphere and transferred to it.[222]

In retrospect, the interactive gaze of the embodied agent is designed to simulate – but not to be seen as equal to – that of a human. As Figure 30 shows, the agent's gaze is under the control of the other person. And this "gaze of the other" has been anticipated by the designer. Whereas in cinema the spectator is able to accept the perspective of the camera as its own and thus reaffirm the point of view of the filmmaker, in the case of the embodied agent the human user has to interact according to the choices that were made during the design process.

Thus, human gaze is reconfigured in accordance with the basic principles of the computing machine, as Friedrich Kittler points out with regard to the technology of eye-tracking: "I would almost assume, that with these trackings of the famous eye movements, it is precisely not the human anymore who is the observer, but who, for the first time, is the one being observed. [...] Eyes and mouth, that are widely regarded as the last realms of the so-called intimacy, are becoming fed into the logic of feedback loops, which is not ours, but that of the machine"[223]. If feminist critique is considered, then the device can no longer be understood as "alien". Instead, like the materialization of cinema, this device results from the co-constructive process of technology and culture. Yet amidst this similarity to cinema's materialization, the interaction setting of the embodied agent changes and differs from the spectatorship in the cinema.

The new quality of the "interactive gaze" is closely related to further aspects, such as the permeability of the screen and the relation of touch and gaze.

It is not only that the organization of the looking-relation changes, it is also that the role of the screen becomes different. In various academic fields, the computer screen is characterized as a mirror, and thereby as an evocative object that informs postmodern concepts of self and identity[224]. Virtual reality technology

---

[222] The master/servant or master/slave dichotomy can be found in various layers of computational devices – master and slave, for example, are terms for primary and secondary hard drives (for a discussion of renaming them, see *http://www.cnn.com/2003/TECH/ptech/11/26/master.term.reut*, checked on 20/12/2013). Within AI, one often finds the following quote by Aristotle, which gets used for marking the liberating aspects: "There is only one condition in which we can imagine managers not needing subordinates, and masters not needing slaves. This condition would be that each (inanimate) instrument could do its own work, at the word of command or by intelligent anticipation [...] as if a shuttle should weave of itself, and a plectrum should do its own harp playing." See: *http://ieet.org/index.php/IEET/more/walker20060101*, checked on 20/12/2013.

[223] "Ich würde fast vermuten, dass bei diesen Abtastungen der berühmten Augenbewegungen [...] eben nicht mehr der Mensch der Beobachter ist, sondern zum ersten Mal der Beobachtete wird. [...] Augen und Mund, die ja weithin als letzte Refugien der sogenannten Intimität gelten, werden also eingespeist in eine Rückkopplungslogik, die nicht unsere, sondern die der Maschine ist." (Kittler 1992 quoted in: Scherffig 2005, p. 4)

[224] See e.g. educational science: Meyer-Drawe (1996), computer science: Nake (2004); psychology: Turkle (1984).

travels along narratives exemplified by the *Alice's Adventures in Wonderland* sequel, *Through the Looking-Glass*. In *Through the Looking-Glass*, Alice sees the family's living room in the mirror and wonders what this world on the other side might be like: "Let's pretend there's a way of getting through into it somehow [...] Let's pretend the glass has got soft like gauze, so that we can get through" (Carroll 1992b, p. 113). Within computer science, the notion of the "display as a looking-glass" (Nake 2004) is an idea(l) that can be traced back to the early years of graphic data processing and representation. What thus enters the agenda is the simulation of reality, which will eventually be inseparable from the world beyond the display (Sutherland 1965, pp. 507–508). The setting of virtual reality stresses the interactive character of the mirror as a functioning technology. In an extrapolation of the cinema screen, the characters of virtual reality, or rather those of mixed reality, step out of the screen: a three-dimensional space is formed where humans and virtual characters interact. The human spectator has to leave the comfortable seat of the auditorium as she/he is drawn into the cybernetic feedback loop – according to the logic of the research field, this claim will eventually extend to the whole human body.

In her analysis of cinema, Laura Mulvey refers, by way of Jacques Lacan's mirror stage, to the reflective quality of the screen. She states that it is interesting that an image lies at the heart of Lacan's formation of the I, or of the interplay of recognition/misrecognition and identification[225]. The power of the cinema oscillates exactly between the position of objectifying the object on screen and the position of identifying with the object on screen. Mulvey writes:

> "Hence it is the birth of the long love affair/despair between image and self-image which has found such intensity of expression in film and such joyous recognition in the cinema audience. Quite apart from the extraneous similarities between screen and mirror (the framing of the human form in its surroundings, for instance), the cinema has structures of fascination strong enough to allow temporary loss of ego while simultaneously reinforcing the ego. The sense of forgetting the world as the ego has subsequently come to perceive it (I forgot who I am and where I was) is nostalgically reminiscent of that pre-subjective moment of image recognition. At the same time the cinema has distinguished itself in the production of ego ideals as expressed in particular in the star system, the stars centering both screen presence and screen story as they act out a complex process of likeness and difference (the glamorous impersonates the ordinary)." (Mulvey 1989b)

So, when the cinematic setting produces a space and a technology that spans between ego loss and production of the ideal ego, what kind of mirroring effect does the Virtual Human have? The image that is here produced is one that sets out to be "more than a pretty face", its codes reach beyond surface level, and this results in

---

225 See Chapter 2.1.1.

animation and pro-active agency. The image in the computing mirror is designed to reflect the human in behavior and appearance, but it also reaches further: it steps out of the mirror and obtains a life of its own.

Ken Hillis views virtual reality technology as a means of pursuing the desire to transcend. He writes: "In order to achieve 'intellectual augmentation' virtually, VR proposes we merge with the object of our gaze that until now has kept us as modern subjects at its beck and call, alternatively enraging us to conquer it as an object or to worship it as God" (Hillis 1996, p. 74).

The idea of merging with, or at least getting very close to, the object on screen poses questions concerning the relation between *touch and gaze*. An interesting take on this presents itself in car assembly scenarios. Since 2004, the Volkswagen Company (VW), in Wolfsburg, Germany, has built two new centers for visualization techniques. Here, new car models get projected in full-scale onto the "powerwall" – a "cave" enables the designers to sit inside the car and experience the usability of it by means of VR technologies. A major part of the construction process thus happens in computer-generated environments. After the design at the visualization center, the car is modeled at the mock-up center and then tested for security[226]. VW uses a VR laboratory developed by the AI Group of the University of Bielefeld, where embodied agents MAX and EMMA were also constructed. One smaller sized predecessor of the lab is the "responsive workbench", a hardware-software unit that uses stereoscopic three-dimensional graphics. A description of the workbench sums up the role vision plays, as well as the co-constructive modeling of user and machine:

> "Virtual objects and control buttons are projected stereoscopically onto a surface of a horizontal table. Users, wearing LCD shutter glasses, can take advantage of 3D vision in a field of about 170cm x 120cm size. Position sensors (one at the side of a pair of shutter glasses and one on the back of a data glove respectively) keep track of the user's eye and hand positions. [...] Depending on application needs various modules can be integrated such as motion, gesture and speech recognition systems. Instead of using a mouse or keys the user handles this environment by actually grabbing and manipulating virtual objects. Because the work action is virtual, human and computer have equal opportunities to manipulate the virtual world." [227]

Christina von Braun characterizes this dominance of vision over other senses as inherent to Christian-Occidental culture and as relevant for the category of gender

---

[226] For more information see: *http://www.volkswagen.de/vwcms_publish/vwcms/master_public/virtualmaster/de3/unternehmen/Innovation/forschung/simulationssysteme0/start.html*, checked on 20/04/2013.
[227] See: *http://www.techfak.uni-bielefeld.de/ags/wbski/Labor/labor_firstgeneration.html*, checked on 20/04/2013.

(Braun 1997, p. 330). She writes: "The Renaissance considered the gaze of the central perspective as a means to avoid touch. With the construction of optical technical devices, however, a way of seeing developed that, in itself, stands for touch. That is, similarly to writing, which has spawned its own images, the sense of vision also creates its own sense of touch"[228]. The technologies of VR exemplify this. The actual object is constructed through the gaze and is obtainable and manipulable through gaze technology. Of interest, within the aformentioned VR setting, is the role of the hand, which wears the data glove that "touches" the object made from light and enables this touch to be experienced as feedback (typically as a vibration). This setting comes close to Ivan E. Sutherland's idea that VR eventually will provide a "mathematical wonderland" in which virtual objects make a claim on physical reality (Sutherland 1965, pp. 507–508). Remarkably, the Virtual Human demonstrates an interface technology that combines oral culture (conversing with the machine through "natural language"), touch, and gaze with the transgression of the display/screen barrier. In this sense, the Virtual Human is the materialization of the "Weltwerdung" ("coming into the world") of computational artifacts.

---

[228] "Der Renaissance mochte das zentralperspektvistische Sehen noch als Mittel dienen, die Berührung zu vermeiden; mit der Entwicklung technischer Sehgeräte entwickelt sich jedoch ein Blick, der für die Berührung selbst steht. D.h. vergleichbar der Schrift, die ihre eigenen Bilder hervorgebracht hat, erschafft auch der Sehsinn seinen eigenen Tastsinn." (Braun 1997, p. 336)

4. Passing as Human[229]

4.1. Uncanny Doppelgängers

4.1.1. The Uncanny Valley

In 1970, roboticist Masahiro Mori published his ideas on how humans react emotionally to artificial beings (Mori 1970). According to Mori, the role model of robotics is the human. In a graphic, he links the trustworthiness of the artifact to its human resemblance.

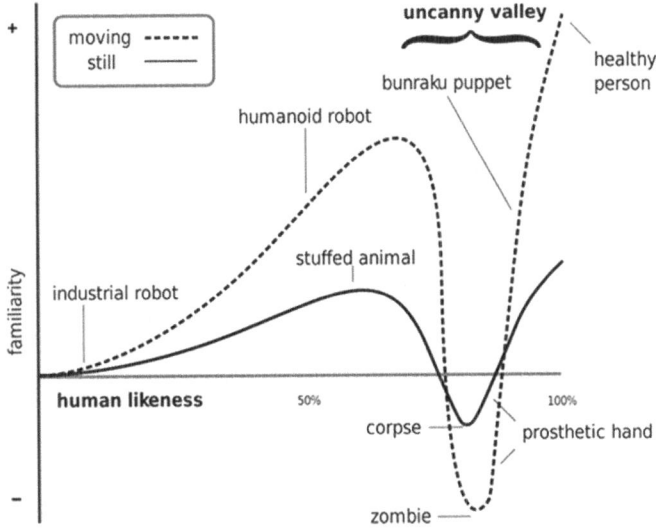

Fig. 32 The Uncanny Valley
(Source: https://upload.wikimedia.org/wikipedia/commons/f/f0/Mori_Uncanny_Valley.svg, checked on 10/11/2014)

Figure Thirty-two shows how, according to Mori, human likeness evokes trust only up to a certain point. If the robot comes very close to appearing human, but

---

229 Some of the findings of this chapter have been previously published in Draude (2011).

of course is still not a "real" human, then minor lapses will produce irritations. On its way to reach the peak of humanness, the robot falls into the depths of the Uncanny Valley. The starting point for Mori's considerations are industrial robots that simulate certain human actions but not human appearance. Adding to this, he differentiates between mobile and immobile objects. The ability to move autonomously, in particular, contributes to the life-likeness of the artifact, but it also adds to its potential creepiness. Most interestingly, the Uncanny Valley addresses matters of life and death. It appears that, even scarier than those who actually *are dead*, are the beings situated *between the two discrete states*: in the abyss, zombies and other undead creatures lurk; the deepest point of the valley is inhabited by those who are *neither dead nor alive*. Mori illustrates this ambiguity by using the example of a prosthetic hand. If the artifact looks like a healthy human hand, but feels cold and alien when touched, it may be experienced as slightly disturbing (at the least) or as horrifying (at the worst). The prosthetic hand can be unsettling precisely because it invokes an encounter with the living dead. According to this, the uncanny is triggered because of the discrepancy between *looking at* and *touching* the object. A further-reaching discussion of the Uncanny Valley effect is lacking in Mori's paper. Still, he wonders: "Why do we humans have such a feeling of strangeness? Is this necessary?" (Mori 1970a). As a roboticist, his perspective is application-oriented. He advises that the design process of anthropomorphic robots should aim for the first peak shown in the graphic, but should not go further. According to his theory, this means that the design of the artificial being, in order to avoid stumbling into the Uncanny Valley, must accept a cutback on life-likeness.

Within the research community, Mori's concept is a controversial object of discussion. While it has been considered non-scientific (Ferber 2003) and questionable (Bartneck et al. 2007), it has also served as inspiration (MacDorman 2007). But even if not addressed explicitly, the Uncanny (Freud 1963) always plays a role when it comes to the design of artificial beings. It serves as a nodal point for the acceptance and the overall impact of artificial beings, such as humanoid robots, embodied interface agents, and computer game figures or avatars. Human characters in animation films, for example, are often considered to fall into the Uncanny Valley when they are designed to achieve a very realistic appearance[230]. Successful movies, in contrast, tend to employ features that are more cartoon-like in order to avoid the effect[231]. Instead of aiming at a copy of the real world, an original aesthetic is created. In social robotics, there exist a variety of possible embodiment forms. When it comes to the Uncanny Valley, the Actroids, lifelike humanoid robots that are designed to explore and challenge the effect, are

---

[230] See discussions on *The Polar Express*, by Robert Zemecki, USA 2004, http://wardomatic.blogspot.com/2004/12/polar-express-virtual- train-wreck_18.html, checked on 01/05/2013.

[231] For example, *Shrek*, by Andrew Adamson, Vicky Jenson, USA 2001.

4.1. Uncanny Doppelgängers

particularly worth mentioning. With silicon bodies and respiratory sounds, this design tries to achieve what is considered the "healthy person status" in Mori's picture. The main developer, Hiroshi Ishiguro of Osaka University, Japan, first took his wife, then his child, and then himself as a model for replication. His work analyzes the concept of "presence"[232]. The doppelgänger status adds to their uncanniness and provokes ethical questions on the cloning of humans. It is worth observing, furthermore, that Ishiguro translates his setting and concept of family into the technological sphere.

Other roboticists, whether aware of it or not, follow Mori's dictum. The MIT humanoid robotics group does not build artifacts that mirror human appearance[233], and the Honda Corporation's humanoids are covered by space suits[234]. Interestingly, an attribution to one gender is very obvious in case of the Actroids, whereas the MIT group seeks to avoid placing the artifact in the binary gender order[235]. Ishiguro's scenario does not work with the latter approach. In the family setting that he chooses, the technological artifact serves as a placeholder within the heteronormative order. Just as in science fiction narratives, such as the movie *A.I.*, his research addresses questions of authenticity, origin (the genealogical order), and, with the focus on "presence", the question of animation.

When it comes to the design of embodied interface agents, the diversity in artifacts is much more limited. Virtual Humans (Magnenat-Thalmann 2004) aspire toward the healthy person status as well. Here, simulating lifelike human behavior and appearance is the goal. Like social robots, Virtual Humans are designed to possess a high degree of autonomy. They are meant to be proactive and to display emotional artificial intelligence. These traits are considered to lead to a behavior that is verbally as well as non-verbally convincing. Scenarios that employ Virtual Humans favor the concept of a shared space, a mixed reality (Kopp et al. 2003). Similar to the story of Alice in *Through the Looking-Glass*, where the mirror serves as an interface that opens up a spatial dimension and provides an imaginary place, the conceptualization of Virtual Humans is driven by narratives that interweave human and non-human actors in a collective environment. Virtual reality – or, furthermore, augmented reality technologies – contribute to the idea that the mirror or screen becomes unnoticeable and eventually disappears completely. New technological scenarios go far beyond the idea of the personal computer and the desktop metaphor[236]. They introduce the idea that computer-generated imagery

---

232 See: *http://eng.irl.sys.es.osaka-u.ac.jp/home/research*, checked on 03/05/2013.
233 See: *http://www.ai.mit.edu/projects/humanoid-robotics-group*, checked on 30/01/2013.
234 See: *http://www.honda-robots.com/english/html/p3/frameset2.html*, checked on 13/01/2013.
235 See: MIT Humanoid Robotics Group, FAQs *http://www.ai.mit.edu/projects/humanoid-robotics-group*, checked on 13/01/2013.
236 See: The "Universal Fan Fest" project, which is part of Japan's bid submitted to football's world governing body FIFA.

leaves the bound space of the machinery and tilts over into physical space. Conceptually, this reverses Alice's wonderland. Instead of Alice (the user) entering a fantasy world *Through the Looking-Glass* (computer screen), fictional artifacts enter the real world. As an example, I referred to Coca-Cola's *Avatar* film advertisement[237], which plays with the idea that an arrow shoots out of the computer display right into the user's room, where it hits a wall. As I have noted, this move relates to Ivan E. Sutherland's early notion of the "ultimate display", which "would, of course, be a room within which the computer can control the existence of matter. A chair displayed in such a room would be good enough to sit in. Handcuffs displayed in such a room would be confining, and a bullet displayed in such a room would be fatal. With appropriate programming such a display could literally be the Wonderland into which Alice walked" (Sutherland 1965, pp. 507–508). The ability of the computer, a semiotic machine that executes code, to turn the display "soft like gauze" changes with the interaction scenario. In a military setting, a main application and development area of VR/AR, the technology actually may produce a fatal bullet (Livingston et al. 2002). Thus, the boundaries between virtual and real are always under negotiation (Hansen 2006, p. 1).

In the case of artificial beings, this tilting point – particularly the contested zone between virtual and real reality – is of interest. The embodiment of the Virtual Human is linked to questions of materiality, imagery, and their concomitant agency. Embodied software agents literally are "Lichtgestalten", or luminous figurations. In contrast to robots, they cannot move through physical space and knock things over or grab something. It is precisely the agents' on-screen or projected visual form of embodiment that seems to free them from the constraints that come with having a material body. As stated above, Mori names the discrepancy between looking at and touching the artifact as one major source of irritation. With the interface agents, touching is impossible – a human cannot shake a Virtual Human's hand. However, even this experience is under reconstruction with vibrating feedback technologies[238].

That these artifacts nevertheless are viewed as valid interaction partners can be regarded as a shift in the relation between the visual and the tangible. In Manovich's terms, this is described as a process of transcoding. It points at a broader sociocultural reconceptualization, where "new visualization techniques transform the material body into a visual medium" (Balsamo 2002, p. 223). Nowadays, Mori's example of the prosthetic hand falls short when it comes to ex-

---

http://www.google.com/hostednews/afp/article/ALeqM5gNVZsxBSbgXx268O16flQfqXOs_w and http://www.youtube.com/watch?v=HFudH8GtcKE, checked on 07/01/2014.
237 See Chapter 3.3.1.
238 See the tangible hologram projector, which was presented at SIGGRAPH 2009. http://www.nextnature.net/2009/08/tangible-hologram-projector/, checked on 26/05/2013.

plaining the potentially uncanny effect of Virtual Humans. And, because this gap between look and feel is not the only means of producing disturbing artifacts, further considerations will be taken into account below.

4.1.2. Doubles

In Thomas Melle's play *The Heart is a Lousy Hustler*[239], from 2010, one of the protagonists, Jenni, proclaims in the first act: "Avatare sind so passé" – that is, "avatars are so over."

This is a remarkable exclamation for a figuration on stage, who itself comes alive via the interplay of acting, writing, stage direction, and audience reception. Similar to stage personas, avatars can be described as material-semiotic embodiments (Haraway 1997, p. 129) in the context of computing. And even the idea of the interface as a stage, where computer-generated beings interact, has found entry into the field (Laurel 1986). Depending on the design goal, the computer-generated persona represents a user online (in case of the avatar) or serves as an autonomous interaction partner (in case of the embodied agent). Either way, it forms an animated representation of the human, a machinic doppelgänger, which is mainly experienced through audio-visual output.

In a way, Virtual Humans are like ghosts. The term avatar, with its religious origin[240], highlights the transcendent nature of the virtual doppelgänger. The adoption of the term in order to denominate programmers or user representatives in forums, games, and online-worlds is not a coincidence. The virtual counterpart, like the religious concept, presents a dematerialized form of embodiment. The avatar speaks of the wish to overcome the restraints of the physical world; it exemplifies the desire "to leave and beat the meat", as it is called in Cyberpunk fiction (Draude 2001).

Of course, the goal of embodied interface agent research is not to construct metaphysical devices, but to make computer usage easier. Anthropomorphism is a means of reaching a broader bandwidth in the interaction: the human body, or here its simulation, serves as a medium that is presumed to produce a direct and more intuitive form of information exchange. As I have elaborated, the special character of Virtual Humans becomes clearer when their origin is reconsidered. As intermediary between the human and the abstract levels of computing technology, an in-

---

239 "Das Herz ist ein lausiger Stricher" - debut performance Theaterhaus Jena, Germany, 25/02/2010, see: *http://www.theaterhaus-jena.de/Das-Herz-ist-ein-lausiger-Stri.390.0.html*, checked on 20/05/2013.
240 See Chapter 3.1.2.

terface agent needs to address both worlds. Modes of simulating humans in computing fall under the logic of "the translation of the world into a problem of coding" (Haraway 1991a, p. 164), and this problem stems from the character of the computer as a "semiotic machine" (Nadin 2007).

This is of importance not only when it comes to designing interfaces. The shift is constitutive for the whole area of techno- and life-sciences and must be viewed as a general sociotechnical transformation (Heintz, Benz 2001; Schinzel 2004). What is noteworthy about computers is that they do not process material objects as other machines might do, they process semiotic representations – descriptions of objects, bodies, and environments. Earlier, I described the cycle of abstraction and remodeling that needs to take place, and that – following the works of Frieder Nake – is comprised of steps like formalization, standardization, and executability. Nake stresses the special character of the "algorithmic sign" – a sign that is simultaneously interpreted by the computer and by the user. The computer and the human thus participate in an ongoing process of sign/signal exchange and interpretation/processing (Nake 2001). According to Donna Haraway, artificial intelligence research is marked by an epistemological shift whereby "organisms and machines alike were repositioned on the same ontological level [...], the process by which something functioned as a sign" (Haraway 1997, p. 128). Manovich further defines virtuality as "the cultural perception that material objects are interpenetrated by information patterns" (Manovich 2000, p. 69) and thus argues that, rather than a projective mirror, computer based simulation imagery is like a virus, "which reflects who we are, while infecting us with its own alien logic" (Manovich 2000, p. 32). It is essential to note that, within this process of computing, reduction is only one way of characterizing abstraction. Simultaneously, there takes place a kind of doubling effect that is inherent to the procedure of semioticizing. Simply put, a new world is created through formalized language. Thus, the very principles of computer science encourage procreation (Nake 1993a, pp. 12–13). Especially with artificial intelligence technologies, the constructive character of language becomes viable. The algorithmic sign obtains a circulating and relational character; it is derived from the world, but it has formative effects as well. From this perspective, the Virtual Human almost literally re-sensualizes abstract technology by providing it with a "Zeichenhaut" – in order to become computable, all matters must grow a skin (*Haut*) of signs (*Zeichen*) (ibid.). Anthropomorphic agents present a very interesting solution for the mediation process that takes place at the interface. With their body made out of signs, they are constructed to close the gap between humans and machines. This oscillating, in-between status is a reminder of ghosts, in the sense that there emerges a dematerialized body that lives in both worlds – the world of the living (humans) and the world of the dead (machines).

4.1. Uncanny Doppelgängers

Like a stage persona, the embodied agent/avatar/Virtual Human evolves from text – both figurations are scripted. But, unlike a stage persona, computer code is a specific form of text, a formalized and rule-oriented text, which needs to be processed and executed in order to work. The embodiment of the interface agent is bound through words, through the semiotic machine. Throughout my analysis, one major question has been: What kind of mirror does the computer demonstrate, and how can the reflective objects produced by this mirror be described? John Cayley, for example, asks whether the computer (screen) can be considered a mirror at all. In order to provide an answer, he continues to point out the specific character of the computer:

> "The answer to this question hinges on two further questions. A mirror 'runs by itself' – no need for it to be started up or attended to – and generates what is agreed to be a more or less perfect reflection. [...] The programmaton (computer system) transmits, stores, and manipulates. Does it also run by itself, generating objects that we recognize as perfect and adequate images? [...] Recording technologies – devices of writing – introduce images of and in time without, necessarily, producing anything other than the persistent 'mirror images' of objects that would otherwise be momentary, ephemeral. As such, these recording devices could, as varieties of time-sensitive mirrors, run by themselves without intervention. However, once a complex surface is programmed to manipulate the images it receives, reflects, and records, then the radical restructuring of image and time emerges as more than trivial and expected; it emerges as something that must be accounted for. The mirror distorts. It reveals, in fact, that it was always distorted, always preprogrammed in a particular way (to reflect 'perfectly' or make a 'perfect' record)." (Cayley 2003)

The body of the agent with which the human interacts is one that resembles the cinematic image. It is a moving light projection. Unlike a character in a film, however, the embodied agent serves as an interactive device. The human's actions have impact on how the agent reacts; pro-activeness and semi-autonomy are set as research goals. At least conceptually, the agent is a doppelgänger with its own life and agency. The degree to which this is realized depends on the interaction setting and the design of the technology. As a helpful application, the agent should not transgress certain borders, but the fear of overstepping is always there – it arises from the desired autonomy of the artifact. The call for papers for a workshop, called "Creating Bonds with Humanoids", states that:

> "In order that the user perceives and accepts the ECA as a companion, the ECA too, should maintain such a relationship. Tying and maintaining these bonds is highly related to the

engagement between interactants. But engagement does not mean pervasiveness. Humanoids should not invade the user's working space, nor should they intervene at any time"[241].

The media theorist Friedrich Kittler writes about the doppelgänger theme in Romanticism, where the "double" is produced by the words of the poet. Increasing alphabetization eventually led to the finding that words produce not foreign bodies but means of identification (Kittler 1997, p. 89). Kittler furthermore points out that words serve as "storage media" – in fact, words were the only storage media at that time (ibid.).

Following this, the embodied interface agent produces a figuration that brings together both technologies – the written double (or, for that matter, any literary character) and the phenomenon of the cinematic image – and takes them one step further. The computer serves as a productive mirror, one whereby narrations become alive. What is considered human finds entry, in the form of formalized descriptions, into the computational world. With the construction of the virtual human, these scripts become processable and executable and result in animation. Writing and imagery thus reemerge in the form of a figuration that is supposed to gain an independent existence and that may even step outside the mirror/interface. With these new traits, the Virtual Human oscillates between life/animation/functioning and death/inanimation/non-functioning. For this, the relation between sign and the body is of rather far-reaching importance. It is precisely such importance that is proposed by the following rereading of the experimental setting of the Turing Test.

4.2. Counting as Machine – Counting as Human: Rereading the Turing Test

4.2.1. The Gender Imitation Game

In the research field of embodied interface agents, a successful interaction scenario is characterized by the agent's ability to pass as a believable interaction partner. The fact that humans need to trust their virtual counterpart and feel comfortable with it (Ruttkay 2004) brings up the topic of the Uncanny Valley effect, even if it is not discussed explicitly. Under no circumstances should the artifact arouse uncanny or unsettling feelings. Thus, in research, a high level of trust and believability is interlinked with the goal to design the Virtual Human as lifelike as possible.

---

241 See: Creating bonds with humanoids, AAMAS 2005 workshop CFP. *http://www.iut.uni-vparis8.fr/~pelachaud/AAMAS05*, checked on 10/04/2013.

Even if not addressed as such, the technological mirroring of the human always invokes and recites a web of identity-establishing categories that includes gender and interdependent markers (ethnicity, cultural background, age, sexual orientation etc.). Unsurprisingly, a believable virtual doppelgänger is linked to a believable performance of gender. For the construction of anthropomorphic interface agents, it has even been stated that transgressing the human-machine boundary seems less threatening than transgressing the cultural order of gender (Bath 2002; Lübke 2005). Or, put differently, it seems more acceptable to mix artificial and real life than to question heteronormative gender relations.

It is of interest, then, that one of the most classic papers of artificial intelligence research interweaves the human-machine boundary with the cultural order of the two genders. The Turing Test, proposed in 1950, challenges the ability of a computer to engage in human-like conversation. While various critics have analyzed the notions of machine and intelligence that Turing develops (Searle 1984; Weizenbaum 1983), others (Hayles 1999) have stated that the gender relevance of this "founding narrative of cybernetics and artificial intelligence"[242] is, for the most part, neglected whenever the test is mentioned today. In the first version of the paper, *Computing machinery and intelligence*, Alan Turing starts by inventing the "Imitation Game", which "is played with three people, a man (A), a woman (B), and an interrogator (C) who may be of either sex. The interrogator stays in a room apart from the other two. The object of the game for the interrogator is to determine which of the other two is the man and which is the woman. He knows them by labels X and Y, and at the end of the game he says either 'X is A and Y is B' or 'X is B and Y is A'" (Turing 1950). Thus, before Turing develops a scenario for human-machine interaction, he invents a gender imitation game, in which different roles are attributed to each gender. The role of the woman is to be of assistance to the interrogator, and Turing suggests she should do that by being truthful. At the same time, it becomes clear that this may just as well cause confusion, because the man might equally claim to be the woman. In fact, in the course of the game, both players try to convince the interrogator that they are the woman. Turing then suggests replacing the original question, "Can machines think?", with the question, "What will happen when a machine takes the part of A in this game?" (ibid.). Following this, the imitation of the woman by the man may be replaced by the imitation of the woman by the machine. By doing so, the test produces a gender-biased scenario, but it also introduces the notion of "doing gender" (Butler 2004), of gender as a performance rather than a fixed, given state.

---

242 "Gründungsnarrativ von Kybernetik und Künstlicher Intelligenz" (Bath 2002, p. 85)

Turing thus suggests, first of all, that a man may transgress his original gender attribution. He then, in a second step, links this transgression to the overcoming of the human-machine boundary. In order to understand the impact of the test, it is important to consider how Turing arrives at this intersection of gender/machine performance. Here, the character of the computer as a semiotic machine, along with the relation between materiality and the (algorithmic) sign, plays a crucial role. With the gender imitation game, Turing suggests a split between the human body and the sign. He describes an experiment in which references to the human body should be eliminated as far as possible. The answers in the game must be delivered by way of typewriter, because handwriting is too close to the human body and might be a giveaway. The gendered coding of the human voice would equally pose a threat to the success of the game. In the test setting, it is the corporeality of embodiment that threatens to reveal which player is human and which is the machine – just as such corporeality reveals, in the original imitation game, which player is the woman and which is the man. In other words, according to the Turing Test, the sign is treated – just as it is in typewritten language – as freed from the connotations, restraints, and limits that an embodied existence brings along. In the course of the test, embodiment can mean either the physical materiality of the machine or the human body. It is this decoupling of the sign and the human body that makes it possible to attribute a rather radical, subversive potential to the 1950s Turing Test. As I have stated above, the test is gender-biased, and, from a historico-cultural perspective, it is no coincidence that female embodiment and the machine's performance are superimposed (Kormann 2006). Nevertheless, the test does introduce a certain form of gender queering that is acted out by the man[243]. Following this, the test suggests that the heteronormative gender order is a symbolic order all along. Or, put differently:

> "This construction necessarily makes the subject into a cyborg, for the enacted and represented bodies are brought into conjunction through the technology that connects them. If you distinguish correctly which is the man and which the woman, you in effect reunite the enacted and the represented bodies into a single gender identity. The very existence of the test, however, implies that you may also make the wrong choice. [...] What the Turing test 'proves' is that the overlay between the enacted and the represented bodies is no longer a natural inevitability but a contingent production, mediated by a technology that has become so entwined with the production of identity that it can no longer meaningfully be separated from the human subject." (Hayles 1999, p. xiii)

---

[243] This is even more interesting against the background of Turing's life, his sexual orientation, and the sufferings he had to endure because of it (Hodges 1992).

Early cyberfeminist discourse welcomed exactly this potential of new technology, namely that of subverting common gender codes by disarranging naturalized assumptions on bodies and identities (for one example see Stone 1991). The deconstructive possibilities that the virtual mirror provides, on the other hand, may be experienced as disturbing and thus allow a deeper insight into what is happening at the borders of the Uncanny Valley.

To sum up, the possibly uncanny artifacts of artificial intelligence research point to a provocative connection between the gender order and computer science's basic principles. At first glance, the situation seems paradoxical: the logic of computing translates the human body into a construct, and this move could serve as an entry point for the deconstruction of stereotypical identity concepts. With end products like the Virtual Human, the idea of a lifelike human copy gets favored. Just as in Mori's graph, anthropomorphic artificial beings seek to gain the status of a healthy person. In effect, this goal leads to an idealized, hyperconformist image of the human, rather than to the construction of diverse, flexible forms of virtual embodiment. With the Virtual Human, a mostly unquestioned state of naturalness is pursued. And precisely this naturalizing effect of the artifact is used to mask the working modes of the underlying technological device (Braun 2001, p. 103). It is important to keep in mind that the setting of the Turing Test is established through reference to the cultural gender order, but that it still introduces gender as a performance and therefore disrupts the nature-culture dichotomy. Turing reaches this point by freeing the scenario from the constraints of embodiment. He made it clear, for instance, that "no engineer or chemist claims to be able to produce a material which is indistinguishable from the human skin. It is possible that at some time this might be done, but even supposing this invention available we should feel there was little point in trying to make a thinking machine more human by dressing it up in such artificial flesh" (Turing 1950).

With social robots and Virtual Humans, however, this task of bringing embodiment back into the picture is precisely the goal. Accordingly, the original setting of the Turing Test is changed into a face-to-face situation, and this brings about an important epistemological shift. Effectively, it is now the case that not only the output of the body, but also the body itself, should be able to trick the audience. The "artificial flesh" in which the Virtual Humans are "dressed up" is, in appearance and behavior, always already gendered artificial flesh.

It is precisely at this point that the uncanny re-enters the stage, as the following remark by Justine Cassell shows:

"One way to think about the problem[244] that we face is to imagine that we succeed beyond our wildest dreams in building a computer that can carry on a face-to-face Turing test. That is, imagine a panel of judges challenged to determine which socialite was a real live young woman and which was an automaton (as in Hoffmann's 'The Sandman'). Or, rather, perhaps to judge which screen was a part of a video conferencing set-up, displaying an autonomous embodied conversational agent running on a computer. In order to win at the Turing test, what underlying models of human conversation would we need to implement, and what surface behaviors would our embodied conversational agent need to display?" (Cassell 2000b, p. 2).

In this new, adapted version of the Turing test, the uncanny emerges in reference to E.T.A. Hoffmann's famous story, *The Sandman*[245]. In contrast to more common virtual forms of embodiment, such as computer game characters or avatars, the Virtual Human is conceptualized as an autonomous interaction partner. Due to the state of research, embodied agents are currently not integrated into everyday environments. Consequently, in order to illustrate the potential of these embodied agents, research material will often make use of examples from films and literature. Using *The Sandman* as a vision not only draws attention to the gendered implications of the human-machine boundary, it also points to the possible uncanniness of the artificial being. For the most part, dystopian threads of science fiction are neglected when used as an example for research. *The Sandman*, in particular, produces a picture that is not very uplifting. Why is it, then, that Cassell recites this romantic story in which Nathanael, the user in interaction with the machine Olimpia, dies in the end and the artifact gets dismantled? What can be learned from this for a broader conception of human-humanoid interaction?

4.2.2. Ambiguous Positions at Peril:
The Case of Olimpia and the Virtual Human

Transferred to the area of computer science, *The Sandman* tells a story of user and artifact. In the narration, the male protagonist Nathanael gets frustrated with his fiancée Clara, mainly because she rejects the ceaseless flow of his ongoing poetic recitations. He encounters the artificial being Olimpia and, being unaware of her factitiousness, falls in love with her. In the course of the novel, the roles of the real-life young woman Clara and that of the automaton Olimpia transpose. Exactly as envisioned in the Turing Test, the woman gets replaced by the machine. Subsequently, Nathanael experiences Olimpia as warm and caring, whereas the character of Clara, for him, reverses. But this only happens for Nathanael. Olimpia, who in

---

244 She is referring to the problem of human-computer interaction.
245 *Der Sandmann (Hoffmann 2006 [1817])*.

the perspective of all the others in the story remains cold and machine-like, serves as a projection space for him. She truly represents a desiring machine[246].

When it comes to the encounter between Nathanael and Olimpia, it is his agency that animates the object. The fact that his lips spread warmth to hers, that the spark of his eyes activate hers, is noteworthy for the field of human-computer interaction, where the ability of the user to construct a meaningful scenario should not be underestimated. For a short moment, even Nathanael experiences the uncanny effect that Mori describes with the prosthetic hand, but he quickly manages to overcome the Uncanny Valley: "Olympia's hand was as cold as ice; he felt a horrible deathly chill thrilling through him. He looked into her eyes, which beamed back full of love and desire, and at the same time it seemed as though her pulse began to beat and her life's blood to flow into her cold hand" (Hoffmann 2006 [1817], p. 37)[247]. In this story, human-machine interaction is established and stabilized through acting out a heterosexual relationship. Olimpia's passing of the Turing Test depends on whether its/her gender performance is convincing enough to superimpose the machine character. As stated above, Olimpia passes only in relation to Nathanael, all the others experience her as uncanny. Siegmund, Nathanael's friend, is extremely worried and voices his concerns about Olimpia:

> "Nevertheless, it is strange that many of us think much the same about Olympia. To us – pray do not take it ill, brother, she appears singularly stiff and soulless. Her shape is well proportioned – so is her face – that is true! She might pass for beautiful if her glance were not so utterly without a ray of life – without the power of vision. Her pace is strangely regular, every movement seems to depend on some wound-up clockwork. Her playing and her singing keep the same unpleasantly correct and spiritless time as a musical box, and the same may be said of her dancing. We find your Olympia quite uncanny, and prefer to have nothing to do with her. She seems to act like a living being, and yet has some strange peculiarity of her own." (ibid., p. 40)

Hence, Olimpia's computability and rule-orientation do not simply make her boring and predictable – they make her fall into the Uncanny Valley. Olimpia is accused of merely pretending to be a lifelike being, which here means: she only pretends to be a woman.

In Sherry Turkle's work on the computer as a *Second Self*, it is the machine's origin, in particular, that renders the anthropomorphic artifact as uncanny. She states that: "A being that is not born of a mother, that does not feel the vulnerability of childhood, a being that does not know sexuality or anticipate death, this

---

246 In the cyberpunk novel *Idoru* the virtual woman, Rei Toei, is an "aggregate of subjective desire" (Gibson 1996).
247 Here: English translation by John Oxenford. *http://www.fln.vcu.edu/hoffmann/sand_e.html*, checked on 15/02/2013.

being is alien" (Turkle 1984, p. 311). Sherry Turkle, furthermore, did interviews and ethnographic research to see how children react towards computing technology and artifacts like robots or on-screen characters. A collection of statements reads like this:

> "The robots know what they are doing, but they are not alive; they would be alive, if they had bodies; they are alive, because they have bodies; they would be alive, if they had feelings; they are alive as insects are alive; they could be alive if they left the computer behind and switched to America Online; they are alive until the computer is turned off, then they are dead; they are not alive, because nothing in the computer is real; the digital beings of the 'Sims' games are not alive, but they are close; they would be alive, if they could speak; they would be alive, if they could travel; they are alive, but not 'real'; they are not alive, because they have no bodies; they are alive, because they can have babies, and finally, the words of an eleven-year-old child, which is relatively new to 'Sim Life', they are not alive because these babies have no parents: 'You see them, and the game tells you, that they have mothers and fathers, but I don't believe it. They are only numbers, not really mother and father.'"[248]

Indeed, in many science fiction narratives humanoids search for some kind of belonging, which at most times results in a quest for proof of their own genealogical identity[249]. This point is not made to support oppositions of natural origins in contrast to artificial ones. I am referring to this in order to point out the way the boundary between human and artifact is drawn: the entrance into the human world is interwoven with the cultural order of the two genders. On one side, there are organic heterosexual reproduction, vulnerability, fear of death, and the finiteness of life, which define humanity; on the other, beings like Olimpia hold the power to transgress this "life cycle" (Turkle 1984, p. 311), but they pay for this by risking to appear non-human, uncanny, and alien.

In order to unravel the entanglement that the Uncanny Valley effect, the cultural order of gender, and the human-artifact relation produce, several threads can be taken up. For example, Karin Esders, in an article on *Digital Beauties*, states that the virtual character is made uncanny due to its incapacity to be traced back

---

248 "Die Roboter wissen, was sie tun, sind aber nicht lebendig; wären lebendig, wenn sie Körper hätten; sind lebendig, weil sie Körper haben; wären lebendig, wenn sie Gefühle hätten; sind lebendig, so wie Insekten lebendig sind; könnten lebendig sein, wenn sie den Computer verließen und zu America Online wechselten; sind lebendig, bis der Computer ausgeschaltet wird, dann sind sie tot; sind nicht lebendig, weil nichts im Computer real ist; die digtalen Wesen der 'Sim'-Spiele sind nicht lebendig, aber beinahe; sie wären lebendig, wenn sie sprechen könnten; sie wären lebendig, wenn sie reisen könnten; sie sind lebendig, aber nicht 'real'; sie sind nicht lebendig, weil sie keine Körper haben; sie sind lebendig, weil sie Babys kriegen können, und schließlich, in den Worten eines elfjährigen Kindes, das relativ neu in 'Sim-Life' ist, sie sind nicht lebendig, weil diese Babys keine Eltern haben: 'Man sieht sie, und das Spiel sagt einem, daß sie Mütter und Väter haben, aber das glaube ich nicht. Es sind nur Zahlen, nicht wirklich Mutter und Vater.'" (Turkle 1999, p. 100)
249 See Chapter 2.3.2.

to a material body. For her, the generally hyperconformed appearance of Virtual Humans derives from their lack of material reference and bodily distinctiveness, which real human subjects inevitably possess (Esders 2007, p. 101). This inevitable richness of the materiality of real world bodies presents the potential to induce moments of resistance and leads to a variety of forms of embodiment and identity concept. Esders' findings link the uncanny to the origin of the artifact, to its modes of construction. Additionally, her analysis poses questions concerning the role of the material and the semiotic.

According to Mori, humanoids fall into the Uncanny Valley if they reach a high degree of human likeness but still produce minor lapses. Hence, "virtual beings embody a state of 'as well as' and of 'neither - nor'"[250], and this points not only to the potential to recode and transgress what is considered human, but also to disturbances in the realm of gender.

In his classic essay on the uncanny effects of *The Sandman*, Sigmund Freud defines "the uncanny" as "that class of the frightening which leads back to what is known of old and long familiar" (Freud 1963, p. 46)[251]. The uncanny, in this view, is something that has been repressed and then re-enters the stage. In Mori's overview, the undead appears to be even more frightening than the dead corpse. One cannot help but wonder why that is. It is understandable that humans fear death, but why is the state between life and death so scary?

The positioning of technological artifacts between two states, their being "neither flesh nor fowl" (Akrich 1992), adds to the ghost-like quality that characterizes their uncanniness. In Mori's valley, the (un)dead are gathering. In a broadened conception, this "immense system of death" (Cixous 1976, p. 543) represents the abject, the outcast, the monstrous – in short, it is that which threatens human identity. Following Judith Butler, and as was noted earlier in reference to science fiction narratives[252], the process of obtaining an intelligible form of subjectivity goes hand in hand with the heteronormative ordering system. For the production of the uncanniness of Virtual Humans, the interconnection of gender and melancholia is of special interest (Butler 1997). According to Butler, it is crucial to note that when it comes to the formation of the gendered self, the taboo against homosexuality is the founding prohibition[253]. In short, the construction of a heteronormative gender identity is always based on the primary loss of the homosexual object of desire. This repressed lost other, which can neither live nor be mourned, is

---

250 "Die virtuellen Figuren verkörpern das Sowohl-als-auch und das Weder-noch [...]" (Esders 2007, pp.101-102).
251 Translation: *http://www.rae.com.pt/Freud1.pdf*, checked on 13/01/2013.
252 See Chapter 2.3.2.
253 Freud characterizes the formation of the ego as melancholic structure. The child has to give up the desire for its parents because of the incest taboo. Butler argues, however, that the taboo against homosexuality precedes the incest taboo (Butler 1990, p. 64).

incorporated as a part of the formation of the self. To grasp the concept of the doppelgänger[254], Steve Garlick suggests that Freud's concept of the uncanny be linked to Butler's theory of identity formation. If Butler's concept of identity formation is taken seriously, Garlick argues, the gendered body itself can be considered a haunted house, for it incorporates the lost other (Garlick 2002, p. 870). According to Freud, the uncanny (*unheimlich*) oscillates between the home (*das Heim*) and the strange (*un-heimisch* = not home). The relation between private and public places is rich with gendered connotations. In the Western, middle-class culture of the 1950s, for example, the family home was considered to be the area for women, and those who stepped out of this ordering system were regarded as threatening (Esders 2007). In the research area of Virtual Humans, the simulation of human appearance and behavior stands for ease of use and trust. Their embodiment can be seen as a housing that transforms abstract computing modes into something comfortable and makes the user feel more at home with the technology. This points to another possible explanation for why so many artificial beings in science are conceptualized as female.

Hélène Cixous provides a deeper analysis of the relation between artificial figurations, death, and the uncanny. Against a Freudian background, she addresses the question of what it actually is that comes back to haunt the human in the form of Olimpia – or, in this case, the form of the Virtual Human. In a rereading of Freud's article, she points out that Freud marginalizes the meaning of Olimpia and focuses instead on Nathanael. According to her, however, the key to understanding the uncanny lies in Olimpia's role as a hybrid and intermediary. She links Olimpia's uncanniness to her position between human and machine, between life and death:

> "It is the between that is tainted with strangeness. Everything remains to be said on the subject of the Ghost and the ambiguity of the Return, for what renders it intolerable is not so much that it is an announcement of death nor even the proof that death exists, since this Ghost announces and proves nothing more than his return. What is intolerable is that the Ghost erases the limit which exists between two states, neither alive nor dead; passing through, the dead man returns in the manner of the Repressed. [...] In the end, death is never anything more than the disturbance of the limits. [...] Olympia is not inanimate. The strange power of death moves in the realm of life as the Unheimliche in the Heimliche, as the void fills up the lack." (Cixous 1976, p. 543)

Cixous understands the ghost as a representation of death. Hence, "the direct figure of the uncanny is the Ghost" (Cixous 1976, p. 542), for it makes an "impossible representation" possible. She asks:

---

[254] In reference to Jaques Derrida, Steve Garlick introduces the doppelgänger as the revenant – that is, as something or someone that comes back.

4.2. Counting as Machine – Counting as Human: Rereading the Turing Test

"Why would death have this power? Because of its alliance with scientific uncertainty and primitive thought. 'Death' does not have any form in life. Our unconscious makes no place for the representation of our mortality. As an impossible representation, death is that which mimes, by this very impossibility, the reality of death. It goes even further. That which signifies without that which is signified. What is an absolute secret, something absolutely new and which should remain hidden, because it has shown itself to me, is the fact that I am dead; only the dead know the secret of death. Death will recognize us, but we shall not recognize it." (Cixous 1976, p. 543)

It is exactly the erasing of the limits that Cixous describes and the transference of this transgression onto the realm of the symbolic gender order to which the Virtual Human caters. With its intermediate character, it not only questions the boundaries of life and death, it also opens up the possibility of transgender options. The potential uncanniness of the Virtual Human makes sense when it is accepted that identity formation is a process, and not simply a fixed state or a natural inevitability. Rather, the forming of a self must be viewed as an ongoing performative act in which the subject recites intelligible norms. The notion of gender as an activity, as a way of doing gender, also leaves some space for breaches and lapses of gender regulations. What the Turing Test does is exemplify the deconstructive potential of computer science by introducing gender and machineness as valid players in the game. The deconstructive power is amplified by the semiotic character of the computer, which – in the process of becoming an object of computing – splits sign and materiality and rearranges them in the end. *No matter what is ascribed to you, in the test you may perform drag.* Against this background, the Virtual Human does not just fill the void between human and computer, it also represents the space between man and woman. And this may be experienced as uncanny and even threatening, given how intelligible identity concepts are gained.

Earlier, I stated that the Virtual Human interface – and this is also valid for the case of Hoffmann's Olimpia – is likely to produce a paradoxical situation. On one hand, the very existence of cyborg beings threatens the nature-culture dichotomy; on the other, this blurring of strict boundaries nourishes the need to stabilize the symbolic gender order rather than to dissolve it. It is the strict following of this ordering system that offers to the artifact the promise of reaching the status of a human subject.

The Virtual Human already is defined as a hybrid – it cannot take additional risks by transgressing a norm so central to Western culture. This seems to be even truer since the artifact already lives with a secret: following the goal of the research field, it has to hide its machine-like origin. As Olimpia illustrates, such an agenda is likely to produce lapses and errors. This is not because the artifact is designed badly, but rather because the underlying working modes of computerization will always shine through. The case of Olimpia tells, among other things, a story of how the idea of being human gets re-established in the face-to-face Turing Test. And computability, standardized behavior, predictability, and formalization are traits that have been sourced out to the machine. The gendered artificial flesh is then used to conceal these characteristics.

But the artificial housing provided by this flesh also introduces dimensions that are unintended by the designers. Remarkably, *The Sandman* introduces a story is that is rather disturbing from a technological point of view – it ends with the human user dying and the artifact getting destroyed. This dystopian aspect is neglected when the story is cited in computing. One reason for this may be that the reference to this narration speaks of the desire to overcome "the between that is tainted with strangeness", to give the story a different end. Virtual Humans, with their ghost-like quality, bring along promises of transcendence, of living forever. These artificial beings make a claim on how emotions are conceptualized and on how visual relations are realized – their design manages life. As Cixous states, artificial beings also introduce uncanniness: "Hence, the horror: you could be dead while living, you can be in a dubious state" (Cixous 1976, p. 545). Against the background of computing, humanness becomes the object of computation itself. The computer program is a text that, in concept, is executed without end. It ceaselessly returns. Therefore, the embodied agent transports the promise not only to manage life, but also to manage death, to make the dubious state computable.

Read against the background of the Lacanian concept, and presuming that humans are able to accept the Virtual Human as a valid mirror image (if the misrecognition of this mirroring is strong enough), we could imagine that death may be beat. But the projected image of the embodied agent, according to Cixous, remains a reminder of death – an uncanny representation. *Alice Through the Looking-Glass* presents a figuration that is able to beat uncanniness by passing through the mirror image. The figuration of the Virtual Human binds the human to the processes of computation and weaves humanness into the cybernetic feedback loop. In the research field of embodied agents, when the artifact is insufficiently believable, this is attributed to the fact that, so far, not enough knowledge about human behavior and appearance has been made available in a rule-oriented, formalized manner (Krämer, Bente 2002, p. 218; Trogemann 2003, p. 286). In this sense, a specific concept of humanness and its accompanying narrations are built into technological systems. Ultimately, the Virtual Human, by promising to overcome materiality and death, participates in a powerful Western escapist fantasy. This label of fantasy can connote either luck or utter dissatisfaction, depending on where you are situated. What can be learned from the narrations that accompany technological artifact production is to take the dystopian aspects, the abject, more seriously. It might very well be that these unwanted side effects – which occur when the interaction goes wrong– are precisely what hold the key to a new way

4.2. Counting as Machine – Counting as Human: Rereading the Turing Test

of thinking about human-artifact relations. They point at issues that need to be addressed.

I have singled out *Alice Through the Looking-Glass* as a successful framing of a user-interface setting (even if the character of Alice is not unproblematic). Just as the human becomes reconstructed, against the background of computing's basic principles, in order to produce the Virtual Human simulation, so Alice, by entering the text, is fed into its logic. I observed earlier, by quoting Sybille Krämer, that the computer is an "interactive mirror of a dynamic world of symbols "[255], where "the world of the mirror receives the status of an independent semiotic representation"[256]. Krämer characterizes simulation as a phenomenon where "a surface-like behavior does not correspond to any analogous deep structure"[257]. But the vigor of the fictional Alice reaches beyond the simulation of the real Alice Liddell. *Alice Through the Looking-Glass* walks right into the heart of the semiotic code – as a result, concepts of time and space, *and* of self and identity, are challenged. Here, at the center of language[258], objects and representations merge and thus it no longer makes sense to differentiate between surface and underlying structure. This move is what the Virtual Human technology exemplifies. Through semiotic de- and reconstruction, it produces a simulation that goes beyond the notion of simulation and makes a powerful claim on reality. The interactive character of the computer and the "Weltwerdung" ("coming into the world") of computational artifacts add to this claim. Perhaps the ultimate Western fantasy of overcoming death has shifted from "leaving behind the meat" towards a semiotic reconfiguration of materiality itself, of literally altering humanness, embodiment, and emotions through code[259]. However strongly this point is made, it is still the case that ideas and realities of embodiment increasingly co-evolve with computing technology. Consequently, future research on humans against the background of computing should seek to include narrations and knowledge that are not as easily translatable into the logic of the computer. Luckily, as Donna Haraway puts it, the world cannot be mastercoded: "Actors come in many and wonderful forms. Accounts of a 'real' world do not, then depend on a logic of 'discovery', but on a power-charged social relation of 'conversation'. The world neither speaks itself nor disappears in favour of a

---

255 "interaktiver Spiegel dynamisierter Symbolwelten" (Krämer 2011, p. 313)
256 "Die Spiegelwelt bekommt den Status einer eigenständigen semiotischen Repräsentation" (Krämer 2011, p. 313)
257 "Einem Oberflächenverhalten korrespondiert keine entsprechende Tiefenstruktur" (Krämer 2011, p. 305). See Chapter 2.2.
258 See end of Chapter 2.1.
259 But then again, maybe this is not a shift, but rather a sign that the program of Western transcendence has arrived at its roots, where words not only produce narrations but also evoke bodies. Cp. "In the beginning was the Word, and the Word was with God, and the Word was God." (The Holy Bible, Johannes 1,1-1)

master coder. The codes of the world are not still, waiting only to be read. The world is not raw material for humanization" (Haraway 1991a, p. 198). And that also means, of course, that the world is not raw material for computerization. The figuration of Alice points out how interesting and poetic it can be to mess with the code in which one was originally written.

Appendix

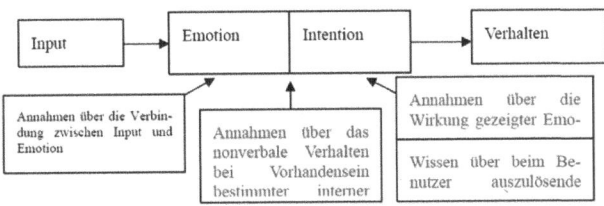

Fig. i Typical Architecture; original version of *Fig. 25*
(Source: Krämer, Bente, 2003)

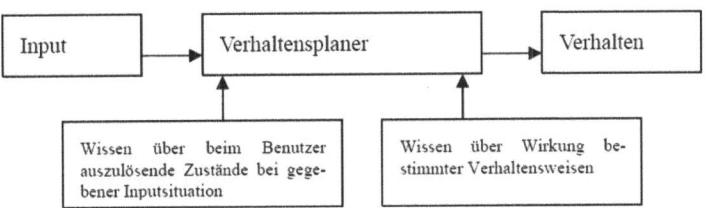

Fig. ii Alternative Implementation of Emotions; original version of *Fig. 26*
(Source: Krämer, Bente, 2003)

Tabelle : Übersicht über Sprechakte, verfolgte Intentionen und zu zeigendes Verhalten

Sprechakt	Intention/zu erreichendes beim Benutzer	Konkretes Verhalten Agent	Zeitaspekt
message_greeting: Das System grüßt den Benutzer, am Anfang der Interaktion	Der Benutzer fühlt sich freundlich und höflich begrüßt	Augenbrauen hoch und Augen 1 Sekunde größer Lächeln Winken (optional) Lächeln Kopf schräglegen (ca. 10 Grad nach rechts)	Beginn der Einblendung Vor Beginn Vor Beginn Nach Begrüßung Nach Begrüßung (für 4 Sekunden)
message_closing: Wird eingesetzt am Ende der Interaktion mit dem Benutzer.	Der Benutzer fühlt sich freundlich verabschiedet	Lächeln	Nach Verabschiedung
message_inform [status: warning]	Benutzer soll Dringlichkeit wahrnehmen	Augenbrauen anheben, Augen größer Hände anheben, Handflächen zum Benutzer (evtl. nur eine Hand heben mit Zeigefinger nach oben)	Gesamtzeit der Äußerung Zu Beginn, dann langsam runternehmen
message_inform [status: busy]	Benutzer soll geduldig bleiben	Kopf geringfügig nach unten neigen	Gesamtzeit der Äußerung

Fig. iii Speech Act Table (Excerpt) ; original version of *Fig. 27*
(Source: Krämer, Bente, 2003)

Bibliography

AAMAS (Ed.) (2002): Proceedings of the first international joint conference on Autonomous agents and multiagent systems, July 15-19, 2002, Bologna, Italy. New York: ACM.

Adam, Alison (1998): Artificial Knowing - Gender and the Thinking Machine. London, New York: Routledge.

Adams, Douglas (1980): The Restaurant at the End of the Universe. New York: Pocket Books.

Akrich, Madeleine (1992): The Description of Technical Objects. In W.E. Bijker, John Law (Eds.): Shaping Technology/Building Society. Studies in Sociotechnical Change. Cambridge: MIT Press, pp. 205–240.

Allen, James F. (1984): Towards a general theory of action and time. In *Artificial Intelligence*, 23 (2), pp. 123–154.

Andersen, P.B. (1990): A Theory of Computer Semiotics. Semiotic approaches to construction and assesment of computer systems. Cambridge: Cambridge University Press (Cambridge Series on Human-Computer Interaction, 3).

Andruszkiewicz, J. L. (2009a): Affordance and Interface Design. Available online at *http://lefthandedpixel.com/wordpress/?p=12*, checked on 4/12/2013.

Andruszkiewicz, J. L. (2009b): Lacan's mirror stage of self awareness. Available online at *http://lefthandedpixel.com/wordpress/?p=5*, checked on 4/12/2013.

Angeli, Antonella de; Bianchi-Berthouze; Nadia (Eds.) (2006): Gender and Interaction: Real and Virtual Women in a Male World. Workshop, AVI 2006 - Advanced Visual Interfaces, May 23-26, 2006, Venice, Italy. Available online at *http://www.informatics.manchester. ac.uk/~antonella/gender/papers.htm*, checked on 5/10/2014.

Anzieu, Didier (1991): Das Haut-Ich. Frankfurt am Main: Suhrkamp.

Appadurai, Arjun (1996): Disjuncture and difference in the global cultural economy. In Arjun Appadurai: Modernity at Large. Minnesota: University of Minnesota Press, pp. 27–47.

Argyle, Michael; Cook Mark (1976): Gaze and mutual gaze. Cambridge: Cambridge University Press.

Ballard, Allen B. (1973): The education of black folk. The Afro-American struggle for knowledge in white America. New York: Harper Row.

Ball, Gene; Breese, Jack (2000): Emotion and Personality in a Conversational Agent. In Justine Cassell (Ed.): Embodied conversational agents. Cambridge Mass.: MIT Press, pp. 189–219.

Balsamo, Ann (2002): On the Cutting Edge: Cosmetic Surgery and the Technological Production of the Gendered Body. In Nicholas Mirzoeff (Ed.): The visual culture reader. 2. ed. London, New York: Routledge, pp. 223–233.

Balsamo, Anne Marie (1995): Forms of Technological Embodiment: Reading the Body in Contemporary Culture. In Mike Featherstone, Roger Burrows (Eds.): Cyberspace / Cyberbodies / Cyberpunk: Cultures of Technological Embodiment. London: Sage Publications, pp. 215-238.

Balsamo, Anne Marie (1996): Technologies of the Gendered Body. Reading Cyborg Women. Durham: Duke University Press.

Barad, Karen (2003): Posthumanist Performativity: Toward and Understanding of How Matter Comes to Matter. In *Signs: Journal of Women in Culture and Society,* 28 (3), pp. 801–831.

Barbrook, Richard; Cameron, Andy (1997): Die kalifornische Ideologie - Wiedergeburt der Moderne. Available online at *http://www.heise.de/tp/issue/downloadcgi? artikelnr=1007*, checked on 3/5/2013.

Bartneck, C.; Kanda, T.; Ishiguro, H.; Hagita, N. (2007): Is the Uncanny Valley an Uncanny Cliff? In IEEE (Ed.): The 16th IEEE International Symposium on Robot and Human Interactive Communication, 2007. RO-MAN 2007. IEEE. Jeju, pp. 368–373.

Bath, Corinna (2002): Was können uns Turing-Tests von Avataren sagen? Performative Aspekte virtueller Verkörperungen im Zeitalter der Technoscience. In Astrid Epp, Niels C. Taubert, Andrea Westermann (Eds.): Technik und Identität. Bielefeld (IWT-Paper, 26), pp. 79–99.

Bath, Corinna (2009): De-Gendering informatischer Artefakte. Grundlagen einer kritisch-feministischen Technikgestaltung. Dissertation, Bremen. Open-Access-Veröffentlichung der Dissertation (Informatik). Staats- und Universitätsbibliothek Bremen. Available online at *http://nbn-resolving.de/urn:nbn:de:gbv:46-00102741-12*, checked on 3/1/2015.

Bath, Corinna (2010): Emotionskonzepte in der neueren Softwareagentenforschung – Von grundlegender Kritik zu feministischer Technologiegestaltung? In Mechthild Koreuber (Ed.): Zur Geschlechterforschung in Mathematik und Informatik. Eine (inter)disziplinäre Herausforderung. 1st ed. Baden-Baden: Nomos (Schriften des Heidelberger Instituts für Interdisziplinäre Frauen- und Geschlechterforschung (HIFI) e.V, 8), pp. 187-204.

Becker, Christian; Kopp, Stefan; Wachsmuth, Ipke (2004): Simulating the emotion dynamics of a multimodal conversational agent. In André E, Dybkjær L, Minker W, Heisterkamp P (Eds): Lecture Notes in Computer Science (LNAI), Affective Dialogue Systems - Proceedings of the Tutorial and Research Workshop, ADS 2004. Heidelberg, Berlin: Springer-Verlag, pp. 154–165.

Beer, Gilian (2012): Mannigfaltigkeiten der Zeit. Die Alice Bücher. In Hubertus Gaßner, Annabelle Görgen-Lammers, Christoph Benjamin Schulz (Eds.): Alice im Wunderland der Kunst. Ausstellung: "Alice im Wunderland der Kunst", Hamburger Kunsthalle, Galerie der Gegenwart, 22. Juni bis 30. September 2012. Ostfildern: Hatje Cantz, pp. 138–144.

Berners-Lee, Tim; Hendler, James; Lassila, Ora (2001): The Semantic Web. A new form of Web content that is meaningful to computers will unleash a revolution of new possibilities. In *Scientific American* 284 (5), pp. 34-43.

Black, John B.; Kay, Dana S.; Soloway, Elliot M. (1987): Goal and Plan Knowledge Representations: From Stories to Text Editors and Programs. In John M. Carrol (Ed.): Interfacing Thought. Cognitive Aspects of Human-Computer Interaction. Massachusetts: MIT Press, pp. 36–60.

Bødker, Susanne (1990): Through the Interface: A Human Activity Approach to User Interface Design: CRC Press.

Boehner, Kirsten; DePaula, Rogério; Dourish, Paul; Sengers, Phoebe (2005): Affect: From Information to Interaction. In Olav Bertelsen, Niels Olof Bousin, Pete Krogh, Morton Kyng (Eds.): Critical Computing – Between Sense and Sensibility. The Fourth Decennial Aarhus Conference. Aarhus, pp. 59–68.

Boella, Guido; van der Torre, Leendert (2005): Enforceable Social Laws. In Virginia Dignum, Frank Dignum, Sven Koenig (Eds.): Proceedings of the Fourth International Joint Conference on Autonomous Agents and Multi Agent Systems. New York: ACM.

Both, Göde (2011): Agency und Geschlecht in Mensch/Maschine-Konfigurationen am Beispiel von Virtual Personal Assistants. Diplomarbeit. Humboldt-Universität zu Berlin, Berlin. Mathematisch-Naturwissenschaftliche Fakultät II. Available online at *http://edoc.hu-berlin. de/docviews/abstract.php?id=39114*, checked on 21/06/2013.

Boukricha, Hana; Wachsmuth, Ipke (2011): Empathy-Based Emotional Alignment for a Virtual Human: A Three-Step Approach. In *Künstliche Intelligenz* (2011) 25, pp.195–204.

Bovenschen, Silvia (1995): Die imaginierte Weiblichkeit. Frankfurt am Main: Suhrkamp.

Bowlby, John ([1950] 1995): Maternal Care and Mental Health. 2nd. Northvale, NJ; London: Jason Aronson.

Bratman, Michael E. (1987): Intentions, Plans and Practical Reason. Cambridge, Mass.: Harvard University Press.

Braun, Christina von (1997): "Ceci n'est pas une femme." Blick und Berührung. In Wildwasser Bielefeld e.V. (Ed.): Der aufgestörte Blick. Multiple Persönlichkeiten, Frauenbewegung und Gewalt. Bielefeld: Kleine Verlag GmbH, pp. 330-347.

Braun, Christina von (2001): Versuch über den Schwindel. Religion, Bild, Schrift, Geschlecht. Zürich: Pendo.

Braun, Christina von (2006): Gender, Geschlecht und Geschichte. In Christina von Braun, Inge Stephan (Eds.): Gender-Studien. Eine Einführung. 2., aktualisierte Aufl. Stuttgart, Weimar: Metzler, pp. 10–51.

Braun, Christina von (2012): Der Preis des Geldes. Eine Kulturgeschichte. Berlin: Aufbau.

Braun, Christina von; Dietze, Gaby (Eds.) (1999): Multiple Persönlichkeit. Krankheit Medium oder Metapher? Frankfurt a. M.: Verl. Neue Kritik.

Brennan, Susan E. (1990): Conversation as Direct Manipulation: An Iconoclastic View. In Brenda K. Laurel (Ed.): The Art of Human-Computer Interface Design, pp. 393–404.

Brennan, Susan E. (1991): Conversation with and through computers. In *User Modeling and User-Adapted Interaction* (Volume 1, March 1991), pp. 67–86.

Brooks, Edward; Ovid (2010): The Metamorphosis of Ovid: Vol. I--Books I-VII. Charleston, South Carolina: Nabu Press.

Bush, Vannevar (1945): As we may think. In *The Atlantic*. Available online at http://www.theatlantic.com/doc/194507/bush, checked on 14/01/2013.

Butler, Judith (1990): Gender Trouble: Feminism and the Subversion of Identity. New York: Routledge.

Butler, Judith (1993): Bodies That Matter: On the Discursive Limits of "Sex". New York: Routledge.

Butler, Judith (1997): The Psychic Life of Power: Theories in Subjection. Stanford: Stanford University Press.

Butler, Judith (2004): Undoing Gender. Oxford, UK: Taylor & Francis.

Cahun, Claude (2007): Disavowals or cancelled confessions. London: Tate.

Card, Stuart K.; Moran, Thomas P.; Newell, Allen (1983): The psychology of human-computer interaction. Hillsdale, N.J.: Erlbaum.

Carroll, Lewis (1992a): Alice's Adventures in Wonderland. In Lewis Carroll: Alice in Wonderland. Ware, UK: Wordsworth Editions Limited (reprinted), pp. 1–104.

Carroll, Lewis (1992b): Through the Looking-Glass and What Alice Found There. In Lewis Carroll: Alice in Wonderland. Ware, UK: Wordsworth Editions Limited (reprinted), pp. 105–198.

Cassell, J.; Bickmore T.; Vilhjalmsson H.; Yan H. (2001): "More Than Just a Pretty Face: Conversational Protocols and the Affordances of Embodiment." In *Knowledge-Based Systems* 14, pp. 55-64.

Cassell, Justine (1998): Storytelling as a Nexus of Change in the Relationship between Gender and Technology: A Feminist Approach to Software Design. In Justine Cassell, Henry Jenkins (Eds.): From Barbie to Mortal Kombat. Gender and computer games. Cambridge, Mass: MIT Press, pp. 298-326.

Cassell, Justine (Ed.) (2000a): Embodied conversational agents. Cambridge Mass.: MIT Press.

Cassell, Justine (2000b): Nudge Nudge Wink Wink: Elements of Face-to-Face Conversation for Embodied Conversational Agents. In Justine Cassell (Ed.): Embodied conversational agents. Cambridge Mass.: MIT Press, pp. 1–27.

Cayley, John (2003): Inner Workings. Code and representations of interiority in new media poetics. Available online at *http://www.brown.edu/Research/dichtung-digital/2003/issue/3/ Cayley.htm*, checked on 17/02/2013.

Cixous, Hélène (1976): Fiction and Its Phantoms: A Reading of Freud's Das Unheimliche (The "uncanny"). In *New Literary History*, Vol. 7, No. 3, Thinking in the Arts, Sciences, and Literature, pp. 525–548.

Cohen, Michael F.; Colburn, R. Alex; Drucker, Steven M. (2000): The Role of Eye Gaze in Avatar Mediated Conversational Interfaces. Microsoft Research Publications: MSR-TR-2000-81.

Coleman, Tracy (2011): Avatāra. Oxford Bibliographies. Available online at *http://www.oxfordbibliographies.com/view/document/obo-9780195399318/obo-9780195399318-0009.xml*, checked on 26/08/2013.

Collins, Patricia H. (1991): Black feminist thought. Knowledge, consciousness, and the politics of empowerment. Reprint. New York: Routledge (Perspectives on gender, 2).

Corbató, Fernando J.; Merwin Daggett, Marjorie; Daley, Robert C. (1962): An Experimental Time-Sharing System. Scanned and transcribed by F. J. Corbató from the original SJCC Paper of May 3, 1962. Edited by Massachusetts Institute of Technology Computation Center. Available online at *http://larch-www.lcs.mit.edu:8001/~corbato/sjcc62/*, checked on 13/10/2013.

Coy, Wolfgang (2008): Auf dem Weg zum "Finalen Interface". Ein medienhistorischer Essay. In Hans Dieter Hellige (Ed.): Mensch-Computer-Interface. Zur Geschichte und Zukunft der Computerbedienung. Bielefeld: transcript, pp. 309–321.

Cregan, Kate (2006): The sociology of the body. Mapping the abstraction of embodiment. London: Sage.

Crenshaw, Kimberlé W. (1991): Mapping the Margins: Intersectionality, Identity Politics, and Violence against Women of Color. In *Stanford Law Review* 43 (6), pp. 1241–1299.

Crutzen, Cecile M.K. (2003): ICT-Representations as Transformative Critical Rooms. In Gabriele Kreutzner, Heidi Schelhowe (Eds.): Agents of Change. Virtuality, Gender, and the Challenge to the Traditional University. Opladen: Leske + Budrich (Technik und Kultur), pp. 87–106.

Damasio, Antonio R. (1994): Descartes' Error: Emotion, Reason, and the Human Brain. New York: Grosset / Putnam Press.

Degele, Nina; Schmitz, Sigrid (2010): Embodying - ein dynamischer Ansatz für Körper und Geschlecht in Bewegung. In Nina Degele (Ed.): Gendered Bodies in Motion. Opladen, Farmington Hills, Mich: Budrich UniPress, pp. 13–36.

Descartes, René (1966, c1961): Essential works. New York: Bantam Books.

Deuber-Mankowsky, Astrid (2001): Lara Croft - Modell, Medium, Cyberheldin. Frankfurt am Main: Suhrkamp.

Deuber-Mankowsky, Astrid (2007): Praktiken der Illusion. Kant, Nietzsche, Cohen, Benjamin bis Donna J. Haraway. Berlin: Vorwerk 8.

Diaz, Jesus (2010): iPad is the Future. Available online at *http://gizmodo.com/5506692/ipad-is-the-futureEdited*, checked on 10/01/2014.

Dijkstra, Edsger W. (1989): On the cruelty of really teaching computing science. In *Communications of the ACM*, Vol. 32, pp. 1398 - 1404.

Domingue, John; Martins, Maria; Tan, Jaicheng; Stutt, Arthur; Pertusson, Helgi (2002): Alice: Assisting Online Shoppers through Ontologies and Novel Interface Metaphors. In Asuncin Gmez-Pez, V. Richard Benjamins (Eds.): Knowledge Engineering and Knowledge Management: Ontologies and the Semantic Web. 13th International Conference, EKAW 2002 Sig enza, Spain, October 14, 2002 Proceedings. Berlin, Heidelberg: Springer-Verlag (Lecture Notes in Computer Science, 2473), pp. 335–351.

Dourish, Paul (1999): Embodied Interaction: Exploring the Foundations of a New Approach to HCI. Available online at *http://www.dourish.com/embodied/embodied99.pdf*, checked on 10/04/2013.

Dourish, Paul (2001): Seeking a Foundation for Context-Aware Computing. In Human-Computer Interaction, Vol. 16, Issue 2, pp. 229-241.

Dourish, Paul (2004): Where the action is. The foundations of embodied interaction. 1. MIT Press paperback ed. Cambridge, Mass.: MIT Press (A Bradford book).

Draude, Claude (2001): Cyberfeminismus. Netzkultur, Neue Technologien und Feministische Strategien. Magistra Arbeit, Universität Bremen.

Draude, Claude (2011): Intermediaries: reflections on virtual humans, gender, and the Uncanny Valley. In: AI & SOCIETY: Volume 26, Issue 4, 2011, pp. 319 – 327.

Draude, Claude; Wajda, Kamila; Maaß; Susanne (2014): GERD - Ein Vorgehensmodell zur Integration von Gender & Diversity in die Informatik. In Anja Zeising, Claude Draude, Heidi Schelhowe, Susanne Maaß (Eds.): Vielfalt der Informatik - Ein Beitrag zu Selbstverständnis und Außenwirkung. Bremen: Staats- und Universitätsbibliothek Bremen, Open Access. Available online *http://nbn-resolving.de/urn:nbn:de:gbv:46-00104194-14*, checked on 08/02/2014; pp. 197-283.

Eglash, R. (1995): African Influences in Cybernetics. In C. Hables Gray (Ed.): The Cyborg Handbook. With assistance of H. Figueroa-Sarriera, S. Mentor. London, New York: Routledge, pp. 17-28.

Elkins, James (1997): The Object Stares Back: On the Nature of Seeing. A Harvest book. San Diego: Harcourt Brace.

Esders, Karin (2007): Trapped in the Uncanny Valley: Von der unheimlichen Schönheit künstlicher Körper. In Heike Paul, Alexandra Ganser (Eds.): Screening Gender. Geschlechterszenarien in der gegenwärtigen US-amerikanischen Populärkultur. Berlin: Lit (Erlanger Studien zur Anglistik und Amerikanistik, 9), pp. 97–115.

Esposito, Elena (2003): Fiktion und Virtualität. In Sybille Krämer (Ed.): Medien - Computer - Realität. Wirklichkeitsvorstellungen und Neue Medien. Frankfurt am Main: Suhrkamp, pp. 269–296.

Fausto-Sterling, Anne (2002): Sich mit Dualismen duellieren. In Ursula Pasero, Anja Gottburgsen (Eds.): Wie natürlich ist Geschlecht? Gender und die Konstruktion von Natur und Technik. 1st ed. Wiesbaden: Westdeutscher Verlag, pp. 17–64.

Featherstone, Mike; Burrows, Roger (Eds.) (1995): Cyberspace / Cyberbodies / Cyberpunk: Cultures of Technological Embodiment. London: Sage Publications.

Ferber, Dan (2003): The Man Who Mistook His Girlfriend for a Robot. University of Texas at Dallas, The Institute for Interactive Arts and Engineering. Available online at *http://www.popsci.com/scitech/article/2003-08/man-who-mistook-his-girlfriend-robot*, checked on 23/09/2013.

Forstall, Scott (2010): The Apple iPad. Webvideo. Available online *at http://www.gearlive.com/news/article/q110-apple-ipad-tour-video/*, checked on 27/08/2013.

Fraser, Mariam; Greco, Monica (Eds.) (2004): The body. A reader. London; New York: Routledge.

Freud, Sigmund (1951): Femininity. London: Hogarth Press (Complete Psychological Works, Standard Edition, 22).

Freud, Sigmund (1963): Das Unheimliche. Aufsätze zur Literatur. Frankfurt a. M.: Fischer (Fischer-Doppelpunkt, 4).

Freud, Sigmund (2010): Drei Abhandlungen zur Sexualtheorie. Hamburg: Nikol.

Gal, Uri (2008): Boundary Matters: The Dynamics of Boundary Objects, Information Infrastructures, and Organisational Identities. Dissertation. Case Western University, Ohio. Available online at https://etd.ohiolink.edu/ap/10?0::NO:10:P10_ACCESSION_NUM:case1202807329, checked on 28/02/2014.

Garlick, Steve (2002): Melancholic Secrets: Gender Ambivalence and the Unheimlich. In Psychoanalytic Review (89), pp. 861-876.

Georgeff, Michael; Pell, Barney; Pollack, Martha; Tambe, Milind; Wooldridge, Michael (1999): The Belief-Desire-Intention Model of Agency. Available online at http://www.csc.liv.ac.uk/~mjw/pubs/atal98b.pdf, checked on 30/05/2013.

Gibson, William (1995): Neuromancer. London: Harper Collins.

Gibson, William (1996): Idoru. New York, London: Penguin.

Goleman, Daniel (1995): Emotional Intelligence. New York: Bantam Books.

Grosz, Elizabeth (2004): Refiguring Bodies. In Mariam Fraser, Monica Greco (Eds.): The body. A reader. London, New York: Routledge, pp. 47–51.

Hables Gray, C. (Ed.) (1995): The Cyborg Handbook. With assistance of H. Figueroa-Sarriera, S. Mentor. London, New York: Routledge.

Hagemann-White, Carol (1988): Wir werden nicht zweigeschlechtlich geboren. In Carol Hagemann-White, Maria Rerrich (Eds.): FrauenMännerBilder. Männer und Männlichkeit in der feministischen Diskussion. Bielefeld, pp. 224–235.

Halberstam, J. Jack (2005): In a Queer Time and Place: Transgender Bodies, Subcultural Lives. New York: New York University Press.

Hansen, Mark B. N. (2006): Bodies in code. Interfaces with digital media. New York, NY: Routledge.

Hanson, Rowland (2010): Windows is called windows. But Why? Webvideo by Laura Foy, April 26, 2010. Available online at http://channel9.msdn.com/shows/ButWhy/Word-is-named-Word—But-Why, checked on 10/2/2014.

Haraway, Donna J. (1991a): A Cyborg Manifesto: Science, Technology, and Socialist-Feminism in the Late Twentieth Century. In Donna J. Haraway (Ed.): Simians, Cyborgs and Women. The Reinvention of Nature. New York, London: Routledge, pp. 149–182.

Haraway, Donna J. (1991b): Situated Knowledges: The Science Question in Feminism and the Privilege of Partial Perspective. In Donna J. Haraway (Ed.): Simians, Cyborgs and Women. The Reinvention of Nature. New York, London: Routledge, pp. 183–202.

Haraway, Donna J. (1997): Modest_Witness@Second_Millenium.FemaleMan©_Meets_Onco-Mouse™. Feminism and Technoscience. New York, London: Routledge.

Hark, Sabine (2005): Queer Studies. In Christina von Braun, Inge Stephan (Eds.): Gender@Wissen. Ein Handbuch der Gender Theorien. Köln, Wien: Böhlau, pp. 285-303.

Hayles, Katherine N. (1999): How We Became Posthuman. Virtual Bodies in Cybernetics, Literature, and Informatics. Chicago: The University of Chicago Press.

Hayward, Philip (1993): Situating Cyberspace: The Popularisation of Virtual Reality. In Philip Hayward, Tanja Wollen (Eds.): Future Visions: New Technologies of the Screen. London: British Film Institute Press, pp. 180–204.

Heintz, Bettina (1993): Die Herrschaft der Regel. Zur Grundlagengeschichte des Computers. Frankfurt: Campus-Verlag.

Heintz, Bettina; Benz, Arnold (2001): Mit dem Auge denken. Strategien der Sichtbarmachung in wissenschaftlichen und virtuellen Welten. Zürich: Ed. Voldemeer (Theorie - Gestaltung, 1).

Hellige, Hans Dieter (2008): Krisen- und Innovationsphasen in der Mensch-Computer-Interaktion. In Hans Dieter Hellige (Ed.): Mensch-Computer-Interface. Zur Geschichte und Zukunft der Computerbedienung. Bielefeld: transcript, pp. 11–92.

Heylen, D.; van Es, I.; Nijholt, A.; van Dijk, A. (2003): Controlling the Gaze of Conversational Agents. In J.C.J van Kuppevelt; V. Dybkjaer; N.O. Bernsen (Eds.): Advances in Natural Multimodal Dialogue Systems, Kluwer Series on "Text, Speech and Language Technology", Vol. 30. Alphen aan den Rijn: Kluwer Acad. Publ., pp. 245-262.

Hillis, Ken (1996): A Geography of the Eye: The Technologies of Virtual Reality. In Robert Shields (Ed.): Cultures of Internet - Virtual Spaces, Real Histories, Living Bodies. London: Sage Publications, pp. 70–98.

Hodges, Andrew (1992): Alan Turing: The Enigma. London: Random House.

Hoffmann, E. T. A. (2006 [1817]): Der Sandmann. Die schönsten und schaurigsten Erzählungen. Düsseldorf: Albatros.

Hofmann, Jeanette (1997): Über Nutzerbilder in Textverarbeitungsprogrammen - Drei Fallbeispiele. In Meinolf Dierkes (Ed.): Technikgenese. Befunde aus einem Forschungsprogramm. Berlin: Ed. Sigma, pp. 71–96.

HUMAINE (2004): HUMAINE (Human-Machine Interaction Network on Emotion) Network of Excellence in the EU's Sixth Framework Programme, IST (Information Society Technologies) Thematic Priority IST-2002-2.3.1.6 Multimodal Interfaces. Available online at *http://emotion-research.net/projects/humaine/aboutHUMAINE*, checked on 14/05/2013.

Hutchins, Edwin L.; Norman, Donald A.; Hollan, James D. (1986): Direct Manipulation Interfaces. In Donald A. Norman, Stephen W. Draper (Eds.): User Centered System Design. New Perspectives on Human-Computer Interaction. Hillsdale, New Jersey: Lawrence Erlbaum Associates, pp. 87–124.

Iida, Fumiya (Ed.) (2004): Embodied Artificial Intelligence. International Seminar Dagstuhl Castle Germany July 7-11 2003 Revised Selected Papers. Berlin, Heidelberg: Springer-Verlag (Lecture Notes in Computer Science).

Isbister, Katherine; Doyle, Patrick (2002): Design and Evaluation of Embodied Conversational Agents: A Proposed Taxonomy. In AAMAS 2002 Workshop on Embodied Conversational Agents – let's specify and evaluate them! , Bologna, Italy.

Ive, Jony (2010): The Apple iPad. Webvideo. Available online at *http://www.gearlive.com/news/article/q110-apple-ipad-tour-video/*, checked on 27/08/2013.

Jagose, Annamarie (1996): Queer Theory. An Introduction. New York: New York University Press.

John, Bonnie E. (2003): Information Processing and Skilled Behavior. In John M. Carroll (Ed.): HCI models, theories, and frameworks. Toward a multidisciplinary science. San Francisco, Calif.: Morgan Kaufmann (The Morgan Kaufmann series in interactive technologies), pp. 55–100.

Kaplan, E. Ann (1997): Looking for the Other. Feminism, Film, and the Imperial Gaze. New York, London: Routledge.

Kay, Alan (1984): Computer software. In *Scientific American* 251(3), pp. 53–59.

Keller, Evelyn Fox; Longino, Helen E. (1996): Feminism and science. Oxford: Oxford University Press.

Kittler, Friedrich A. (1997): Romanticism - Psychoanalysis - Film: A History of the Double. In Friedrich A. Kittler, John Johnston (Eds.): Literature, media, information systems. Essays. Amsterdam: Gordon & Breach (Critical voices in art, theory and culture), pp. 85–116.

Kittler, Friedrich A.; Johnston, John (Eds.) (1997): Literature, media, information systems. Essays. Amsterdam: Gordon & Breach (Critical voices in art, theory and culture).

Klages, Mary (2001): Jaques Lacan. Available online at *http://www.colorado.edu/English/courses/ENGL2012Klages/lacan.html*, checked on 04/01/2014.

Knudsen, Susanne (2006): Intersectionality - A Theoretical Inspiration in the Analysis of Minority Cultures and Identities in Textbooks. Caught in the Web or Lost in the Textbook. Available online at *http://www.caen.iufm.fr/colloque_iartem/pdf/knudsen.pdf*, checked on 23/02/2014.

Koivunen, Anu; Paasonen, Susanna (Eds.) (2001): Conference proceedings for affective encounters. Rethinking embodiment in feminist media studies. Turku: University of Turku, School of Art, Literature and Music, Media Studies, published in association with the Finnish Society for Cinema Studies (Series A / University of Turku, School of Art, Literature and Music, Media Studies, 49).

Kopp, Stefan; Wachsmuth, Ipke; Lessmann, Nadine; Jung, Bernhard (2003): Max - A Multimodal Assistant in Virtual Reality Construction. In *Künstliche Intelligenz* (4), pp. 11–17.

Kormann, Eva (2006): Textmaschinenkörper. Genderorientierte Lektüren des Androiden. Amsterdam [u.a.]: Rodopi (Amsterdamer Beiträge zur neueren Germanistik, 59).

Krämer, Nicole C.; Bente, Gary (2002): Virtuelle Helfer: Embodied Conversational Agents in der Mensch-Compuetr-Interaktion. In G. Krämer N. C. &. Petersen A. Bente (Ed.): Virtuelle Realitäten. Göttingen: Hogrefe, pp. 203–225.

Krämer, Nicole C.; Bente, Gary (2003): Brauchen Interface Agenten Emotionen? In Gerd Szwillus, Jürgen Ziegler (Eds.): Mensch & Computer 2003. Interaktion in Bewegung. 1st ed. Stuttgart [u.a.]: Teubner (Berichte des German Chapter of the ACM, 57), pp. 287–296.

Krämer, Sybille (1988): Symbolische Maschinen. Die Idee der Formalisierung im geschichtlichen Abriß. Darmstadt: Wissenschaftliche Buchgesellschaft.

Krämer, Sybille (2011): Simulation und Erkenntnis. Über die Rolle computergenerierter Simulationen in den Wissenschaften. In *Nova Acta Leopoldina* (377, Bd. 110), pp. 303–322.

Krüger-Fürhoff, Irmela Marei (2005): Körper. In Christina von Braun, Inge Stephan (Eds.): Gender@Wissen: Ein Handbuch der Gender-Theorien. Köln: Böhlau, pp. 66–88.

Lacan, Jaques (1977): The mirror stage as formative of the function of the I as revealed in psychoanalytic experience. Delivered at the 16th International Congress of Psychoanalysis, Zürich, July 17, 1949. In Jaques Lacan: Écrits. A selection. New York: Norton.

Lakoff, George; Johnson, Mark (1999): Philosophy in the flesh. The embodied mind and its challenge to western thought. [Reprinted]. New York: Basic Books.

Lance, B. Marsella S. and Koizumi D. (2004): Towards Expressive Gaze Manner in Embodied Virtual Agents. Autonomous Agents and Multi-Agent Systems Workshop on Empathic Agents, 2004. Available online at *http://www.isi.edu/~marsella/lance-aamas.pdf*, checked on 26/09/2013.

Lanier, Jaron (1998): A Vintage Virtual Reality Interview. Available online at *http://www.jaronlanier.com/vrint.html*, checked on 25/09/2013.

Latour, Bruno (2002): Wir sind nie modern gewesen. Versuch einer symmetrischen Anthropologie. Frankfurt am Main: Fischer-Taschenbuch-Verl. (Fischer: Forum Wissenschaft, 13777).

Laurel, Brenda K. (1986): Interface as Mimesis. In Donald A. Norman, Stephen W. Draper (Eds.): User Centered System Design. New Perspectives on Human-Computer Interaction. Hillsdale, New Jersey: Lawrence Erlbaum Associates, pp. 67–85.

Laurel, Brenda (1990a): Interface Agents: Metaphors with Character. In Brenda K. Laurel (Ed.): The Art of Human-Computer Interface Design, pp. 355–365.

Laurel, Brenda K. (Ed.) (1990b): The Art of Human-Computer Interface Design. Apple Computer, Inc.

Lauretis, Teresa de (2000): Alice Doesn't. Feminism, Semiotics, Cinema. 7th ed. Bloomington: Indiana University Press.

Lee, Jehee; Chai, Jinxiang; Reitsma, Paul S. A.; Hodgins, Jessica K.; Pollard, Nancy S. (2002): Interactive Control of Avatars Animated with Human Motion Data. Association for Computing Machinery. Available online at *http://www.cs.uu.nl/docs/vakken/manim/papers/paper05.pdf*, checked on 19/10/2013.

Lee, Jinha (2013): Reach into the computer and grab a pixel. Available online at *http://www.ted.com/talks/jinha_lee_a_tool_that_lets_you_touch_pixels.html*, checked on 19/10/2013.

Leigh Star, Susan; Griesemer, James R. (1989): Institutional ecology, "translation", and boundary objects. Amateurs and professionals in Berkeley's museum of vertebrate zoology, 1907-39. In *Social Studies of Science* 19, pp. 505–524.

Lewis, C. S.; Baynes, Pauline (2000): The complete chronicles of Narnia. New York: HarperCollins.

Livingston, Mark A.; Rosenblum, Lawrence J.; Julier, Simon J.; Brown, Dennis; Baillot, Yohan; Swan II, J. Edward et al. (2002): An Augmented Reality System for Military Operations in Urban Terrain. Proceedings of Interservice / Industry Training, Simulation & Education Conference (I/ITSEC) 2002. Orlando, Florida. Available online at *http://people.cs.vt.edu/~jgabbard/publications/iitsec02.pdf*, checked on 18/12/2013.

Lübke, Valeska (2005): CyberGender. Geschlecht und Körper im Internet. Sulzbach, Taunus: Ulrike Helmer.

Luck, Michael; McBurney, Peter; Shehory, Onn; Willmott, Steve (2005a): Agent Based Computing. Agent Technology Roadmap Draft - A Roadmap for Agent Based Computing: AgentLink.

Luck, Michael; McBurney, Peter; Shehory, Onn; Willmott, Steve (2005b): Agent Link Roadmap. (Draft). University of Southampton. Available online at *http://www.agentlink.org*, checked on 30/05/2013.

Lupton, Deborah (1995): The Embodied Computer/User. In Mike Featherstone, Roger Burrows (Eds.): Cyberspace / Cyberbodies / Cyberpunk: Cultures of Technological Embodiment. London: Sage Publications, pp. 97-112.

Maaß, Susanne (1984): Mensch-Rechner-Kommunikation. Herkunft und Chancen eines neuen Paradigmas. Dissertation. Universität Hamburg, Fachbereich Informatik.

MacDorman, Karl F. (2007): Charting the Uncanny Valley: Do Looks Matter? Karl F. MacDorman presents on the uncanny valley at the 2007 NMC Summer Conference (June 6-9, 2007, Indianapolis), Indiana University School of Informatics. Edited by AndroidScience. Available online at *http://www.youtube.com/watch?v=-eRcs0T4arw*, checked on 6/11/2013.

Macho, Thomas (2002): Narziß und der Spiegel. Selbstrepräsentation in der Geschichte der Optik. In Almut-Barbara Renger (Ed.): Narcissus. Ein Mythos von der Antike bis zum Cyberspace. Stuttgart/Weimar: Metzler. Available online at *http://www.gestaltung.hs-mannheim.de/designwiki/files/4891/macho_narziss%20und%20der%20spiegel,%202002.pdf*, checked on 12/10/2013, pp. 13–25.

Magnenat-Thalmann, Nadia (Ed.) (2004): Handbook of virtual humans. Chichester: Wiley.

Manovich, Lev (2000): Alien Vision: Simulation of Life and the History of Illusion. In Erkki Huhtamo (Ed.): Alien Intelligence. Catalogue. Kiasma - Museum of Contemporary Art: Helsinki, pp. 26-33.

Manovich, Lev (2001): The Language of New Media. Massachusetts: MIT Press (Leonardo).

Meek, James (1995): Intelligent agents, Internet information and interface. In *Australian Journal of Educational Technology* (11(2)), pp. 75–90.

Meyer-Drawe, Käte (1996): Menschen im Spiegel ihrer Maschinen. München: Wilhelm Fink Verlag.

Minsky, Marvin (2006): The Emotion Machine. Commonsense Thinking, Artificial Intelligence, and the Future of the Human Mind. New York: Simon & Schuster.

Moravec, Hans (1995): Mind children. The future of robot and human intelligence. Cambridge: Harvard Univ. Press.

Morgan, D. H. J.; Brandth, Berit; Kvande, Elin (2005): Gender, bodies, and work. Aldershot, Hampshire, England, Burlington, VT: Ashgate.

Mori, Masahiro (1970): Bukimi no tani. The uncanny valley (K. F. MacDorman & T. Minato, Trans.). (Originally in Japanese). In *Energy* 4 (7), pp. 33–35.

Mulvey, Laura (1989a): Afterthoughts on 'Visual Pleasure and Narrative Cinema' inspired by King Vidor's Duel in the Sun (1946). In Laura Mulvey Visual and other Pleasures. Houndmills: Macmillian, pp. 29–38.

Mulvey, Laura (1989b): Visual Pleasure and Narrative Cinema. In Visual and Other Pleasures. Houndmills: Macmillian, pp. 14–26.

Nadin, Mihai (1996): Der bessere Computer ist unsichtbar. In Dr. Dotzler Medien Institut (Ed.): Computer Art Faszination. Frankfurt am Main, pp. 209–212.

Nadin, Mihai (2007): Semiotic Machines. In *The Public Journal of Semiotics* (1(1)), pp. 85–114.

Nake, Frieder (1992): Informatik und die Maschinisierung von Kopfarbeit. In Wolfgang Coy, Frieder Nake, Jörg M. Pflüger, Arno Rolf, Jürgen Seetzen, Dirk Siefkes, Reinhard Stransfeld (Eds.): Sichtweisen der Informatik. Theorie der Informatik. Berlin: Vieweg, Friedr., & Sohn Verlagsgesellschaft mbH, pp. 181–201.

Nake, Frieder (Ed.) (1993a): Die erträgliche Leichtigkeit der Zeichen. Ästhetik, Semiotik, Informatik. Baden-Baden: AGIS-Verlag (Internationale Reihe Kybernetik und Information, 18).

Nake, Frieder (1993b): Von der Interaktion. Über den instrumentalen und den medialen Charakter des Computers. In Frieder Nake (Ed.): Die erträgliche Leichtigkeit der Zeichen. Ästhetik, Semiotik, Informatik. Baden-Baden: AGIS-Verlag (Internationale Reihe Kybernetik und Information, 18), pp. 165–189.

Nake, Frieder (2000): Begegnung im Zeichen. Köln: Salon Verlag (Jahrbuch 4). In *Entwerfen*, pp. 174–186.

Nake, Frieder (2001): Das algorithmische Zeichen. In Kurt Bauknecht, Thomas A. Brauer, Wilfried Mück (Eds.): Informatik 2001. Tagungsband der GI/OCG Jahrestagung 2001. (2), pp. 736–742. Available online at *http://www.agis.informatik.uni-bremen.de/ARCHIV/Publikationen/ Algor.ZeichenWienText.pdf*, checked on 6/09/2013.

Nake, Frieder (2004): The Display as a Looking-Glass. Zu Ivan E. Sutherlands früher Vision der grafischen Datenverarbeitung. In Hans Dieter Hellige (Ed.): Geschichten der Informatik. Visionen, Paradigmen, Leitmotive. Berlin, Heidelberg: Springer-Verlag, pp. 339–364.

Nass, Clifford; Isbister, Katherine; Lee, Eun-Ju (2000): Truth is beauty: researching embodied conversational agents. In Justine Cassell (Ed.): Embodied conversational agents. Cambridge Mass.: MIT Press, pp. 374–402.

Norman, Donald A. (1986): Cognitive Engineering. In Donald A. Norman, Stephen W. Draper (Eds.): User Centered System Design. New Perspectives on Human-Computer Interaction. Hillsdale, New Jersey: Lawrence Erlbaum Associates, pp. 31–61.

Norman, Donald A. (1987): Cognitive Engineering - Cognitive Science. In John M. Carrol (Ed.): Interfacing Thought. Cognitive Aspects of Human-Computer Interaction. Massachusetts: MIT Press, pp. 325–336.

Norman, Donald A. (1988): The design of everyday things. New York: Basic Books.

Norman, Donald A. (2005): Emotional design. Why we love (or hate) everyday things. New York: Basic Books.

Norman, Donald A.; Draper, Stephen W. (Eds.) (1986): User Centered System Design. New Perspectives on Human-Computer Interaction. Hillsdale, New Jersey: Lawrence Erlbaum Associates.

Orland, Barbara; Scheich, Elvira (Eds.) (1995): Das Geschlecht der Natur. Feministische Beiträge zur Geschichte und Theorie der Naturwissenschaften. Frankfurt am Main: Suhrkamp.

Ortner, Shery B. (1972): Is Female to Male as Nature Is to Culture? In *Feminist Studies* 1, 1972 (2), pp. 5–31.

Ortony, Andrew; Clore, Gerald L.; Collins, Allan (1988): The Cognitive Structure of Emotions. Cambridge: Cambridge University Press.

Ovid: Metamorphoses. Available online at *http://www.poetryintranslation.com/PITBR/Latin/ Metamorph3.htm#_Toc64106192*, checked on 16/08/2013.

Paiva, Ana; Vala, Marco; Blanco, Gabriel (2011): Providing Gender to Embodied Conversational Agents. In H. Högni Vilhjálmsson et al. (Ed.): IVA 2011, LNAI 6895. IVA 2011. Berlin, Heidelberg: Springer-Verlag, pp. 148–154.

Papapetros, Spyros (2012): On the animation of the inorganic. Art, architecture, and the extension of life. Chicago, London: University of Chicago Press.

Paula S. Rothenberg (Ed.) (2004): Race, Class, and Gender in the United States. New York: Worth Publishers.

Pausanias; Jones, William Henry Samuel; Ormerod, Henry Arderne; Wycherley, Richard Ernest (191835): Pausanias Description of Greece. London, New York: W. Heinemann; G. P. Putnam's sons.

Pelachaud, C.; Carofiglio, V.; Carolis, B. de; Rosis, F. de; Poggi, I. (2002): Embodied Contextual Agent in Information Delivering Application. In AAMAS (Ed.): Proceedings of the first international joint conference on Autonomous agents and multiagent systems July 15-19, 2002, Bologna, Italy, pp. 758-765.

Perry, Lynellen D. S. (1996): ACM Crossroads Student Magazine. Available online at *http://www.acm.org/crossroads/xrds3-1/emotware.htm*, checked on 20/05/2013.

Petri, Carl Adam (1983): Zur "Vermenschlichung" des Computers. In *GMD-Spiegel* 3 (4), pp. 42–44.

Pflüger, Jörg (2004): Konversation, Manipulation, Delegation: Zur Ideengeschichte der Interaktivität. In Hans Dieter Hellige (Ed.): Geschichten der Informatik. Visionen, Paradigmen, Leitmotive. Berlin, Heidelberg: Springer-Verlag, pp. 367–408.

Pflüger, Jörg (2008): Interaktion im Kontext. In Hans Dieter Hellige (Ed.): Mensch-Computer-Interface. Zur Geschichte und Zukunft der Computerbedienung. Bielefeld: transcript, pp. 323–390.

Kulms, Philipp; Krämer, Nicole C.; Gratch, Jonathan; Kang, Sin-Hwa (2011): It's in Their Eyes: A Study on Female and Male Virtual Humans Gaze. In H. Högni Vilhjálmsson et al. (Eds.): IVA 2011, LNAI 6895. Berlin, Heidelberg: Springer-Verlag, pp. 80–92.

Pias, Claus (2000) »›noisy, narrow-band devices‹. Prolegomena zur Animationsgeschichte des Computerspiel(er)s«. In: Kai-Uwe Hemken (ed.), Bilder in Bewegung. Traditionen digitaler Ästhetik. Köln (DuMont) 2000, pp. 222-235.

Picard, Rosalind W. (1997): Affective Computing. Cambridge, Mass.: MIT Press.

Picard, Rosalind W. (2003): Affective Computing: Challenges. Edited by Affective Computing Group. MIT (Massachussetts). Available online at *http://affect.media.mit.edu/pdfs/03.picard.pdf*, checked on 06/05/2013.

Plant, Sadie (1997): Zeros and Ones: Digital Women and the New Technoculture. New York: Doubleday.

Pokahr, Alexander; Braubach, Lars; Lamersdorf, Winfried (2002): Dezentrale Steuerung verteilter Anwendungen mit rationalen Agenten. Universität Hamburg, FB Informatik, Verteilte Systeme und Informationssysteme. Available online at https://vsis-www.informatik.uni-hamburg.de/getDoc.php/publications/241/pokahr_kivs05_revised.pdf, checked on 3/3/2014.

Prendinger, Helmut; Ishizuka, Mitsuru (Eds.) (1998): Life-Like Characters. Tools, Affective Functions, and Applications. Berlin, Heidelberg: Springer-Verlag (Cognitive Technologies).

Rao, Anand S.; Georgeff, Michael P. (1995): BDI Agents: from theory to practice. In MIT (Massachussetts) (Ed.): Proceedings of 1st International Conference on Multi-Agent Systems (ICMAS'95). Cambridge, Massachusetts; London, England: MIT Press, pp. 312-319.

Rehm, Matthias; André, Elisabeth (2005): Where do they look? Gaze Behaviors of Multiple Users Interacting with an Embodied Conversational Agent. In T. et al Panayiotopoulus (Ed.): IVA 2005, LNAI 3661. Berlin, Heidelberg: Springer-Verlag, pp. 241–252.

Reif, Gerald (2001): Intelligente Agenten. Available online at http://www.iicm.edu/greif/node12.html, checked on 30/05/2013.

Rockwood, Alyn; McAndless, Janet (1999): "Through the Looking Glass": The Synthesis of Computer Graphics and Computer Vision. In IEEE MultiMedia, vol. 06, no. 3, pp. 8-11.

Rolf, Arno (2003): Interdisziplinäre Technikforschung und Informatik - ein Angebot für einen analytischen Orientierungsrahmen. In Technikfolgenabschätzung – Theorie und Praxis 12 (3/4), pp. 59–67.

Rommes, Els (2002): Gender Scripts and the Internet - The Design and Use of Amsterdam's Digital City. Enschede: Twente University Press.

Rowbotham, Judith; Stevenson, Kim (2003): Behaving badly. Social panic and moral outrage - Victorian and modern parallels. Aldershot: Ashgate.

Rumpf, Ewald (1999): Spiegel und Introspektion. Verabschiedung der Diplomanden. Universität Kassel. Kassel. Available online at http://www.ewald-rumpf.de/psychologie/texte/spiegel-und-introspektion/, checked on 27/10/2013.

Ruttkay, Zsófia (2004): From brows to trust. Evaluating embodied conversational agents. Zsófia Ruttkay (ed.) Dordrecht: Kluwer Acad. Publ. (Human-computer interaction series, 7).

Schelhowe, Heidi (1997): Das Medium aus der Maschine. Zur Metamorphose des Computers. Frankfurt am Main, New York: Campus.

Schelhowe, Heidi (2005): Interaktionen - Gender Studies und die Informatik. In Heike Kahlert, Barbara Thiessen, Ines Weller (Eds.): Quer denken - Strukturen verändern. Gender Studies. Wiesbaden: VS Verlag.

Scherffig, Lasse (2005): It's in Your Eyes. Gaze Based Image Retrieval in Context. With assistance of Hans H. (ed.) Diebner: ZKM | Institute for Basic Research.

Scherke, Katharina (2009): Auflösung der Dichotomie von Rationalität und Emotionalität? Wissenschaftssoziologische Anmerkungen. In Sabine Flick (Ed.): Emotionen in Geschlechterverhältnissen. Affektregulierung und Gefühlsinszenierung im historischen Wandel. Bielefeld: transcript (Gender studies), pp. 23–43.

Schiebinger, Londa L. (1999): Has feminism changed science? Cambridge, Mass: Harvard University Press.

Schiebinger, Londa L. (2000): Feminism and the body. Oxford, New York: Oxford University Press (Oxford readings in feminism).

Schinzel, Britta (2004): Epistemische Veränderungen an der Schnittstelle Informatik und Naturwissenschaften. In Britta Schinzel, Sigrid Schmitz (Eds.): Grenzgänge - Genderforschung in Informatik und Naturwissenschaften. Königstein/Taunus: Ulrike Helmer, pp. 30–49.

Schott, Gareth (2011): The production of machinima: A dialogue between ethnography, culture and space. In *International Journal of Business, Humanities and Technology* Vol. 1 No.1, pp. 113-121.

Sculley, John; Byrne, John A. (1987): Odyssey. Pepsi to Apple...: a journey of adventure, ideas, and the future. New York: Harper & Row.

Searle, John R. (1975): A Taxonomy of Illocutionary Acts. In Keith Gunderson (Ed.): Language, mind, and knowledge. Minneapolis: University of Minnesota Press (Minnesota studies in the philosophy of science, 7), pp. 344–369.

Searle, John R. (1984): Minds, Brains and Science. Cambridge, Mass.: Harvard University Press.

Selfridge, Oliver (1997): Agents: from Pandemonium to ... whither? Available online at *http://www.almaden.ibm.com/almaden/npuc97/1997/selfridge.htm*, checked on 19/09/2013.

Sengers, Phoebe; Boehner, Kirsten; David, Shay; Kaye, JJ (2005): Reflective Design. In Proceedings of the 4th Decennial Conference on Critical Computing: Between Sense and Sensibility CC '05 (Aarhus, Denmark). New York: ACM Press. Available online at *http://www.nyu.edu/projects/nissenbaum/papers/reflectivedesign.pdf*, checked on 14/04/2013.

Shabot, Sara Cohen (2006): Grotesque Bodies: A Response to Disembodied Cyborgs. In *Journal of Gender Studies* 15 (3), pp. 223–235.

Shneidermann, Ben (1982): The Future of Interactive Systems and the Emergence of Direct Manipulation. In *Behavior and Information Technology*, Vol. 1 No.3, pp. 237–256.

Simon, Gérard (1992): Der Blick, das Sein und die Erscheinung in der antiken Optik. München: Fink.

Simon, Herbert A. (1982 (1969)): The sciences of the artificial. Cambridge, Mass.: MIT Press.

Singh, Munindar P.; Rao, Anand S.; Georgeff, Michael P. (1999): Formal Methods in DAI: Logic-Based Representation and Reasoning. In Gerhard Weiss (Ed.): Multiagent Systems. A Modern Approach to Distributed Modern Approach to Artificial Intelligence. Cambridge, Massachusetts; London, England: MIT Press, pp. 331–377.

Snow, C.P. (1959): The Two Cultures. Cambridge: Cambridge University Press.

Stephenson, Neal (1992): Snow Crash. New York: Bantam Bell.

Stone, Sandy (Allucquere Rosanne) (1991): Will the Real Body Please Stand Up? In Michael Benedikt (Ed.): Cyberspace: First Steps. Cambridge Mass.: MIT Press, pp. 81-118.

Suchman, Lucy A. (1987): Plans and situated actions. The problem of human-machine communication. Cambridge: Cambridge Univ. Press.

Suchman, Lucy A. (2005): Agencies in Technology Design: Feminist Reconfigurations. Workshop on Gendered Innovations in Science and Engineering, Stanford University, April 15-16, 2005. Lancaster University. Available online at *http://www.lancs.ac.uk/fss/sociology/papers/suchman-agenciestechnodesign.pdf*, checked on 31/03/2013.

Sutherland, Ivan E. (1965): The Ultimate Display. In Proceedings of IFIP Congress, pp. 506–508.

Sutherland, Ivan E. (2003 (1965)): Sketchpad: A man-machine graphical communication system. Edited by Alan Blackwell, Kerry Rodden. University of Cambridge, Computer Laboratory (Technical Reports, 574). Available online at *https://www.cl.cam.ac.uk/techreports/UCAM-CL-TR-574.pdf*, checked on 01/06/2015

Tatai, Gábor; Laufer, László; Csordas, Annamária; Kiss, Árpád; Szaló, Attila (2003): The Chatbot Who Loved Me. Embodied Conversational Characters as Individuals, Workshop at AAMAS 2003, Melbourne, Australia. Available online at *http://citeseerx.ist.psu.edu/viewdoc/download?doi=10.1.1.97.3826&rep=rep1&type=pdf*, checked on 24/01/2015.

Theweleit, Klaus (1986): Buch der Könige. Orpheus und Eurydike: Stroemfeld/Roter Stern.

Torres, Obed E.; Cassell, Justine; Prevost, Scott (1997): Modeling Gaze Behavior as a Function of Discourse Structure. In Proceedings of the First International Workshop on Human-Computer Conversations, Bellagio, Italy. Available online at http://www.media.mit.edu/gnl/publications/obed_bellagio_97.pdf, checked on 26/09/2013.

Trogemann, Georg (2003): Mit Hand und Fuß - Die Bedeutung der nonverbalen Kommunikation für die Emotionalisierung von Dialogführungssystemen. In Christian Lindner (Ed.): Avatare - Digitale Sprecher für Business und Marketing. Heidelberg, Berlin: Springer-Verlag, pp. 269-290.

Turing, Alan M. (1948): Intelligent Machinery. National Physical Laboratory Report. Digital facsimile of the original typescript. Available online at http://www.alanturing.net/intelligent_machinery, checked on 24/09/2013.

Turing, Alan M. (1950): Computing machinery and intelligence. In *Mind*, pp. 433–460.

Turkle, Sherry (1984): The Second Self. Computers and the Human Spirit. New York: Simon & Schuster.

Turkle, Sherry (1995): Life on the Screen. Identity in the Age of the Internet. New York: Simon & Schuster.

Turkle, Sherry (1999): Computertechnologien und multiple Bilder des Selbst. In Christina von Braun, Gaby Dietze (Eds.): Multiple Persönlichkeit. Krankheit, Medium oder Metapher? Frankfurt a. M.: Verl. Neue Kritik, pp. 86–104.

Turner, Bryan S. (1984): The body and society. Explorations in social theory. Oxford, UK, New York, NY, USA: B. Blackwell.

Turner, Bryan S. (2012): Routledge handbook of body studies. Abingdon, Oxon, New York: Routledge (Routledge international handbooks).

Van der Hoek, Wiebe; Roberts, Mark; Woolridge, Michael (2005): Knowledge and Social Laws. In Virginia Dignum, Frank Dignum, Sven Koenig (Eds.): Proceedings of the Fourth International Joint Conference on Autonomous Agents and Multi Agent Systems. New York: ACM, 674-681.

Vinayagamoorthy, Vinoba; Garau, Maia; Steed, Anthony; Garau, Mel Slater Maia Anthony Steed (2004): An Eye Gaze Model for Dyadic Interaction in an Immersive Virtual Environment: Practice and Experience. In *Computer graphics forum: journal of the European Association for Computer Graphics* (23), pp. 1–11.

Wachsmuth, Ipke (2010): "Ich, Max". In Tilmann Sutter, Alexander Mehler (Eds.): Medienwandel als Wandel von Interaktionsformen. Wiesbaden: VS Verlag für Sozialwissenschaften / GWV Fachverlage, Wiesbaden, pp. 135–157.

Waldenfels, Bernhard (2003): Experimente mit der Wirklichkeit. In Sybille Krämer (Ed.): Medien - Computer - Realität. Wirklichkeitsvorstellungen und Neue Medien: Suhrkamp, pp. 213–241.

Walker, John (1990): Through the Looking Glass. In Brenda K. Laurel (Ed.): The Art of Human-Computer Interface Design, pp. 439-448.

Warner, William B. (2001): Computable Culture and the Closure of the Media Paradigm. Telepolis - Heise Online. Available online at http://www.heise.de/tp/r4/artikel/11/11377/1.html, checked on 03/10/2013.

Weber, Jutta (2003): Turbulente Körper und emergente Maschinen. In Jutta Weber, Corinna Bath (Eds.): Turbulente Körper, soziale Maschinen. Feministische Studien zur Technowissenschaftskultur. Opladen: Leske + Budrich (Studien interdisziplinäre Geschlechterforschung, 7), pp. 119–136.

Weber, Jutta; Bath, Corinna (2004): 'Social' Robots & 'Emotional' Software Agents: Gendering Processes and De-gendering Strategies for 'Technologies in the Making'. Talk at the international symposium Gender Perspectives Increasing Diversity for Information Society Technology. June 24-26 2004. Bremen. Extended Paper, unpublished.

Weigel, Sigrid (2005): Phantombilder: Gesicht, Gefühl, Gehirn zwischen Messen und Deuten. In Oliver Grau (Ed.): Mediale Emotionen. Zur Lenkung von Gefühlen durch Bild und Sound. Frankfurt am Main: Fischer-Taschenbuch-Verl ([Fischer-Taschenbücher], 16917), pp. 242–276.

Weiss, Gerhard (Ed.) (1999): Multiagent Systems. A Modern Approach to Distributed Modern Approach to Artificial Intelligence. MIT (Massachussetts). Cambridge, Massachusetts; London, England: MIT Press.

Weizenbaum, Joseph (1983): ELIZA: a computer program for the study of natural language communication between man and machine. In Communications of the ACM. 25th Anniversary Issue. 26 volumes (1), pp. 23–27.

Weizenbaum, Joseph (1984): Kurs auf den Eisberg. München, Zürich: Piper.

Wetterer, Angelika (2002): Arbeitsteilung und Geschlechterkonstruktion. "Gender at work" in theoretischer und historischer Perspektive. Konstanz: UVK (Theorie und Methode. Sozialwissenschaften).

Whiteside, John; Wixon, Dennis (1987): Discussion: Improving Human-Computer Interaction. In John M. Carrol (Ed.): Interfacing Thought. Cognitive Aspects of Human-Computer Interaction. Massachusetts: MIT Press, pp. 353–365.

Wiesner, Heike; Kamphans, Marion; Schelhowe, Heidi; Metz-Göckel, Sigrid; Zorn, Isabel; Drag, Anna et al. (2004): Gender Mainstreaming in „Neue Medien in der Bildung". Leitfaden. Universität Bremen; Universität Dortmund. Bremen; Dortmund (GM im BMBF-Programm "Neue Medien in der Bildung - Förderbereich Hochschule"). Available online at *http://dimeb.informatik.uni-bremen.de/documents/projekt.gender.GMLeitfaden.pdf*, checked on 13/02/2014.

Wilde, Oscar (1993): The picture of Dorian Gray. Charlottesville, Virginia: University of Virginia Library.

Winograd, Terry (1998): The Design of Interaction. In Peter J. Denning, Robert M. Metcalfe (Eds.): Beyond Calculation. The Next Fifty Years of Computing. New York: Copernicus; Springer, pp. 149–161.

Wooldridge, Michael (1997): Agent-based software engineering. In IEE Proceedings Software Engineering, 144 (1), pp. 26–37.

Wooldridge, Michael (1999): Intelligent Agents. In Gerhard Weiss (Ed.): Multiagent Systems. A Modern Approach to Distributed Artificial Intelligence. Cambridge, Massachusetts; London, England: MIT Press, pp. 27–73.

Wooldridge, Michael (2008): An Introduction to MultiAgent Systems, 2nd ed. New Jersey: John Wiley and Sons Ltd.

Woolf, Jenny (2010): Mystery of Lewis Carroll: Discovering the Whimsical, Thoughtful, ar Sometimes Lonely Man Who Created Alice in Wonderland: St. Martins Press.

Wundt, Wilhelm (1913): Elemente der Völkerpsychologie. Grundlinien einer psychologisc' Entwicklungsgeschichte der Menschheit. Leipzig: Kröner.

Zakin, Emily (2011): Psychoanalytic Feminism (Summer 2011 Edition). The Stanford Encyclop of Philosophy. Edited by Edward N. Zalta. Available online at *http://plato.stanforc archives/sum2011/entries/feminism-psychoanalysis*, checked on 17/08/2013.

Zeising, Anja; Draude, Claude; Schelhowe, Heidi; Maaß, Susanne (Eds.) (2014): Vielfalt der Informatik - Ein Beitrag zu Selbstverständnis und Außenwirkung. Bremen: Staats- und Universitätsbibliothek Bremen. Available online *http://nbn-resolving.de/urn:nbn:de:gbv:46-00104194-14*, checked on 08/02/2014.

Zong, Yuang; Dohi, Hiroshi; Ishizuka, Mitsuru (2000): Emotion Expression Functions attached to Multimodal Presentation Markup Language. Tokyo Technical University. Available online at *http://www.miv.t.u-tokyo.ac.jp/MPML*, checked on 13/09/2013.